GOLF IN SCOTLAND:
THE HIDDEN GEMS

by Bob and Anne Jones

[Scotland's Hidden Gems: Golf Courses and Pubs
2016 Revision]

TABLE OF CONTENTS

INTRODUCTION: A BEGINNING

In Fort Augustus, Scotland, we stopped at the Tourist Information Bureau, the "I" of Scotland we term it, to make reservations for a few days ahead in yet another town. The girl behind the desk knows just the place for us in Crieff. "It's the best place in all Perthshire," she exclaims, "and it's got the awards to show it." She lets us know it will take at least an hour to confirm our lodging and suggests a place we might want to "...have a wee bite of lunch."

Thanking her and wishing her luck at getting us a bed in the best of Perthshire, we take our leave and head for lunch in the direction she indicated. Our first question after leaving the "I" is, "Perthshire? What's Perthshire?" A quick stop at the car retrieves the map which shows Perthshire. "Stirling to Perth and up towards the Highlands," says Anne with a little authority, after all, she's been map reader now for about 1500 miles. We both hope the Tourist Bureau girl reserves it for us.

Tossing the map back into the car, we strike out on foot towards our lunch goal, a place called something like the Loch Inn. Before we go half a block we make two discoveries. First, a tour bus lets out in the parking lot in front of us. Hordes of tourists--well, at least a dozen or two--hustle off the bus and rush over, cameras clicking and whirring, to a bridge ahead of us. Second, we discover the reason for the shutter-bugging: the bridge crosses the Caledonian Lock. As we work our way to the bridge, my camera clicking, we see several medium sized pleasure craft working their way along the lock.

There across from us is our objective, the Lock Inn and Gilliegorm Restaurant. The inn turns out to be a positively quaint pub with an enticing selection of single malt scotches, real ales on tap, interesting soup specials, and a friendly barkeep who allows me to shoot a couple of interior photos, including one of him wiping a glass. Trite, maybe, but definitely quaint.

The walk back to the "I" to check on our Perthshire lodging yields a pair of surprises. The first is just across the lock from our lunch pub. A small museum dedicated to the Caledonian Locks provides insight into the history and significance of the system. Even a ten minute stroll through the museum is enough to make us more appreciative of what we've been seeing. The second event is one of those easily missed or overlooked happenings that enrich our lives if we let them. As Anne and I approach the Tourist Bureau office, I spy a dog in a stone-fenced and iron-gated yard across the road. Though I consider myself a "dog person" (having raised and raced Siberian Husky sled dogs for twelve years), what attracted my attention is the red ball in the mouth of the black and white Aussie standing at the gate. As a pedestrian, probably from the tour bus, walks close to the gate the Aussie tips her head (so coyly I'm sure it is a she) and drops the ball so it bounces in front of the approaching person. He looks first at the dog and then at the ball which has rolled in front of him. He picks up the ball and throws it back over the gate and continues his walk. The dog chases the ball, grabs it, mauls it a little, then scampers back to the gate, ball in mouth, to wait for the next walker who can be enticed into playing ball. Clever, these Scottish Aussie dogs!

Back at the "I" the girl greeted us all smiles. "I've got great news. You're booked into Merlindale in Crieff. It was awarded Best B&B in Perthshire."

This hour-and-a-half visit to Fort Augustus was so typical of our trips to Scotland over the past twelve years. Surprise, discovery, friendliness, history, beauty, and more surprises. As we immersed ourselves in the culture, Anne and I fell in love with Scotland. Anne has Scottish and Irish ancestry and I have Welsh (and we both have a little English heritage which we don't admit to when in Scotland, Ireland, or Wales). Definitely in Scotland we both feel so comfortable, so at home, so connected.

It was early in our first visit in September 2000 that we started to feel the connection. We had just finished playing golf at West Linton GC, a lovely 1890 built track set in the middle of the Borders countryside, and were sitting in the Golden Arms Pub sipping a coke and sharing a bag of crisps (chips) with a golden retriever and a Heinz 57 pub mutt. The piano next to us had a note on it which read: "I like to be played. Please feel free." We gave each other that look that after thirty-five years of marriage says, "You're thinking the same thing, aren't you." I said, "Wouldn't it be fun to write about this...the golf...the pubs...the dogs?" Anne replied, "You do the writing and I'll help with the research."

From that kernel of an idea, and after several trips to Scotland with golf every chance we could, eating in pubs for most meals, this book was born. *Scotland's Hidden Gems: Golf Courses and Pubs* was researched by two newly retired teachers and golfing duffers making their first excursions in international travel.

Update to this Edition: Since publishing this first book in 2005 we have written two other golf travel guides (*Ireland's Small Greens* in 2007 and *Hidden Gems II: Scotland and Wales* in 2009) and have finished a book of travel stories, *Ten Years of Travels in Scotland, Ireland, England and Wales*. This second edition of *Scotland's Hidden Gems* (updated in 2016) is presented in a different format and has expanded information about the golf courses in the first edition plus the addition of several more courses. Pubs, restaurants, tearooms, B&Bs, and attractions are listed in relation to the area of the golf courses. All the information has been checked and updated to the best of our ability right until the time of publication. We hope you enjoy the great hidden jewels of Scottish golf!

MAP OF SCOTLAND

CHAPTER ONE: SOME QUESTIONS AND A FEW ANSWERS

Eilean Donan Castle

If this is a book of information, questions must be asked and answers must be sought. The questions come easily, but the answers are sometimes harder to find. Let me answer some of the most important questions.

First, **why the connection between golf and pubs?** Besides the simple fact that both Anne and I enjoy golf and food and drink there are some deeper connections. Both golf and pubs create their own cultures and those cultures overlap. Golfers, since the first shepherd hit a rock with a crooked stick into a rabbit hole, have wanted to "share" their good shots and their tragedies with anyone who would listen (and many who couldn't care less). What better place to share than over a pint or a dram (or both) at the neighborhood watering hole, the pub. After spending more than three hours making a fool of yourself on the links, fighting gorse and gentle Scottish breezes (right!), many golfers find they need a pint to drown their sorrows or a dram to warm up their bones...or both!

Second, **why did we choose to concentrate on golf courses which we call hidden gems?** We have played often at the upscale courses in the States, like Hilton Head, Pinehurst, Marcos Island, and Kapalua, but we often find the more interesting courses are the unsung, unknown local courses. For example, a favorite of ours is the public course in Moab, Utah, the Moab Golf Club. It's a wonderful desert-style course where the deep green of the fairways contrasts with the surrounding red-rock canyon walls. This course won't make many "best course" lists in the mainstream golf media, yet it is full of interesting holes, beautiful vistas, it's inexpensive and uncrowded.   In short, a great golfing experience.   We found this true in Scotland as well.   As majestic as is the Gleneagles Kings Course, the Crieff Ferntower Course only twelve miles away can provide as satisfying a golfing experience at less than a fourth the price. The difference between the famous and the unknown courses is often the amount of their advertising budget and the non-golfing amenities they offer.

Acquaintances from our home club return from golf tours in Scotland and Ireland talking about the famous courses they played, or about the tour group members they played with. We come home talking about the fascinating golf we found and about the posties (postal workers) we played with at St Fillans, or about the late night round at Crieff Dornock when I was the only player on the course. Others come back with tales about the extravagant fees at Royal Turnberry, Troon, or Loch Lomand.   We come home extolling the enjoyable, inexpensive golf found all over Scotland.

As for pubs, Edinburgh and Glasgow have some lively, historic pubs which shouldn't be missed. For instance, the

Golf Tavern in Edinburgh looks out onto the links and has good English-style pub grub served in comfortable surroundings. Anne and I enjoyed a delicious courgette (baby zucchini) and Stilton soup at the Bad Ass Bistro next door to Dirty Dick's just off the Royal Mile. We enjoyed it, though, with hundreds of other tourists. Many of those visitors missed the opportunity to eat lunch at the more hidden Myrtle Inn outside of Callander with a lovely elderly woman who each day takes her one meal out at the inn.

Out of the way golf and pubs put us in touch with the real Scotland populated with real Scots. As Robert Frost said in "The Road Not Taken," "...that has made all the difference."

A third question fair to ask is, **what do we mean by hidden or out-of-the-way?** For golf courses there are easy answers. "Out-of-the-way" means a course that is not on the British Open Rota, one that doesn't require a tee time reserved a year in advance, or one that is not in a metropolitan area. Courses which are out-of-the-way include some famous courses like Royal Dornoch, Machrihanish, or Crail, as well as courses only locals know much about like Comrie or Dalmally. Out of the way pubs are even easier to define. If it's not in Edinburgh, Glasgow, Dundee, Aberdeen, or Inverness, then it's fair game for this book.

Next we should note **what we looked for in both pubs and golf courses.** With over 595 golf courses in Scotland (probably 450 or more fitting the description of out-of-the-way) and many times that number of pubs in Scotland, how did we select and deselect for this book?

In pubs we include only those we've visited in our Scotland travels. We include only those that have something positive to recommend them. We haven't found too many pubs we haven't enjoyed, but there were some, like one in Golspie, where we said, "Let's not bother to tell anyone about this one." We looked at several considerations when evaluating a pub for inclusion:

- Menu; breadth and uniqueness

- Libations; particularly numbers of beers, ales, and malt whiskies
- Atmosphere or style
- Service; friendliness and efficiency
- Wholesomeness; a general feeling of "would I bring my mother here"

[Note to the Second Edition: We have expanded our definition of pubs to include restaurants, cafes, tearooms, and coffee shops.]

For golf courses, again we stick to courses we've played during our first five years of visits and some we've played since *Hidden Gems II* was published. Though most courses have something to recommend them, we've played one or two we couldn't find enough good about. Again we designed a list of criteria:

- Quality of shots; both interest and playability
- Condition of the course
- Availability to visitors
- Beauty of the course and/or surroundings
- Cost and value for dollar

These criteria for pubs and golf courses had to add up to a place that both Anne and I, with our different perspectives, could recommend.

Now that you have an idea of the **WHY** and the **WHAT** of this book, a final question might relate to **HOW we gathered the information here presented.** Certainly, we haven't explored every corner of the country but we have covered quite a bit of ground, often more than once. We tried to visit different eateries and play different courses but often found we just had to return to a favorite. We couldn't possibly go to the Black Isle without a stop at Fortrose and Rosemarkie GC. Anytime we are in the West Linton area we stop by the Golden Arms, if not for dinner, then at least for a brew or a dram.

The question-asking and note-taking often meant we got strange looks from pub patrons, wait staff, or course attendants. Though we got quizzical expressions we never had an instance when we didn't enjoy full cooperation from business people. In several cases when I'd ask for information about a golf course, the professional, secretary, or club captain would give me a copy of the written history of the course (often published as centenary histories).

Now, with some of the questions out of the way, join us as we prepare for a brief tour of some of the hidden gems of Scottish golf courses and pubs.

CHAPTER TWO: Things You Need to Know about Scottish Golf, Pubs, Driving, and Touring

Southerness Golf Course

On our very first day in Scotland we ended up spending a couple of hours in downtown Glasgow's shopping district. After a long plane ride and hassles finding our first lodging, the first things we wanted was a drink and a snack other than airplane peanuts or pretzels. We stopped at the first pub we could find, took a seat in a booth, and sighed, "Our first Scottish pub!" Then we waited, and we waited. With, I'm sorry to say, typical American impatience we began to think we'd never get served. About that time we woke up from our travel-addled stupor enough to see that others were served when they went to the bar. Off I trundled and ordered drinks and a snack. Almost before I returned to the booth a waitress had brought our drinks. That was our first of many "I-wish-I'd-known-that-before" examples.

This chapter is dedicated to what we wish we'd known before our first trip.

GOLF

Golf isn't the same in Scotland as it is in America. It will help to understand some of the ways golf in Scotland may differ from golf at home. Here are some aspects of, for want of a better term, Scottish golf culture.

The Courses

1.To play golf you must find the courses. We've discovered several resources you should get to help you navigate the country looking for golf courses. Obviously, you need a good map or atlas. *Frommer's Road Atlas of Britain* (we took out England, Wales, and Northern Ireland) clearly describes routes and pinpoints golf courses. *Scotland A-Z: Visitor's Atlas and Guide* has also been a helpful reference. A more specialized resource is the *Official Guide to Golf in Scotland* (published yearly by VisitScotland) is available for free at almost any Tourist Information Centre. The guide has details about each course and some notes on directions

2. Course design and toilets are important, perhaps more important than directions to the course, especially if you're over fifty. Many eighteen hole courses, except the most modern, are out-and-back designs. The first nine holes play away from the clubhouse and the second nine play back to the clubhouse. This means that you cannot just play nine as you can on most courses in the States. Playing only nine would

put you at the furthest point away from the clubhouse. It also means that you best be well relieved before you begin your round or be prepared to answer nature's call in nature. Many Scottish courses, both nines and eighteens, lack toilet facilities on the course. At Pitlochry Golf Club there is a ladies' port-a-potty (port-a-loo to the Scots) on the tenth hole, but none for men. On the thirteenth at West Linton GC is a convenient stand of trees (with a path leading to the center) awaiting the needy golfer. I personally don't find anything wrong with the system or lack of it and Anne has adapted well, but it is an important detail to know if you're going to play in Scotland.

3. Perhaps the shortage of toilets forewarns the scarcity of drinking water as well. Many of us are used to water fountains or jugs of water spaced throughout our rounds. In Scotland water fountains are few and far between. Crieff Ferntower GC has drinking water between the ninth and tenth holes, but then it has toilets there too. Pitlochry GC has a pipe with water flowing out into a ditch. A metal cup there is chained to a post next to a sign which reads, "Drinking Water." I bet the water was straight out of a spring, but Anne wouldn't let me try it. I didn't argue. [Choose your battles.] Plan to carry water on most courses.

4. Don't expect to ride in carts (called "buggies") on Scottish courses. In Scotland golf is a walking sport. On several of the more well known courses, such as Royal Dornoch, buggies are only available with medical certification. Those courses which do have buggies may have a limited number available (St Fillans GC has only two buggies). In fact, a number of the smaller courses didn't even have pull carts (called "trolleys") for hire. Be prepared to carry your clubs if you want to play those courses. Thankfully for those not used to carrying, the weather is cooler in Scotland and it's usually the short nine-hole courses which don't have trolleys.

5. Another amenity hard to find on Scottish golf courses, especially the older courses, are yardage markers.

Some courses will mark at 150 yards to the green and some will have markers at 100 yards as well. Smaller courses may have no markers at all. Golf is a different game when every sprinkler head doesn't indicate the yardage. In Scotland you can either use a range finder or learn to judge distances by eye. Many 18-hole courses do now offer for sale Stroke Saver books ($3 to $5 each) with hole-by-hole descriptions. If the course has markers, be sure to check whether the markers indicate distance to the front or the middle of the green--it can easily mean a difference of two to three clubs on a hole.

6. Many of the courses you play in Scotland will be flat and easy to walk, especially links courses built on the land that links the sea to the land. Be prepared, though, for Scottish descriptors such as "undulating." Peebles GC is considered an undulating course, but it is a pretty stiff climb to the top, then it drops down and climbs back up again. Read "undulating" as "hilly," and at the "hilly" Pitlochry GC, the Switzerland of Scottish golf, consider renting a mountain goat to haul your clubs.

7. A fascinating feature of the old Scottish courses, especially the village nine-hole tracks, is that holes often cross over other holes. At Corrie GC on the Isle of Arran the first fairway crosses the second near the tee and the ninth near the green. We played several courses where we had to be aware of golfers on other crossing holes. Check a map of the course so that you are forewarned. I didn't pay enough attention at Whiting Bay GC and after teeing off on one hole walked right into the landing area for tee shots from another hole. The golfers yelled a warning at me and apologized, but it was I who should have apologized. Check the course carefully.

8. Finally, the courses in Scotland are categorized by the types of terrain over which they play. In the States most of our courses are designated as parkland or forest courses. In the Southwest we play on desert courses. What will you play

on in Scotland? We've noted and use as descriptors several different types of courses (briefly described):

Parkland: a mixture of pasture, meadows, and forest.
Linksland: played on and in the dunes next to the sea.
Moorland: a combination of tough grasses, heather, and gorse or whins.
Heathland: similar to moorland, but drier with more heather and often birch forest.
Clifftop or Seaside: played beside the sea, but usually on high plateaus with more parkland or moorland vegetation.
Inland: a combination of park, moor, and heath.

Playing the Course

1. Don't expect to always find a pro shop on the smaller courses. Most will have some sort of clubhouse or changing rooms, but amenities of a pro shop (golf balls, pencils, snacks, etc.) may not be available. Often no attendant is available to collect fees. Instead, you may find an "honesty box," a place in which you put fees before you go out to play the course. Scorecards are usually near the honesty box as well as sign-in sheets and tickets (receipts). At Tarbat GC near Tain in northern Scotland we couldn't find the honesty box in the office, but we did find a sign-in sheet and with it money from players ahead of us. We signed in, left our money, took a ticket and a scorecard, and went to play. After our round I visited with two locals on the first tee who asked if we'd found the honesty box all right. I said I hadn't. We both went into the open office and he showed me the box in the corner. I showed him the sign-in sheet, the money from the group ahead, our money, and money from a group behind still sitting on the office desk. Honesty Box: out-of-the-way Scotland, yes; in the US, I don't think it would work.

2. On the subject of paying and playing it may be important to note that many nine-hole courses offer only an all

day ticket price. For Anne and I it made nine holes at Innerleithen GC a little pricey (£20 or about $35 each). While we only had time for nine, that price was good for play all day. Eighteen or 36 holes for $35 is a decent price. The all day ticket is a very good deal if you can play more than one round, but not for only nine holes. Then, it is Scotland, and you are on vacation, and who else do you know who can say they've played Anstruther GC on Fife?

3. If you want to play some famous or famous out-of-the-way courses be prepared to show a handicap certificate. At Machrihanish, Royal Dornoch and North Berwick we were asked to prove we had handicaps of no more than 24 for men and 32 for ladies. Boat of Garten say they require a certificate, but they never asked for it. We take both our current USGA GHIN cards which show our Handicap Index and our membership card for our home club (though we've only used it once and that was in England--see Silloth on Solway GC). Be prepared.

4. It is a good idea as well to be prepared with plenty of ammunition. Gorse or whins eats golf balls (and hands and feet if you try to retrieve balls), heather eats balls, and so does most of the rough in Scotland. You'll find acres of gorse, whins, heather, and rough on the courses you'll play. The ocean seems to pluck balls out of the air--it doesn't seem to, it does! Be prepared to lose golf balls in more than your usual quantity. At one hole on Anstruther GC on Fife I launched two balls straight into the firth and bounced another off the fairway into the firth. I still think of it as a fantastic hole. Plan that you may lose two or three (for a low to mid-handicapper) balls per round. Those days you don't lose that many means more for the next round. Don't get cocky, though! I played the first sixteen holes at the tough Royal Dornoch with the same ball. On the 17th I thought I might make the whole round with same ball. Of course, that was the wrong way to think. I could swear that ball eating gorse bush just jumped into the middle

of the fairway to grab my ball. Golf balls are expensive in Scotland, so plan to bring plenty.

5. Speed of play is a concern for golfers everywhere. In the States five or six hour rounds are not unheard of, and four hour rounds seem to be the target. In Scotland that four hours is far too slow. We've seen Scots walk off the course because the round was approaching four hours. Anne, I, and Jacky (our B&B host) worked hard one day to stay ahead of two 75-year-old Scottish newlyweds who carrying their clubs. Scots also believe in the "honors" system. Quick play and honors may not seem compatible, but if you're ready to shoot when it's your turn, the round can move right along. Two other conditions may account for speedy play in Scotland. First, Scots play often as a two-ball (pairs or couples) without pairing up. A twosome can move more quickly than a foursome. Not as many players may be on the course, but those who are move faster. Second, when we've played with Scots the tendency is to give numerous putts. It made more sense when the handicap system used in Scotland was explained to me. Of most importance, the only scores used to calculate handicaps are scores in competitions. That means that the casual round (called a "bounce" round) is not considered an official round. The unintended effect is quicker play. Be careful when you come home though; after a month of Scottish golf we are much less tolerant of slow play at home.

6. Though golf won't be cheap in Scotland (especially considering the currency exchange rate), costs can be kept reasonable. Some courses offer special prices at twilight or after a certain time in the afternoon. Playing at those times can save 25-50 percent. Another way to save up to half your fees is to take advantage of various reduced-price offers. Certain regions offer special reduced fee passes for courses in the area. For instance, a *Borders' Freedom of the Fairways Passport* gives special three or five day golf breaks. Other areas have similar deals. On a wider scale, several two-for-

one schemes allow you to play many courses for half price. Green Fee Savers is one we've used for several years to get half priced golf in both Scotland and Ireland. Check on line or at participating golf clubs.

7. Finally, our most important suggestion is to play "vacation golf." By this we mean have fun, enjoy the golf and the surroundings, and don't get bothered about score or performance. One of my worst golfing days was at the lovely Boat of Garten GC in the Highlands. I played terribly--so badly, in fact, that I actually quit playing and just walked with Anne for a hole and a half, then dropped a ball and just chipped and putted. Whether from bad biorhythms or too much driving doesn't matter. I hated my golf, but I loved the course. I count Boat of Garten as one of my favorite courses. Whatever it takes to have fun is what we suggest you do: Take a mulligan (as long as it doesn't slow play), drop one instead of hunting through the heather, dismiss penalties for unknown hazards, etc.

What to Bring to Golf

1. Think about the golf clothes you'll want to bring. Shorts can probably be left at home no matter what time of year. It may be warm enough for shorts occasionally, but they are not a necessity. Rain clothes and umbrellas (*brollies*) are. If playing in the spring or fall, long john tops (maybe even bottoms) are not a bad idea; they're lightweight and layer well. I've often been thankful that I had two or three pieces of rainwear (two zip jackets and a pullover), a warm hat with ear flaps, and winter gloves. Rain gloves (which work best when wet) are a savior on many trips. Plan to play at 60 degrees in the sun, and at 40 degrees with 30 miles per hour wind and rain, all in one round. It helps if your golf clothes double as touring clothes as well.

2. There are ways to pack light on clubs, too. On some trips Anne and I will share one bag and each take six or seven

clubs and a putter. Sure, we get into situations where we are under or over-clubbed, but that's a fun challenge. Especially with current airline luggage charges, it can be easier and cheaper to take one golf bag. Another suggestion, made by golfer/analyst Johnny Miller, is to take your driver, putter, and one favorite club, and then rent. Sounds good, but be warned that some of the rental sets at small courses are in poor condition. However you do it, you can pack light and still play golf.

3. Finally, plan to take a camera (even a point-and-shoot throwaway). The Scottish courses and countryside are beautiful with sites on the courses (castles, ruins, standing stones, monuments, water fountains, etc.) that you won't see other places and will want to show your friends. Memory is cheap, so take plenty of pictures.

PUBS

A dramatic difference exists between the pubs of Scotland and the services they provide to the community and the taverns or bars in the States. For the most part, at least with pubs we'll be recommending, you can forget the image of a seedy dark bar with down-on-their-luck patrons huddled behind their cheap booze (B-grade movies help create wonderful images). These bars occur in Scotland but most of the town public houses (where the term "pubs" came from) are friendly establishments which serve as eating and meeting places, as well as drinking places. Here is some advice to help you enjoy your Scottish pub experiences: [Note to the 2nd Edition: For this edition we have included far more restaurants and tearooms than in the first edition. Pubs are still fun and pub food is improving, but tearooms, cafes, and restaurants expand eating options greatly.]

1. Don't expect typical American bar or restaurant service is a pub. You may get it, but more often than not you'll be expected to take care of yourself. Many establishments

will have menus sitting at the bar or posted on the wall. That's a clue that you may have to ask for service or put in your order at the bar. In most cases the meal or drinks will be brought to your table. At one pub, though, the drinks were simply bought to the closest part of the bar with the indication that I should pick them up. Whether a wait-staff is helping you or you are ordering at the bar, don't be afraid to ask for what you need (e.g.., sauces, water, etc.). We now have no problem with this system. We usually sit down to see what a particular pub will do, and then go with the flow. It is good to know that you can sit in a pub practically forever and no one will bother you.

2. When your food does come it will be Hot! All hot food is served really hot in Scotland, on hot plates. Plan on time for the food to cool, especially soup. This is not just microwaved (zapped) hot food slapped on a plate; it's hot food placed on an oven-heated plate. Perhaps it's because Scotland has a relatively cool climate, but whatever the reason, be prepared, food will be HOT!

3. Expect to be given ample settings of tableware. Silverware and serviettes (napkins) come with each course and then are taken away. To me it sometimes seems wasteful. I could use that fork and knife for a starter and the main course. In almost all cases the wait-staff will take it away and replace it with fresh. Don't be surprised or bothered by this.

4. While you will get plenty of silverware, you won't get much water or ice. Ask for a coke and you may get a can and a glass with no ice. Ask for a coke with ice and you may get a cube or two in the glass. In most areas in the States water is served with all restaurant meals. In Scotland you need to ask for tap water unless you want to pay for bottled. We get plenty of water when we ask for a jug of water. Our first trip to Scotland was our first trip out of the country, so we wanted to be prepared. I bought a heavy water jug with charcoal filter so we would be safe. Duh! Scotland is famous for its wonderful

water--the main ingredient in Scotch whisky. We never used the water jug (it's still tucked away in a closet someplace waiting for our trip to Africa). In Scotland we've never had any ill effects from the water or food. You have to ask for the water.

5. Expect both dogs and children in the pubs. These are family places and in most both dogs and children are welcome. We've never seen a discourteous dog in a pub; they've all been well-behaved. Some have belonged to the pub and others to patrons. We can't say we haven't seen ill-behaved children in pubs, but it is unusual. Fairly liberal laws govern when children can be in pubs. About the only incident that gnawed at me was when in a pub in Lamlash (Isle of Arran) I watched a boy of about eight get a pint for his dad. I had to remind myself that this is a different culture.

6. Three notes about food are in order. First, the daily or nightly specials at a pub are often the best bet for quality and price. Most of the time we've been very pleased with what was listed as the "special." Secondly, the quantity of food in Scotland's pubs is such that you can often get away with just ordering two starters. But if you do, be sure you specify that you want them as starters and not main entrees. In one hotel pub (not one we recommend in this book) I ordered soup and another starter. I ended up being charged for the second starter as a main because I could have shared the potatoes and veg that came on the side with Anne's main course. Be specific. Third, also be specific if you plan to share something. At the Byre Bistro in Kenmore (a very pleasant pub which is no more) we ordered the pate´ starter. We each got our own starter. To be clear we needed to say that we wanted to share one pate´ starter.

7. If you enjoy *Uisge Beatha*, the Water of Life, Scotch whisky, we have a suggestion that might add to your pub visits. At different places we'll ask the barkeep to select a whisky for us--maybe his favorite or one representative of the area. It's a good way to start a conversation and it has yielded

interesting results. About half the time we've done this we've been given Highland Park by the barkeep. If you want a little adventure and you can see the pub has a good selection of single malts, try it.

8. Lastly, we offer some advice on tipping. Many guidebooks say it isn't necessary or expected. This is changing. In a pub where you basically serve yourself, no tips are necessary. After talking to many wait-staff, though, we found that tips are becoming a more important part of their income. For limited service, a pound on the table may be enough. In a pub or restaurant with full service fifteen percent of the bill should be left as a tip. It may be a sign that some of Scotland's quaintness is vanishing.

DRIVING

To find the hidden gems of golf and pubs you will have to drive. That means the steering wheel will be on the right-hand side of the car, the rearview mirror is to the driver's left, the cars are coming at you from what you perceive to be the wrong side. In our trips to Scotland I've driven more than 70,000 miles in rental cars. In that time I've hit bushes on the left a couple of times, hit one fence at a corner (no damage to the car or the fence), and scared passengers or myself only a few times. I did fold up an outside mirror by scraping a rock bridge in Ireland, but driving in Ireland is a completely different experience. These experiences have led us to offer some advice that we wish we'd had heeded before first driving in Scotland.

1. Obviously, drive on the left. Don't think of it as the "wrong side," but as the "other side." Driving on the left has a major implication: Look Right! One of the harder ideas to grasp when walking or driving is that you must look to the right because that's where the traffic will be. I like the Glasgow airport's approach which marks all crosswalks, "Look Right."

2. When parking pay attention to the lines on the side of the road. Double lines means no parking and single lines mean limited parking. Other than that, anything goes. You'll see cars parked both directions on both sides of the street. In some places you'll see cars parked on the sidewalk. The system makes sense. Why let a parking space go to waste simply because it's on the other side of the street? Take it, but then remember to drive on the left.

3. Scots will park on both sides of a road and they will stop any place they want. I have passed up many fine photo opportunities because I couldn't get myself simply stop the car unless there was a pullout. We approached one car stopped in our lane on a narrow two lane road as its driver read a map. I waited until the road ahead was clear and then pulled around. It's really not a problem, just not our usual way.

4. Plan on paying significantly more for gasoline (petrol). Petrol is far more expensive in the UK than in the States. I'm not very good at converting litres to gallons, but I figure we've paid between $6.00 and $10.00 a gallon depending upon the current exchange rate. Believe me, when we get home we don't complain about our gas prices for a long while.

5. Plan more time than you think to drive from one place to another. The roads in Scotland, though superior to Ireland's, are still small and narrow without much room at the edges. Twenty miles of back roads in America may take only twenty minutes. In Scotland twenty miles of back roads may take you thirty or forty minutes. Plan accordingly.

6. Learn to love traffic circles or roundabouts. We are starting to see this type of traffic control system in the Sates, but it is well in use in Scotland. Instead of approaching a corner with cross traffic, you'll come to a circular road usually around a small island. Traffic enters the circle from the right and exits left onto roads coming off the circle. Three to five

roads may spoke off the roundabout. Your jobs are to enter the circle without disturbing the flow of traffic and exit onto the proper road. Most of the time stop signs are not present where you enter but you are expected to yield to traffic from the right. Remember, you're going left around the circle. After you've driven through a few roundabouts they make more sense. I find they are very efficient. It did take Anne (the navigator) and me (the driver) a while to agree on how to give directions. At first Anne would say to turn right towards such-and-such. She would be reading the map and seeing the turns as right off the circle, but in reality all the exits are left. Finally, we agreed that she would direct me to "take the second road" or "the second left." Traffic circles are scary at first, but with use will come comfort. Besides, one of the beauties of roundabouts is if you don't take your turn the first time, just go around the circle again.

7. Lastly, when you find yourself driving on single-track roads follow the proper etiquette when passing oncoming vehicles. The car nearest the pullout or passing place gives way. If the pullout is on your side (the left) pull into it and stop until the other car passes. If the pullout is on the other side (the right) but you are closest, stay on your side and stop across from the center of the pullout and let the other car use it to get around you.

I feel quite comfortable now driving in Scotland. It only takes a few minutes on their roads to be comfortable again. I find that the Scottish drivers are courteous, even if they do drive very fast. One final trick: Have your navigator hold the map up high enough so all the locals know you're a tourist. They'll forgive a lot.

[Note to the New Edition: Bringing a UK compatible GPS or renting one from the car rental company makes driving in Scotland much easier. All the golf courses we list in the book include the six digit post code which is all you have to input into the GPS to get directions to the courses. As useful as GPSs are, it is still a good idea to have a good road atlas.]

TOURING

Whether golf is your primary reason to visit Scotland or a sidelight you will most probably do "that tourist thing." We offer a couple of hints to aid you as you tour the many sights of Scotland.

1. The **National Trust for Scotland (NTS)** and **Historic Scotland (HS)** are two umbrella trusts working to preserve Scotland's places and buildings of historic significance. Battlefields, castles, nature preserves, gardens, and buildings of historic importance are a few of the sights maintained. To pay for the work of restoring and maintaining these antiquities a small admission is often charged. Make use of the National Trust and Historic Scotland bargain tickets. When you visit your first site maintained by NTS or HS you may choose to buy a limited membership (usually three-day, seven-day, or 14-day) or a yearly membership. These memberships allow you entrance into all the sites under the auspices of that organization. If you intend to visit several of the sites maintained by that group, the price of the membership will pay for itself. Also note that your NTS or HS membership may be good for entrance into sites in England, Wales, and Northern Ireland Be aware, though, some of the most popular facilities (Glamis Castle, for example) are privately maintained; your trust memberships won't help you at these.

2. As I mentioned in the Introduction, the Scottish Tourist Information Bureau ("The I"), located in almost every village of size is a great resource for the traveler. Here you can book lodging for a small fee, get loads of free information about the country or region, buy maps and books, get postcards and stamps, and ask for directions. The staff is always friendly and helpful. Almost all maps will designate

which villages or towns have an "I." For the golfer, be sure to pick up the yearly *Official Guide to Golf in Scotland*.

3. With ATMs on almost every corner (only a slight exaggeration), it's not necessary to take a large amount of cash (British pounds) with you.   Credit cards are almost universally accepted, with the exception of small B&Bs and really small golf courses.   VISA is the most accepted card, followed by Master Card, with others not as popular.   If you plan to rely on credit cards we have an additional hint from our experiences. In our first trips to both Scotland and Ireland we had a bank put a hold on our card. Not because we exceeded any credit limits, but because we weren't making our normal purchases.   We now know to call our credit card companies ahead and let them know when and where we'll be traveling. On vacation you really don't need the frustration of funds suddenly drying up--unless you overspend, and then you deserve it.

With these hints about golf, pubs, driving, and touring in mind, let's now go to Scotland.

Chapter 3: Central Scotland around Crieff

Crieff Ferntower Golf Course

The Old Course at St Andrews is recognized as the Home of Golf. The King's and Queen's courses at Gleneagles may be golf's royalty. Prestwick, Royal Troon, and Turnberry represent golf's heritage, but the gems of Scotland golf, the diamonds, sapphires, and rubies have names like Fortrose and Rosemarkie, Boat of Garten, Shiskine, Killin, Crail, and Crieff. While the world may recognize and honor the grand courses of Scottish golf, golfers would be remiss if they didn't seek out the gems hidden in almost every small community in

Scotland. Here, on these little known and mostly unacknowledged courses, visitors will find scenic beauty, interesting holes, challenging tests, friendly and accommodating staff, eminently fair prices, and, unlike the big name clubs, Scots on the courses.

Perfect examples of Scotland's out of the way golf gems are available nearby the central Scotland community of Crieff. We start our tour of Scotland's hidden gems of golf at a course next door to the famous Gleneagles Resort, host of the 2014 Ryder Cup competition.

AUCHTERARDER GOLF COURSE
The Clubhouse, Orchil Road, Auchterarder, Perthshire
    PH3 1LS
www.auchterardergolf.co.uk 01764-662804
Parkland, 5750 yards, par 69, £30

AMENITIES: Comfortable clubhouse serves a good Guinness after a round--the food is good also. Well stocked golf shop.

COURSE COMMENTS: Auchterarder (meaning "summit of rising ground") GC is a 1913 Ben Sayers 9-hole design which was expanded to 18 in 1979. The parkland course is next to the Gleneagles Resort complex and plays partially next to the PGA Centenary course. The course is mostly flat with only slight elevation changes. None of the numerous bunkers are too severe, but most are strategically placed to be bothersome. The course is an enjoyable track, even for a competition, with fair challenges. The demands of the course, though, start with the well-named first, *Deil's Dyke*. This 376-yard par 4 is nothing spectacular except that on your first shot of the round you must drive between two stands of mature trees and over a stone fence (Devil's Dyke) about eighty yards out. Many a competitive round has been ruined by a wayward first shot bouncing off the trees or the dyke. The 11th, *Roon an Roon*, a 331-yard par 4 is a fun challenge. A sharp dogleg right starts this short hole with a large stand of trees intruding if you try to cut the corner. Trees and a small burn are there if you hit through the fairway. The green is nestled back right. An intimidating hole is *Punch Bowl*, the 205-yard par 3 fourteenth. A large bunker sits right in front of the bowl-shaped green which is very receptive, if you miss the bunker. The course can be busy, but at £30 a rounds, its good value golf.

COMMENTS FROM THE FORWARD TEES: Auchterarder Golf Course is a very playable course, easy to walk, with great visual appeal, and it is a course one can score well on. There are still many challenges, including trees and more trees, bunkers, some water, hills and some slopes. The course is not too long at 5093 yards long with a par of 70. Three of the four par 5s are over 400 yards. The 6th is the shortest par 5. It plays uphill to a fairway which slopes off both sides, jogs right and back at the approach to an elevated green, and is surrounded by three bunkers. The 10th is the same yardage as the 6th but is flat, wide, and straight ahead. There are five par 3s of reasonable lengths with the exception of the 16th which is 182 yards--it's a good challenging hole. We always have this on our list of courses to play if time and weather permits.

ARBROATH GOLF CLUB
Elliot, by Arbroath, Angus DD11 2PE
www.arbroathgolfcourse.co.uk 01241-875837
Links, 5826 yards, par 68, £35

AMENITIES: Clubhouse lounge looks out to the 18th green and serves light meals all day. Nice fully-stocked golf shop is run by PGA pro J. Linsay Ewart.

COURSE COMMENTS: This busy seaside links course has a great pedigree. Designed originally by Old Tom Morris in 1877, the 18-hole course was updated by Troon pro Willie Fernie in 1907. Then in 1931 the famous James Braid was asked to do a redesign. It is the Braid course that you play today. Dunes run the length of the course on the seaward side which means the wind will always be a factor of play. Beside the sea breezes there are more than 70 bunkers in play and the Braid fairway bunkers are penal. Some of the grenade bunkers are deep as well. Greens are moderate size and fairly flat, except near the grenade bunkers. Arbroath has one double green (2nd and 15th). The course has ten burn crossings—several are difficult to see, so check the maps at the tees. A word of caution: the course is not friendly to slicers. There are some pleasant views of the town of Arbroath south of the course.

We loved playing on the Arbroath links and would highlight several holes. The 3rd, *The Dennie*, is a 334-yard par 4. Drive to a fairway narrowed by heavy rough left and farm (OB) right. The approach to the green is made trickier by three bunkers front, left, and right. Stroke index #1 is the 5th. *Mains of Kelly*, a 389-yard par 4, has three bunkers on the left to bother drives. A burn crosses the fairway about 70 yards from a green guarded by traps right and left. A fine par 3 is the 7th, *Corse Hill* at 155 yards. It should be easy as stroke index #17, but three bunkers at the green make the first shot tough. On the back we were drawn to the 13th, *Dowrie*, a 368-yard par 4. With the rail line all down the right (OB) you must stay left with your drive. The second shot will be over (hopefully) the burn which crosses the fairway. Large bunkers on both sides guard the green. Next is *The Secretary* (a memorial hole to an earlier club secretary). This 200-yarder, besides being long, three bunkers guard the green making this a tough hole. The club considers this their signature hole. The 16th, *The Dunes*, is another nice par 3. At 151-yards it is listed as the easiest hole on the course, but with five bunkers around the green it's not that easy. In an area rich in fine golf courses (Carnoustie, Panmure, Montrose), Arbroath GC is definitely a course to add to your itinerary.

FROM THE FORWARD TEES: This is a fun links course on the North Sea which has all the usual links characteristics—hit down the middle and it will roll wherever, many bunkers, short approaches can be putted, ten water crossings. A Stroke Saver or course guide is really a "shot saver" on this course. With a par of 71 the yardage is 5384 yards with three par 5s and four par 3s. The 5th requires some planning so that your approach shot misses the water and the 16th can be very difficult if you miss the green. What's not to like on a good links course—especially on a sunny day.

ALLOA GOLF COURSE (SCHAWPARK)
Sauchie, Alloa FK10 3AX
www.alloagolfclub.co.uk   01259-724476
Parkland, 6200 yards, par 70, £28

AMENITIES: Downstairs lounge and upstairs restaurant have views of the first tee. Good food served all day--open to the public. Golf shop has an excellent selection of equipment.

COURSE COMMENTS: The Alloa Golf Club was established in 1891 and the Schawpark course was designed by famed architect James Braid in 1935. The course you play today has been continuously updated but has essentially remained true to Braid's design.   The lovely tree-lined Schawpark course plays over gently rolling hills beneath the Ochill range of hills. The course is very typical of Braid's style of bunkering with several fore-bunkers and many of the 40 mixed greenside and fairway traps fairly penal.   The well conditioned greens are on the small side with interesting slopes and subtle borrows. There are three ditches to cross, but none are cause for concern, except perhaps the one on the 17th.   Schawpark is characterized by several blind tee shots and a few blind approach shots, but all are well marked. Another characteristic of the club is its friendly members; we felt very welcome when we played. Several holes stand out in our notes on the course. The 1st, *Witch's Well*, a 321-yard par 4, is a good start over a rise to a small green guarded by one trap right. It's an easy start but don't get into the trees that line the fairway.   A fine short par 4 is the 306-yard 3rd called *Quarry*. Drive to the right because the fairway slopes left and drops down near the green.   Bunkers on each side of the green keep you honest. Good chance for a birdie. *Craigbank*, the 371-yard par 4 eighth starts with a tight drive on a slight dogleg right around a prominent tree. The approach is complicated by a Braid fore-bunker about 60 yards from the green. Again two bunkers guard the green. At the 11th, *Deil's Gate*, another blind drive starts the 344-yard par 4. Aim for the post because a good drive is important as five bunkers surround the green. A good one-shotter is *Seven Sisters*, the 170-yard 15th. Drive to an elevated green over a small burn (shouldn't be any problem). Three bunkers front and right and one more left make the green a small target. *Pond's Wood* is the 460-yard par 4 seventeenth. This long, slight dogleg left (near the green) is a tough hole. Long, playing into the wind, and a small ditch in front of the green is what makes the hole hard. Thankfully, there is a saving bunker behind the green. Schawpark is a fun course and one to which we will returning soon.

COMMENTS FROM THE FORWARD TEES: A great walk in the woods best describes this lovely course. It is on the old Schaw family estate. Maureen Mitchell, Ladies Capt. in 2011, told me as we approached the 12th fairway that this spot originally was the tennis courts for the estate. We both spent just a moment imagining the ladies in the 18th century in their long dresses having a tennis match on this site. The fairways are wide and have long runs up and down hills making the course an easy invigorating walk. The greens often run away at the back or are perched on a knoll requiring precision on the approach. The course has a par 73 for ladies with three par 5s on the front and two on the back that range from 394 to 459 yards. Par 3s range from 100 to 155. This is a beautiful challenging course.

BRAEHEAD GOLF COURSE
Cambus, by Alloa, Clackmannanshire FK10 2NT
www.braeheadgolfclub.co.uk 01259-725766
Parkland undulating, 5682 yards, par 68, £30

AMENITIES: Large pleasant lounge in clubhouse. Serves from 11:30—breakfasts, snacks, lunches, full meals, and special Sunday carvery. Nice golf shop with both clothes and clubs.

COURSE COMMENTS: *Brae* in lowland Scottish means "brow of a hill." That name fits this course which was originally designed as a nine-hole course in 1891. The course was redesigned two fields away in 1923 and then later extended to 18. The course you play today is a lovely tree-lined course with some very large old trees. Besides the trees, the hills will affect play. Although the course is not steep, there are long uphill stretches and about half the holes have significant sidehill lies. It's a good course to take an electric trolley. There are more than 35 bunkers, mostly greenside, in play and a couple are fairly steep-sided. Greens are large and several are tiered or significantly scaled. A couple of ditches crossing will affect play, especially on 13 and 16. Try to play in the dry as the course tends to not handle the wet well.

The interesting holes at Braehead start with the 1st, *Newbiggin*, a 312-yard par 4. A fairly blind dogleg left start to your round. Drive about 200 yards staying toward the right, but avoid the bunker on the outside of the turn. Being too far left means a large tree will be in the way of your approach to a green protected by bunkers on both sides. Another good short hole is *Lornshill*, the 311-yard par 4 fifth. The hole climbs to your first good views. The green can't be seen for the first 125 yards and the fairway has trees right and a stone fence left. The green is protected by one bunker on the right. Some of the best views from the course are on the green here. On *Sir James*, the 141-yard par 3 eighth, you hit from an elevated tee to a plateau green with a large gully in front. Long is better than short, and the green is surrounded by three traps. The inward nine starts with *Dunmar*, the stroke index number one hole. This 448-yard par 4 is a long bend left, down and then up. A lovely large tree is trouble on your second or third shot if you are coming in from the left. The green has plenty of tricky pin placements, so the hole needs no bunkers. A long tricky downhill one-shotted is *Burn*, the 16th at 217 yards. A burn (duh!) crosses the fairway about 25 years in front of the green

—be strong or lay back. The large green is protected by two bunkers right and one left. As you play, pay attention to the groups in front of you because there are some tricky spots where the routing isn't clear.

FROM THE FORWARD TEES: This is a big parkland course with lovely views, but it it is hillier than it looks at first. The course plays up and around the right side of the hill which results in many holes sloping to the right. The yardage is fairly long (5483 yards) but the par is 73. The par 5s are long—the 7th is 450 yards uphill and the downhill 12th is 508 yards. Par 3s are short but often quite tricky. The 8th, for example is 146 yards down and then up. The green sits on a small hill with steep sides and a grassy ditch in front. The course is a difficult walk with challenging holes and some great views of the area.

BRECHIN GOLF & SQUASH CLUB
Trinity, Brechin, Angus DD9 7PD
www.brechingolfclub.co.uk 01356-625270
Parkland, 6162 yards, par 72, £32

AMENITIES: The larger, refurbished clubhouse which opened in 2003 has a pleasant lounge with views onto the course. Serves good food all day. The club has a very complete golf shop run by pro Stephen Rennie.

COURSE COMMENTS: Built in 1893 the Brechin Golf Course was improved by James Braid in 1926 and then had a major overhaul in 1993 by John Farrell. The course is a lovely tree-lined track with views of the surrounding farms and hills. The course can be quite windy as we found out on the early September day we played--30 to 40 miles per hour gusts. Sixty-one moderate to penal bunkers protect all the holes. Water is in play at the right of the second and two ponds guard the right side of the third. The greens are well conditioned, speedy with significant breaks not always easy to see. It is also important to note that the course has several dramatic doglegs and you cross over a major highway by a foot bridge twice (not in play).

The second hole is interestingly named *Bruce's Bounty* because of all the balls which slice over the trees into a field of a farmer named Bruce. A fine par 3 is the 129- yard 3rd called *Cowie's Hill.* This tricky one-shotter has a two-tiered green guarded front and left by two bunkers and front and right by two ponds. Take plenty of club here. *Wee Well* is the 344 yard par 4 eighth. The hole is a dogleg left through a gap in the trees. Big hitters can try to go over the trees, but the safe approach is to try to play through the gap which leaves a wedge to a small sloped green. On the back I liked the 12th, *Peter Manson*, a par 3 of 201 yards from the members' tees. A large wide ditch in front of the green makes this hole tough. Bunkers at green level on each side add to the difficulty. The hard 12th is followed by another long 205-yard par 3, but this time there is less trouble. The finishing hole, *Jock's Tee*, is a 316-yard two-shotter. The dogleg right starts with a blind drive. Two fairway bunkers not in view from the tee can grab good drives. The green is protected by bunkers on each side and is tiered. Brechin is a lovely course and fits well with other courses in the area, such as Edzell and Forfar.

COMMENTS FROM THE FORWARD TEES: This golf course has more variety than it seems when you drive into parking lot. It looks very flat and rather back and forth, but isn't at all. A layout map will show you that it is divided into 4 sections as it criss-crossed the road and highway. It has some hills and many trees and also has a few very open flat holes. The variety makes it very interesting and exciting to play. For me part of the charm of this course was playing with two senior members, Les and George. These charming friendly men were such gentlemen that they insisted I ride in the buggy on the uphill walks. So much for burning up the calories of the famous Scottish breakfasts. The course has a par of 72 and is well designed for ladies. There are four par 5's with the 14th being the longest a 447 yards. The par 3s on the first nine are short but have water, bunkers, and uphill challenges. The two on the back are much longer and distance will be the biggest test on these. I am anxious to play this course again.

CHAMPIONSHIP Course

CARNOUSTIE, BURNSIDE LINKS
Links Parade, Carnoustie DD7 7JF
www.carnoustiegolflinks.co.uk 01241-802270
Links, 6028 yards, par 68, £40

AMENITIES: The Carnoustie Hotel, Caledonian Club, and Carnoustie Club each have lounges which serve drinks and food. The Championship and Buddon Clubhouse has a golf shop with tons of souvenirs (not much equipment). Another private shop is across the street. The Burnside Course starter house has a few essentials.

COURSE COMMENTS: Built in 1892 as a 9-hole relief course for the Championship Links, the Burnside Course was extended to 18-holes in 1914. While not the challenge the Championship is, Burnisde is quite enjoyable from the members' tees and testing from the back tees. Forty-seven fairway and greenside bunkers, many penal, call for accurate shotmaking. Three holes have no bunkers. The Barry Burn is in play on four holes and is a serious challenge on the 5th and 17th. Greens are moderate to large with sufficient undulations (without being extreme) to keep you on your toes. Even after a bad spring the greens were in excellent condition. Besides the burn and bunkers, wind and gorse are the main challenges at Burnside. There's much to like about Burnside Links starting with the par 3, 161-yard, 3rd hole called *Fence*. This is a challenging one-shotter with three bunkers, two to the right and one directly in front, protecting green. The tee shot is over a burn, but it is not much of a problem. The green has interesting borrows. *Camp*, is the short 299-yard par 4 sixth. The hole is a dogleg right with five traps on the inside turn and gorse on the outside. A good drive leaves a short iron to a generous green. Next is a par 4 of 346-yards called *Shelter*. The tee shot is narrow with trees left and a bunker about 190 yards out. Stay to the right to have an open shot to the large green guarded on both sides by bunkers. Another good short par 4 is the 10th, *Kopje*. The 283-yard hole begins with a blind drive --aim for the pole. The green has only one small bunker on the right and is one of the flattest on the course. A real birdie opportunity. The 13th is a 359-yard par 4 called *Punchbowl*. Three bunkers, one left and two right, can bother your drive, but it is the blind approach which is more demanding. One bunker front left of the green adds to the challenge. A great two-shotter is *Sinkies*, the 438-yard par 4 seventeenth. Long hitters can try to reach in two with a good drive close to the first burn crossing at about 250 yards from the tee. The prudent play for most is to lay up short of both the first and second burn crossings, the last at about 25 yards in front of the green. No bunkers are needed on this hole. The Carnoustie Championship Course is on everyone's list of Must Play courses, but a chance to play the Burnside Course should not be missed.

FROM THE FORWARD TEES: A very enjoyable links course on a point of land at the convergence of Firth of Tay and the North Sea. It is often windy here as it was the day we played. The course is very playable for all. With the Championship course weaving through and around the Burnside it was sometimes a bit of work to decide where the next flag was, but the course is well signed. The burn and many bunkers provide most challenges, but the links bounces can also set one up in a difficult position. The course is a reasonable length at 5400 yards and has par of 71. There are five par 3s ranging from 127 to 168 yards. The 168 yard par three 14th wasn't as difficult for me as the 9th (127 yards) which was a steep hill with the green situated on top. The par 5s are all over 400 yards, but if you can place the ball in the fairway and get some good roll they can be quite playable. A wonderful day of golf can be had here anytime.

COMRIE GOLF COURSE
Laggan Braes, Comrie, Perthshire PH6 2LR
www.comriegolf.co.uk 01764-670055
Parkland/heathland, 3008 yards (9 holes), par 35, £12

AMENITIES: New comfortable clubhouse is open from 9:00 AM in season and serves snacks and light meals. No golf shop.

COURSE COMMENTS: The scenic Highland Comrie GC climbs for three holes, plays across the top before coming down. The 1891 designed course affords a good view of the Lord Melville Monument nearby. The few bunkers on the course will be troublesome, but the main challenges will be the trees and the rough if you stray off the fairways. Although the course plays in the hills, it is relatively easy to walk. The 3rd, *Quarry*, is a 174-yard par 3 with a tee shot over an old quarry to an elevated green. Miss the green and you can find a big number when you find your ball. I like the 6th called *Monument*. The only par 5 on the course, this 493-yarder plays at the top of the course. The tee shot is down to a moderate fairway and the second is a layup to an opening in the trees and the green beyond. It's a lovely strategic hole on a fine small course.

CRIEFF GOLF CLUB, FERNTOWER COURSE
Perth Road, Crieff PH7 3LR
www.crieffgolf.co.uk 01764-652397
Parkland, 6427 yards, par 71, £30

AMENITIES: Beautiful clubhouse with a great view of the 18th hole. The food is excellent and the lounge is always busy. The separate golf shop, run by PGA professional David Murchty, is one of the best in the area.

COURSE COMMENTS: Old Tom Morris designed the original 9-hole Crieff GC in 1891. James Braid redesigned the course seven years later, and most of this course plays now as the Dornock 9-hole course. The big course, and it is big, was laid out in 1980 and is the course you play as the Ferntower. The fine parkland layout climbs slowly to the top at 14 from where there are great vistas out over Strathearn (the Valley of the River Earn). Some say it's possible to see the Gleneagles Resort complex from the top of the Ferntower course. The holes are well protected by both fairway and greenside bunkers--a few are quite penal. Trees sparsely line all the holes, but they can be bothersome. The biggest challenge of the Ferntower course is the length of the holes. The actual length of the holes may not be extreme, but several of the longer holes play with side sloping fairways so that balls tend to hit and bound down the slope rather than forward. Two good shots on par 4s can still leave a long wedge or more to the green.

The Ferntower layout is classic golf with demanding tee and approach shots. The start, an uphill par 3, is a common feature in Scotland with Peebles and Carnwath's starts coming to mind. The second has a feature you won't find on American courses. About 180 yards out on the right on the downhill par 4 is a set of ancient standing stones known as the Druid Stones. The 7th, *Old Fifteenth*, is one of those long tough par 4s. The 454-yard hole is downhill, but the left sloping fairway takes away significant distance off your shots. Three fairway bunkers and two greenside complicate the hole. The flat green is a welcome relief. On the back the combination of 14 and 15 are impressive. Fourteen, *Ferny Den*, is the top of the course and is a challenging 353-yard two-shotter where you hit from an elevated tee down and then up to an elevated narrow green with bunkers on the downhill side and heavy rough on the up side. A visually enticing challenge. Scary is the next hole, the 377-yard par 4 called *Heather Bank*. The tee shot is a steeply downhill dogleg right with tall trees on the inside and a large bunker straight ahead. A good tee shot will still leave a tight approach between two greenside bunkers. There isn't a weak hole on the Ferntower course. Even the 18th, a 303-yard straight ahead par 4 rated as third easiest can eat your lunch. For some reason I have worked so hard at avoiding the two bunkers on the right that I've pulled my last three tee shots out of bounds on the left. Next round I'm going to tee off with a wedge just to stay in play. The Crieff Ferntower course is always an enjoyable round.

COMMENTS FROM THE FORWARD TEES: Ladies will discover Crieff Ferntower is a fair challenge with slopes, downhill lies, and a gentle climb up the side of the knock.

Ladies tees do not give much advantage over visitor men's tees and the course is long especially compared to other Scottish courses. The challenges last through all eighteen holes. I have played this course many times and am always willing to try again, and especially with a dram in the clubhouse afterwards.

CRIEFF GOLF CLUB, DORNOCK COURSE
Parkland, 2119 yards, par 32, £12

COURSE COMMENTS: Sharing all the amenities of the Ferntower course is the 9-hole Crieff Dornock course. It may be a practice course or a relief course for the Ferntower, but it is a worthy track in it's own right. With the Old Tom Morris/James Braid pedigree, the Dornock course will present some interesting challenges including long par 3s, elevation changes, bunkers, and a pond. If you can't get on or don't have time for the Ferntower course, don't pass up a chance to play this short gem.

GLENBERVIE GOLF COURSE
Stirling Road, Larbert FK5 4SJ
www.glenberviegolfclub.com 01324-562725
Parkland, 6438 yards, par 71, £35

AMENITIES: The clubhouse has three lounges and one dining room and serves good food, but only to members and visiting golfers. Pro Steven Rosie runs a very complete golf shop. The course has a full-sized driving range with excellent teaching facilities.
COURSE COMMENTS: Glenbervie is a fine parkland track designed by James Braid in 1932. The course is the home course of Scottish professional and three time Ryder Cup player John Panton ('51, '53, and '61). A quiet course, Glenbervie is a beautiful tree-lined challenge over rolling hills (never a hard walk). In clear weather there are great views of the surrounding hills, and in any weather the course is still lovely with over 100 species of trees and numerous planted

areas. More than 60 typical Braid bunkers are strategically placed in play, none easy to get out of. The mostly moderate sized greens seem relatively flat, but subtle slopes mean you won't have many truly straight putts. A couple of the greens are tiered and all are well-conditioned. As you play you will face six burn crossings, but only a couple affect shots. One small pond on 12 affects lay-up shots short of the burn. Trees, lovely as they are, will be a major condition of play.

Glenbervie has numerous holes we like, starting with *The Manor*, the 326-yard par 4 third. Tee off down towards a burn 130 yards out. The shot is complicated by two fairway bunkers on the left. The fairway doglegs left and rises slightly towards a small green protected by three bunkers. A slight dogleg right with a double crossing of a burn near the tee box begins the 5th *Ben Cleugh*, a 390-yard par 4. A fore-bunker makes the approach difficult to one of the more sloped greens protected by two more traps. A fun one-shotter is the 7th, *Auchengaw*, which is 211 yards from the medal tees and 179 from the member tees. A bank to the left keeps you straight to a flat, raised green protected by three traps. Straight shots will be rewarded. Stay to the right of the gnarled oak 190 yards out on *The Well*, the 423-yard par 4 twelfth, but watch out for two bunkers on the right. You must cross a burn 90 yards from smallish green with trees left and a bunker right. A fine par 3 is the 19-yard 13th called *Treetops*. The drive is tight between trees to a raised kidney-shaped green with one bunker right and another left. Could be a birdie, if you don't miss your six-foot putt like I did. The 14th hole, *Braid's*, heads back to the clubhouse--we watched several locals end their round at 14 holes. The par four 409-yard hole is long, straight, and slightly uphill with only one fairway bunker. The large green has three levels and is tricky to putt. Classy golf hole. *Joug Tree*, the 507-yard par 5 fifteenth is straight with large, beautiful trees scattered the length to create problems. Your approach must avoid five traps to find a two-tiered green. It's important to note that the green on the 18th is severe enough to be pivotal to many matches. Glenverbie GC is very welcoming to visitors (except on weekends, which are reserved for members) and should be on more people's play list.

COMMENTS FROM THE FORWARD TEES: This is a visually appealing course with wide fairways and over a hundred varieties of trees lining the holes. There are many rolling hills but none will tire your out, they only add interest to this golfing experience. Besides the tree's, there is a burn to cross, doglegs, bunkers, hills and slopes on this course to test your golf. The par 5's are at or over 400 yards. Par 3's are not extremely long, but getting to the green through narrow gaps and between bunkers was never easy. One of the things I like best about this course is that if you miss the fairway and get in trouble in the trees you often find you still have a shot. This course is very playable for women.

GLENISLA GOLF COURSE
Pitrocknie, Alyth, Perthshire PH11 8JJ
www.golf-glenisla.co.uk 01828-632445
Parkland, 6402 yards, par 71, £29

AMENITIES: There is a lovely unique circular glass upstairs lounge in the clubhouse where they serve food during the day and weekend evenings. Grand views of several tees and greens. The small golf shop has all the essentials.

COURSE COMMENTS: The relatively new parkland track is the design work of Tony Wardle, who worked with Robert Trent Jones and Jack Nicklaus. The course is a big hitters course, wide open (it will tighten up a little as the trees grow), with gentle rises and drops. Forty-six bunkers, none too penal thankfully, will challenge your accuracy, but it's a fine sand if you do visit. Six holes have water in play as five ponds and two burns. The greens are large with interesting slopes and contours. When we played they putted very true. The rough is hard to hit out of even though it looks benign. The view of the surrounding hills is lovely, and as we played a spring round we counted six or eight different song birds on the course, and heard a cuckoo's call. Also in the spring a couple of Oyster Catchers nest near the clubhouse and have been known to dive bomb players who came too close to the nest. Local players watch the progress of the yearly brood. When we pulled into the parking lot we noticed that most of the cars had their windscreen wiper blades raised off the windscreen. We didn't know the reason, but followed the pattern and then asked. The secretary of the club told us that the wiper blades are raised so that a couple of local crows, nicknamed Osama and Bin Laden, can't chew the rubber wiper blades. It does give a strange look to the parking lot.

The course is fun from the start. The 1st, *Glenisla*, is a 318-yard par 4, which doglegs right. A good drive leaves a short pitch to the green. Between the second and third holes is a large standing stone. The club has no history to the stone called the Pitcrocknie Stone, but respectfully build the course around it. The 4th, *Dunsinane*, is another short par 4 of only 332 yards, but can be quite challenging with a pond 250 yards off the tee eating up half the fairway. Many second shots will be directly over the pond to a green with two traps behind. A bunker on the right and trees left are the problems on 315-yard par 4 ninth called *Cat Law*. Two more bunkers guard the elevated green. A strategic test is the 13th. A 180 yard layup is all you need on the 359-yard dramatic dogleg right *Devil's Elbow*. The green is protected by mounding and two traps. Key to the hole is a tee shot not blocked by the trees at the turn. Next is *Pudd's Dyke*, and 159-yard one-shotter. You must carry the pond and bunker fronting the green or bail out to the right. The green is almost two tiers. The 17th and 18th can be tough finishing holes. Glenisla makes a pleasant contrast to the tight tree-lined courses at Alyth and Blairgowrie.

COMMENTS FROM THE FORWARD TEES: This parkland course has an open feel and look. As the trees grow the look will change, but the fairways are still wide enough. The course has some hills with more on the back nine than the front. The total yardage of this 18-hole course is 5437 with a par 71. There are three par 5s and four par 3s. The par 5s are very long; 440, 526, and 563 yards. The 12th, the longest of the par 5s, doglegs left at about 200 yards out then climbs slightly. There are also six fairway bunkers to deal with and some mounding on the green. It is the number one handicap hole for both men and women. The par 3s vary in length from 108 to 171 yards. I found the 5th to be the hardest par 3 because between me and the green was a large pond. It only required a carry of 90 yards, but my brain doesn't always believe I can do it. This is a pleasant course that will be fun to play again soon.

KILLIN GOLF COURSE
Killin, Perthshire FK21 8TX
www.killingolfclub.co.uk   01567-820312
Parkland, 2534 yards, par 33, £15/9-holes,
£22/18-holes

AMENITIES: The clubhouse dates from 1922 and is the best bet in town for a pleasant meal. A small golf shop in the clubhouse has most essentials. The course has buggies (what we'd call carts) available and they were handy one year when Anne was playing with a broken toe.

COURSE COMMENTS: The picturesque parkland Killin course is hilly, but not a difficult walk. Designed in 1911 by a group of locals, the course provides great views of the surrounding hills. The rough off the fairways is the biggest trouble on the course, but playing strategically is vital. The holes at Killin GC are all interesting, but some are quite unique. The 4th, *Gully*, is a 370-yard par 4 which starts with a blind shot over a hill to a relatively narrow fairway. The second shot has to go over another hill to a flat green. With two blind shots it's a good idea if you haven't played before to walk up to the top of each hill before your shot. Between the hills at the side of the fairway is an interesting old crank fire bell. Next is *The Dyke*, a 97-yard par 3. This short, challenging hole has a tee shot which must carry a three-foot high rock wall five yards in front of the small green. A bunker left and mound behind (the tee box of 6) complicate the shot. It may look and sound easy, but that rock wall definitely plays with your mind as you hit. The 9th, *Home*, is one of the most impressive finishing holes in Scottish golf. The 506-yard par 5 plays downhill all the way with first and probably second shots half-blind (you can't see the actual landing area, even though you can see the green beyond). Lochay Bridge, the clubhouse, and valley beyond are always in view. Beautiful and demanding. Killin GC may be out-of-the-way, but a round or two here is well worth the effort.

KING JAMES VI GOLF COURSE ("THE ISLAND')
Moncrieffe Island, Perth PH2 8NR
www.kingjamesvi.co.uk 01738-445132
Parkland, 5684 yards, par 68, £24

AMENITIES: A unique course in the middle of thriving Perth, where you must walk by way of footbridge over the River Tay about a third of a mile to the course. After the walk with your clubs the clubhouse is a welcome sight. The lounge has a good view of the 18th green. The small golf shop is well-stocked.

COURSE COMMENTS: Only a few courses in the world are sited on an island in the middle of a river--King James VI GC in Perth, Scotland is one (interestingly enough, another one is in Perth, Australia). The club began in 1858 and the present Old Tom Morris designed track was opened in 1897. The course is flat and prone to be wet [Duh! It's on an island in the middle of a river in Scotland.] with plenty of strategically placed bunkers--a mix of 77 fairway and greenside. Many holes have fairway bunkers left and right at about 180 to 200 yards from the tee, and par 3s have bunkers about 25 yards in front of the greens. Only one hole, the 13th, has no bunkers Two holes (the 11th, a 372-yard par 4, and the 13th, a 171-yard par 3) have large berms in front of the greens and the 11th green is elevated. The 6th, *Spectacles* (named for the shape of the fairway bunker on the right) is a good example of holes on the front. The hole is a straight ahead 317-yard par 4 with plenty of tree trouble on the sides and a two-tiered green guarded by three bunkers. Another typical hole at King James is the 14th, *Corner*. This 358-yard par 4 is a dogleg right where your tee shot needs to avoid the trees on the right to set up an approach to the two-tiered green. Seventeen (named *Hawthorne* for the trees behind the green), a 158-yard par 3, is a challenging short hole. Five bunkers front the moderate sized green. Beware, all the bunkers make the hole look shorter than it is. The course gets many comments about being good value for your green fees.

FROM THE FORWARD TEES: The long walk over the river and past community gardens makes for a unique experience. We learned that the club gets all its supplies delivered by boat--after walking 18 on a very hot day I would have appreciated a boat ride back to the car park. The course is flat with wide fairways. The overall yardage for women is 5478 yards. There are five par 5s and only the 11th is shorter than 400 yards and it has a burn in front of the green. The ditch/burn is in play on 9 through 12, but is especially problematic at the 12th. With a dyke 50 yards and the ditch 135 yards from the tee planning your landing spot becomes very important. Playing King James VI GC is an adventure worth scheduling.

KIRRIEMUIR GOLF COURSE
Sheilhill Road, Kirriemuir, Angus DD8 4LN
www.kirriemuirgolfclub.co.uk 01575-573317
Parkland/heath, 5518 yards, par 68, £36

AMENITIES: Lovely clubhouse has views of the first tee from the lounge. A broad menu of pub food is offered most usual hours. Good quality fare. The clubhouse lounge is only open to members, guests, and day players. Good golf shop is well outfitted.

COURSE COMMENTS: The busy Kirriemuir GC was redesigned by James Braid in 1926. The course is robed in gorse, broom, and trees, but plays fairly wide. Located in the heart of some good golf country, with Carnoustie, Forfar, Panmure, and several other fine courses nearby, the village was the birthplace of *Peter Pan* author J.M. Barrie. The course exhibits strong Braid bunkering with 61 traps in play and most penal--the large bunker on 18 is brutal. Greens are small with subtle borrows which are often difficult to read. Stay below the hole and don't be generous giving putts (unless you're playing with your wife). There is a drinking fountain on the 11th tee, but no water hazards. The course is characterized by several blind tee shots (all have aiming posts) and there are several trees encroaching on approach shots. Your round affords good views of the surrounding farmland and hills and there is a lovely variety of trees on the course.

All the holes at Kirriemuir are interesting, but several stood out after our round. The 4th, *Muirhouses*, is a 335-yard par 4 where you should drive to the right of the marker pole because your ball will run down and slightly left. Avoid the three bunkers around the green and a birdie is possible. The 8th, *Quarry*, is a 154-yard tricky par 3 with three bunkers fronting the green. Take plenty of club here. Be straight on your drive at the 13th, *Ditches*, because a ditch along the right and crossing the fairway diagonally can cause problems on this 391-yard par 4. It takes more club than you think to reach the elevated green. *Caddam* is the short, 285-yard, par 4 fifteenth--one of Kirriemuir's fine short two-shotters. Play for position. Two hundred yards will leave a wedge into a sloping green guarded by two traps. *Braid's Gem*, the 17th, plays downhill 195 yards, so you can hit less club. The hole is tight, though, and a bothersome tree sits just right of the green. Two bunkers front the green as well. The hole is indeed a gem. The 18th is a fine finishing hole. Stay left of the large tree on the right in the fairway in order to attack the green at *Hame*, a 388-yard par 4. Your approach is over one of the deepest bunkers I've ever seen (it crosses almost all the fairway only a few yards in front of the green). The greenskeeper, James Kerry, said it was originally a large ravine, but as golfers chewed it up trying to get out, he thought it would be better as a bunker. Believe me it's hell to get out of that bunker! Kirriemuir is a quality course and deserves wider recognition.

COMMENTS FROM THE FORWARD TEES: A very good course with good views of the hills and Cairngorms.

Kirriemuir has many stands of trees and there is a good mix of play in and out of the trees. Rough, bunkers, and small hills and slopes will keep you on you toes. This course is a good and fair golf challenge. The ladies' red tee markers are often behind the yellow visitor men's tees. You might want to choose to play the yellow makers, which was recommended by our host, James Kerry the superintendent of the course, when we played. You may also want to adjust the overall par since you will be playing about 200 yards less than the card info for the red tees. The par 3s are very doable, and the par 5's are not too long but offer a good test of your golfing skills. The layout of the course is interesting and the setting in the trees with some views over the valley was lovely on the spring day we played. Do stop in the village to see the Peter Pan statue in the town center and visit the J. M. Barrie museum.

MAINS OF TAYMOUTH GOLF COURSE
(aka KENMORE GC)
Mains of Taymouth, Kenmore PH15 2HN
www.kenmoregolfcourse.co.uk 01887-830226
Parkland, 2751 yards, par 70 (for 18), £20/18

AMENITIES: No clubhouse, but a few essentials are available in the reception area where you check in for golf. We suggest the Mains of Taymouth Court Yard Bistro for lunch or dinner (same owners as the golf course).
COURSE COMMENTS: Opened in 1992 this mostly flat forested 9-hole track is now in much better condition than we first saw it. The course is well bunkered with some of the traps quite penal. No water is in play on the course, but stone walls are at 4, 6, and 7. Trees, gentle hills (with some sidehill lies probable), and heavy rough off the generous fairways will be conditions of play. Greens are small and mostly flat, but a few have interesting slopes. The forested course is lovely, especially in the spring and autumn, and the views of the surrounding hills and forest are grand all the time. There are plans for more nearby holiday housing, but they probably won't intrude much on the course. All the holes here are

interesting, but a few are particularly grabbing. The 2nd, *The Roundels*, is a 302-yard par 4 which starts with a shot out of a copse of trees. It's a difficult tee shot because it's so tight you tend to aim toward a tree covered hill to the right of the green. The green doesn't need much protection. *Gallop*, the 507-yard par 5 fourth starts with a tee shot which must clear a stone fence about 150 yards out--shouldn't be a problem, but it is. Three Braid-type bunkers left complicate your approach to the small green. This hole is listed as the most difficult hole on the course. Next we liked the 7th, *Sheepfold*. From the tee on this 145-yard par 3 you look down onto the green fronted by a ditch backed by a stone fence. A bunker right adds difficulty to an already tough shot. Located in the beautiful Scottish hills, Mains of Taymouth GC is a small course definitely worth a visit.

COMMENTS FROM THE FORWARD TEES: Kenmore is situated in the trees along the River Tay with a stone wall crossing three holes. The stone wall presents demanding shot making and planning on holes 4, 6, and 7. On the 4th ladies will have to decide to layup or try to hit over the wall. The par 5s are very long and the par 3s very doable. This nine hole course makes a very good 18-hole round because the holes are challenging and the setting is beautiful.

MUCKHART GOLF COURSE
Drumburn Road, Muckhart, By Dollar,
Clackmannanshire FK14 7JH
www.muckhartgolf.com 01259-781423
Moorland/parkland, 27-holes (3 nines), £30

AMENITIES: Comfortable clubhouse with pleasant lounge and separate golf shop. Each nine-hole layout comes back to the clubhouse.

COURSE COMMENTS: Muckhart Golf Club [misspelled in the first edition -- please accept my apologies] is a fine course (or set of courses) in the central Scotland area. The club has three similar nine-hole layouts any of which can be played to make an 18-hole round (though they usually designate two courses for the day). Naemoor is the newest course and is fairly open with gentle hills. Cowden is the original course and is tighter with more blind shots. The Arndean nine is the most scenic with views over the Forth Valley to the Ochills. All three courses have interesting holes. On the Naemoor course (a little over ten years old and where the trees are starting to mature) we liked the 2nd, *Cauldron Linn*, a 404-yard par 4. The hole doglegs right with tough grass and trees on the inside corner. The second shot here is blind over mounds to a green protected on each side by bunkers. *The Wee Skellum* is the 190-yard par 3 seventh. It's a downhill tee shot to a green sloping left-to-right with a good sized bunker on the left. Tough shot. The Cowden course is the original nine, now over 100 years old and playing as it was built originally. Here the 5th, *Seamab*, is a fine 422-yard two-shotter. A dogleg right with large swales in the fairway, the hole has trees on the right side all along. Your approach shot will be half blind with only the top of the flag visible. The 9th, *Barking Creek*, a 545-yard par 5, is normally played as the 18th on a full round. This is a long finishing hole with a generous fairway which has rough left and OB right. The third shot (for all but the biggest hitters) must contend with a burn about 40 yards from the green. On the Arndean course it is the 5th, *Top of the World*, a 361-yard par 4, which most impresses. The short two-shotter is a tough uphill challenge even with no bunkers. Whether you play nine or 18, and no matter which courses you play, you'll enjoy your golf at friendly Muckhart Golf Club.

MURRAYSHALL CHAMPIONSHIP GOLF COURSE
Scone, Perth PH2 7PH
www.murrayshall.com/golf 01738-551171
Undulating parkland, 6441 yards, par 73, £40

AMENITIES: The facilities of the Murrayshall Hotel means the two courses here have a grand clubhouse with lounge and full restaurant. A well-stocked golf shop services both the Murrayshall Championship course and the Lynecdoch course. Buggies are available for hire.

COURSE COMMENTS: The Murrayshall Championship course is the design work of Hamilton Stutt, grandson of James Braid's chief foreman. The 18-hole parkland course uses natural slopes to provide plenty of elevation change, but the course is never a hard walk. Some very large bunkers will cause problems, but they aren't the main concern. As one golfer said, "If there is a soundtrack to the course it is the clunk of balls hitting trees and golfers swearing." Tiger Woods may get around the Old Course at St Andrews without finding a bunker, but I would defy him to get around either course here without hitting a tree. That said, the course isn't excessively difficult, though it will test all levels of golfers.

Murrayshall is full of good holes. The 3rd, *Pinnacle*, a 478-yard par 5, needs a tee shot to the right to set up the second on this dogleg left. Your approach should avoid the three large bunkers fronting the green. Five looks easy, but the 367-yard par 4 plays tough. Your first shot must set up a second through the gap in the trees with a slope working against you. Demanding. *Dog's Grave*, the 379-yard par 4 seventh, is intriguing. A tree in the center of the fairway--216 yards out--makes the hole challenging. Left of the tree lengthens the second shot which must cross a burn to a sloping green. You can't go very far right on the first shot because OB runs the length of the hole. Be sure to pay respects to the dog graves behind the green. On the 9th, *Devil's Elbow*, you need either a short tee shot of about 200 yards or a big fade to get around the corner on this 498-yard par 5. Be careful of the large bunker left of the green. The most open hole on the course is the 416-yard par 4 thirteenth called *Maidenwells*, but watch out for the 13 bunkers (13 on the 13th) on this one hole--at least ten are in play for the average golfer. Avoid the bunkers and you still face a testing two-tiered green. The Murrayshall course is a good, challenging, well-maintained course.

MURRAYSHALL LYNEDOCH COURSE
Parkland, 5361 yards, par 69, £25

AMENITIES: Same as Murrayshall
COURSE COMMENTS: The Lynedoch course is the easier of the two to get on and is easier to play at well. Built about 20 years after the Marrayshall course, Lynedoch is an undulating course set in beautiful forest lands. The course is a little more open than the championship course, but has several water hazards, 19 bunkers, and plenty of trees still in play. The views are as good or better than the other course. The first three holes are a great, tough start. The 1st, *Two Mile*, is a 369-yard par 4 which seriously doglegs right. Your second shot is over a double gully with two burn crossings. The elevated green has bunkers right and back. The 3rd is a fine short par 3 of only 152 yards. Three bunkers (front, right, left) guard the elevated green. *Douglas Wynd* is the very narrow downhill 12th with a drop-off right and gorse left. Birdie is very possible and so is double-bogey. Lynedoch may not be the challenge of Murrayshall, but it is a fun course to play.

MUTHILL GOLF COURSE
Peat Road, Muthill, Perthshire PH5 2DA
www.muthillgolfclub.co.uk 01764-681523
Parkland, 4673 yards, par 66, £12.50 for 9, £18 all day

AMENITIES: Small clubhouse with light snacks available mostly on weekends. Trolleys are available for hire.
COURSE COMMENTS: The nine-hole Muthill (MOO-thil) golf course was designed in 1911, but folded in 1917 due to the need for the land for agricultural use during the war. The course was reestablished in 1935 and only survived World War II by the club captain's donation. The course has some hills, but is never a difficult walk. Only a few bunkers are in play, but some of them are quite deep. Muthill is a pleasant local course which has some memorable holes. The 4th, *Laverock Lea*, is a 276-yard par 4 which doglegs right about 70 yards from the green. The right side is protected by

trees and several bunkers front the green. *Gowan Lea*, the 393-yard 6th, is the longest hole on the course and plays downhill off the tee (blind). The slightly elevated green is protected by traps. Tougher than it looks, the 197-yard par 3 ninth, *The Loaning*, has a downhill tee shot over the 8th green to small target protected by two deep pot bunkers. If looking for some stress-free golf Muthill GC is a good bet when in the area.

COMMENTS FROM THE FORWARD TEES: Muthill is a delightful 9-hole course with more challenges than it might immediately seem. Bunkers are well placed especially for ladies and the uphill shots seem longer than I expected, especially on the windy day we played. The course is short at 2270 yards (second time around is 2255 which equals 4525 total for 18). It has three par 3s and six par 4s on each nine. Two par 3s are long at 181 and 201 yards and the third is 106 yards. A hint for playing the 3rd is to aim to the left of he hill off the tee and stay to the left side for the best angle into the green. It is easier to see the line on the rest of the holes. This is a good nine hole course with interesting views of the area.

ST FILLANS GOLF COURSE
South Loch Earn Road, St Fillans, Perthshire PH6 2NJ
www.st-fillans-golf.com   01764-685312
Parkland, 5520 yards, par 70, £10/round, £20/day

AMENITIES: Great clubhouse tearoom with outstanding food. In season does weekend special meals for which you have to have reservations. A few golf essentials available in clubhouse.

COURSE COMMENTS: St Fillans GC is the perfect nine-hole course. It can be easy, it can be difficult, but it will always be fun and friendly. The 1903 Willie Auchterlonie design is mostly flat, but the one hill on the course gives a great elevated tee for one hole and adds challenge on three others. Although there are a few bunkers, the main difficulties are the hill and the heavy rough off the fairways. St Fillans is beautifully sited between steep hills and next to lush pastures. Bring you camera!

The club website lists the first as the toughest hole on the course, and although it can be difficult if you mishit left, I think that the 2nd and the 7th are more difficult all the time. The 2nd, *Earnside*, is a 415-yard par 4 which starts with a long carry over heather to an angled fairway. Even a good drive then leaves a long second shot to a small green protected by a wee burn in front and heavy rough all around. For me a par feels like a birdie at this hole. *Earnside* is followed by *St Fillans*, the 279-yard par 4. Tee off from the top of the only hill on the course. Anything mishit short is probably lost in the ferns and bracken. Second shot should be a short wedge to a green protected by two fronting bunkers. With wind behind I have actually driven the green, but I've also found my share of trees and rough on the right. Definitely a fun hole! The 5th is the favorite hole of most club members. *The Bothy* is named for the small croft just off the fairway left and is a challenging 265-yard par 4. The tee shot is over a corner of the hill you tee off of on the 3rd and played around on the 4th. After the blind drive, the second is to an elevated green--short rolls back down or into a bunker, long rolls off into mean nasty rough. Never give a putt on this green. I really like the 7th, at 455 yards it is the longest par 4 in Perthshire. The hole is good, straight forward classic golf with OB on the left, trees and rough on the right, and several fairway bunkers before you reach the large green. Here again, par is like a birdie to me.

I may gush a little about St Fillans GC, but we are members. It's a course you can have fun on the first time, but it will still be a challenge the hundredth time you play. We absolutely love the interesting shots, the magnificent mountain views, the food in the clubhouse tearoom, and the friendly people we meet on the course.

COMMENTS FROM THE FORWARD TEES: I love a round on this course. It feels and looks like it will be easy but don't be fooled. There are trees, heather, a small burn, and the hill to get in your way. The greens can be a challenge because they are different depending on the weather and ground conditions. I love this course and the setting, in a small valley surrounded by rocky hills, makes this one of the loveliest courses in Scotland.

STIRLING GOLF COURSE
Queens Road, Sterling FK8 3AA
www.stirlinggolfclub.com phone
Parkland, 6187 yards, par 72, £30

AMENITIES: Pleasant clubhouse which includes Trevino's Restaurant (open 7:30-11:00 PM).   Clubhouse lounge serves snacks and light meals most usual hours. Well-stock golf shop in the clubhouse.

COURSE COMMENTS: The Stirling GC was built in 1869 and was distinguished to have Young Tom Morris as its first professional.   The course was redesigned in 1966 by Henry Cotton. The course plays below Stirling Castle and the ground, known as "The King's Park," was used as a royal hunting ground. Fifty-one bunkers add difficulty, but we found the rough to be particularly sticky. There are many fine holes at Stirling, including the 320-yard par 4 third, called *Rocking Stone*.   Bunkers left and right make the tee shot a test of accuracy, and the second shot is to an elevated green with a small bunker behind. A long uphill hole is *Tree Out*, the 509-yard 5th. Be careful as you carry the ridge on your second shot because the approach to the green breaks left to right. The green is protected by surrounding trees. *Cotton's Fancy* is the hardest hole at Stirling.   The uphill 384-yard par 4 fifteenth is a dogleg left shaped almost like a fish hook, with the green at the point of the hook. The fairway swings out to the right, but you can go straight at the hole. Beware, though, as the uphill adds length and the rough short of the green is tough. The views of historic Stirling Castle, like the views of Harlech Castle from Royal St David's GC in Wales, is a wonderful distraction.

STRATHMORE RANNALEROCH COURSE
Strathmore Golf Centre, Leroch, Alyth, Blairgowrie
PH11 8NZ
www.strathmoregolf.com 01828-633322
Moorland, 5848 yards, par 70, £32

AMENITIES: The course has a lovely clubhouse and the lounge has several eating areas. Serves tasty meals and you may have to book ahead. There is a small but nicely stocked golf shop where you check-in for golf, a 9-hole practice course (see notes below), and a ten bay covered driving range.

COURSE COMMENTS: The undulating Rannaleroch Course, designed by John Salvesen and opened in 1996, fits its motto as a "Friendly Place to Play Golf." The course, with recent renovations, has been discovered and can be quite busy--it's worth your time to book ahead. This lovely tree-lined, moorland track is player friendly--tough enough to challenge good players and forgiving enough to be fun for a casual round. A mix of 39 fairway and greenside bunkers, none too penal, add some challenge. A small ditch runs beside several holes (OB) and ponds are in play on 5, 6, and 11. Most of the moderate to large greens have gentle borrows and few have distinct tiers. All are easy to putt. The course can be windy and has wiry rough (not too deep), but basically the course is wide open with broad fairways.

There's plenty to like about the Rannaleroch Course starting with the 484-yard par 5 first. Stay to the right of the bunker at the inside corner of the dogleg left. A good drive will allow a go at the green with a hill on the right and a bunker left. The green is fairly flat--a par or birdie opportunity to start your round. The 173-yard par 3 fourth is considered the signature hole by many, though I would choose the 17th. This is a gentle downhill one-shotter with a burn on the right (OB) and two traps left to give it some bite. A fine, fun hole. Next is a 400-yard par 4 where you hit over a pond (only a visual problem) to a right sloping fairway. The second shot may have tree problems on the right. The green has one bunker right, plenty of surrounding mounding, and a pond behind. On the 9th, a 379-yard par 4, stay to the right to cut some distance off this left to right dogleg, but watch out for the bunker about 180 yards out. The green is deep and narrow and slopes back to front with one bunker left. After nine you return to the clubhouse. The 11th is a short dogleg right (280 yards) two-shotter where you should stay left to have a good approach to the friendly green. You can try to drive close to the green, but the best play is a layup and wedge with a chance for birdie. The short par 4 is followed by a relatively short par 5. The 12th at 496-yards is a three-shot dogleg right around twin bunkers. Keep your ball in play and it's a fun hole; stray and the hole will fight you all the way. A classic design and the toughest hole on Rannaleroch is the 433-yard par 4 fourteenth. The hole is a long slight dogleg left with a ditch (OB) all along the left. After a blind tee shot the hole is downhill to a well-guarded two-tiered green. The 17th is a lovely downhill 198-yard par 3 with trees and OB behind the green. Even with a large green and only one bunker right it's trickier than it looks. Bring you camera for this one. In an area rich with good golf (Blairgowrie, Alyth, Forfar) Strathmore's Rannaleroch Course fits right in.

COMMENTS FROM THE FORWARD TEES: We played this course several years ago and at the suggestion of the course secretary we played it again in the spring. Many improvements have been made to the course. The overall yardage of 5539 hasn't changed and is only a few yards less than the yardage for the visitors' tees for men. All four of the par 3s are good challenges, especially visually. The 4th is very memorable; It is a downhill 156 yards with a small burn on the right, two bunkers on the left, and trees behind. Water is in play on two of the other par threes but can be avoided with good tee shots. The 17th is another wonderful par 3 at 189 yards for women. There are four par 5s, one on the front side and 3 on the back, all over 400 yards. Hole 12 is a 475-yard dogleg right with a burn and trees along the left, and trees on the right. The green is up and over a slight rise and tucked in to the right. It is a bit of a bowl with water and a bunker to the left and mounds behind and to the left. It's not a bad idea to walk up and take a look before you hit to the green. Enjoy this friendly pleasant course in the foothills of the Cairngorms.

STRATHMORE LEITFIE LINKS
Parkland, 3332 for 18, par 58, £12 for 9 holes

AMENITIES: Same as for the Rannaleroch Course.

COURSE COMMENTS: Opened in 1995 while the Rannaleroch course was being completed, Leitfie Links (the name refers to the local area of the course) is a 9-hole practice or warm-up course. While the course has no pretensions of being anything more than it is, we enjoyed a quick 18 when we didn't want to get stuck between foursomes on the big course. While there are no bunkers at Leitfie and the greens are relatively flat (a couple are two-tiered), the course was good practice for the short game. A couple of blind drives will add interest as well. Leitfie has some pleasant views of the surrounding farmland, and a couple of holes on the big course are in view. The most challenging holes at Leitfie are the 4th and 8th. The 4th, *Buzzard*, is a 281-yard par 4 which doglegs left around a large copse of trees. If your drive is too short the second shot will be blind as well. Trees on the right can be a problem for slicers. *Partridge*, the 201-yard one-shotter 8th begins with a blind shot over a ridge--be sure the green is clear before driving; golfers leaving the green can be seen as they go through the hedge to nine. If short the approach can also be blind. Lastly, the 9th green is dramatically tiered for a small green on a short (110-yards) hole. If you want a quick nine or eighteen or some short game practice, Leitfie Links can be fun.

STRATHTAY GOLF COURSE
Upper Derulich, Strathtay, Pitlochry PH9 0LR
www.strathtaygolfclub.com 01887-840373
Parkland/heathland, 3826 yards, par 62, £15 all day

AMENITIES: Small clubhouse (for members) with changing rooms open during the day. Honesty box for when no one is around. No golf shop, but trolleys are available, pay at the Honesty Box

COURSE COMMENTS: The short 9-hole course (four par 4s and five par 3s) climbs around a couple of knocks. The course has a few traps, but the elevation changes and the trees should be enough challenge for any golfer. Ladies particularly may struggle when hitting into hill faces and having their ball stop or roll back. Strathtay is a course you will want to play more than once in order to learn it. Among the memorable holes is *Copse*, the 169-yard 3rd which you can play as dogleg par 3 around a copse of trees or be brave and try to go up over the tall beech trees. I rattled a ball around in the trees and managed to chip out and one putt for a par--I'm sure that's not the way the locals will play it. A most challenging hole is the 5th, *Spion Kop* ("the blind summit") which is a 218-yard par 4. Yes, a four of only 218 yards. The hole plays dramatically uphill with the last few yards a 20-foot drop to the green. It has to be seen to be believed. The highest point on the course with good views is at the tee of the 345-yard par 4 sixth, *Cottage*. It's a downhill tee shot to a plateau which leaves a blind second shot to a green in front of Broom Cottage. With the second hole also a dogleg par 3, Strathtay GC is funky, but it is also grand fun!

PUBS, RESTAURANTS, & TEAROOMS

This list and the ones in subsequent chapters give suggestions for lunches, snacks, or dinners. We've eaten in all these and tried to make sure the information is current. Always ask your B&B hosts for current recommendations.

Aberfoyle Golf Course Lounge (pub) in Aberfoyle. For lunch and early dinner it has the best food in town and great prices.

Allanwater Cafe (chip shop) at the north end of the main
street in Bridge of Allan.This ice cream   parlour/chip
shop has been in business for more than a hundred
years. Famous for fish and chips and specialty
homemade ice cream.

#2 Baker Street (pub) at #2 Baker Street in Stirling just down
from the Castle. Good pub food, reasonable prices,
traditional music on some evenings.

The Blue Flax Tearoom on Comrie Road in Crieff, just down
from James Square. Modern tearoom with relaxed
seating. Owners take pride in serving homemade
fare—soup, sandwiches, and sweets.

Breizh (restaurant) on High Street in the heart of Perth's
shopping district. French/Italian bistro which is very
popular with locals. Book ahead or stop in and book
and then continue shopping. Great food, decent prices.

Carbeth Inn (pub) on Stockiemuir Road, Blanefield near
Drymen.   Roadside pub with beer garden once known
as the Halfway House (between Stirling and Glasgow).
Decent pub food, popular with bikers and cyclists.

The Clachan Inn (pub) in Dryman, near Loch Lomand.
Advertised as the oldest licensed pub in Scotland.
Upscale pub food is excellent and reasonably priced.

Ciao Roma (restaurant) in the main shopping area of Perth.
Traditional Italian with full menu.

The Coach House (pub) on the main street of Aberfoyle.
Typical pub menu.   Comfortable refuge on a cold, rainy
afternoon.

The Comrie Cafe on the main street through the village.
Typical tearoom fare, good quality.

Courtyard Bar and Brasserie in The Mains of Taymouth
shops in Kenmore. Modern chalet-style lunchroom and
formal dining restaurant with a very complete menu
and full bar. Great pizza and soups.

Clive Ramsay (restaurant) on the main street of Bridge of
Allan. Bistro named for the owner/chef has an
interesting menu and is always busy.

Cocoa Mountain on High Street in Auchterarder in the middle
of town. Delicious   truffles, hot chocolate to die for,
coffee specialties, and sinful sweets. Forget your
diet, you're on vacation.

Crieff Hotel, Haggis and Sporran (pub) on Perth Road in
Crieff at the east end of the shopping area of town.
Typical hotel pub where the food gets mixed reviews.

The Cross Keys Pub in Kippen on the main road. Old pub
(1703) with low dark ceiling, a couple of rooms, small
tables, and stone fireplace. Broad menu beyond the
traditional pub items (ie., guinea fowl). Friendly pub.

Darnley Coffee House (tea room) on Bow Street in Stirling,
just down from the castle. Housed in the bottom floor
of historic Darnley's House (home to Queen Mary's
second husband) the tearoom is a good lunch stop.
Recommended by castle staff.

Deil's Cauldron (pub/restaurant) just off the main road
through Comrie heading north. A top spot to eat in the
Strathearn Valley. Food is exceptional and the service
matches. Pricey, but a Must Stop.

Delivino's (lunch/tearoom) down from the main square in
Crieff. A deli and wine bar (hence the name) with good
lunches and fantastic sweets. Serves dinners in
season.

Doyle's Cafe and Deli (tearoom) on the main street in
Balfron. A fairly new tearoom with specialty sweets and
sodas. Free WiFi is a bonus.

Drummond Hotel (pub/restaurant) on the main road through
St Fillans just past the golf course. The food was good,
but the service was abysmal--go to the golf course
tearoom instead.

Dun Whinny Coffee Shop (tearoom) on Bridge Street just off
the main road through Callander. Specializes in
homemade bakery goods and soups.

The Forth Inn (pub) in the center of Aberfoyle. Typical pub
food in pleasant surroundings.

Gloagburn Farm Store on the Old Crieff Road between Perth
and Crieff. Farm converted to store and restaurant

with good produce and a small deli. Soups, salads, sandwiches and sweets are the tearoom fare. We've stopped several times.

Habitat Cafe on the town square in Aberfeldy. Award winning tearoom/coffee shop serves great sandwiches as well as specialty sweets. Some of the best coffee we've had in Scotland.

Hansen's Kitchen on the main road (A85) through Comrie. Hansen's is a deli, small grocery, and lunch place. Serves soups, sandwiches, light lunches, and sweets. Best egg mayo sandwich ever on great bread.

The Horn on A9 between Perth and Dundee. Cafeteria and gift shop with plenty of tables. Famous for Best Bacon Roll in the World (bap piled high with Scottish bacon). You have to try the Bacon Roll here at least once.

The Inn at Kippin (pub) on Fore Road in the cute village of Kippin. Large pub menu with interesting selections. Serves large portions for fair prices.

The Joinery (Meigle Cafe & Coffee Shop) on the Square in Meigle. Interesting cafe (good food) and gift shop with friendly, helpful owners.

Killin Hotel and Riverview Bistro (restaurant/pub) on the main road through the village. Classic hotel pub, nicely decorated which serves good food.

Lounge in Crieff (restaurant) on High Street in the heart of the shopping district. Combination coffee shop and bistro-style tapas bar run by Yann and Shari (owners of Yann's). Excellent food and full bar.

Meadow Inn (pub) in Crieff on A823 (road to Perth) at the west end of town. A locals pub with typical, but good pub food.

Old Tudor Coffee Shop & Bistro on Main Street, Auchterarder, in the middle of town. Great sweets and lunch items in a Tudor-style interior.

Paco's Restaurant and Sandwich Bar (restaurant) near the Opera House in Perth's downtown shopping area. Good quality food (huge menu featuring Italian,

American Southwestern, and steaks) at good prices. Can be hectic.

Pip's Coffee House, Ancaster Square, just off the main street in Callander. Typical coffee house or tearoom menu, but the sweets are good.

Port Bar, Lake of Menteith Hotel (pub and restaurant) between the parish church and the boat dock for the small ferry to the priory at the Lake of Menteith. The hotel restaurant is fine dining at a dear price, but the bar has a great menu, and the same chef.

The Quaich Bar on High Street in Crieff. Nice whisky bar with bar and tables up front and dining area in the back. Specializes in tasty burgers as well as other pub fare.

Red Squirrel Cafe (tearoom and art gallery) on High Street, Crieff in the upper part of the shopping district. Some high quality art and sandwiches and sweets. Friendly atmosphere.

Royal Hotel (restaurant) in the middle of Comrie. Elegant dining at affordable prices. Order in the lounge and be taken to your table when the food is ready. The hotel also has a separate lively bar.

Tormaukin Hotel (pub/restaurant) in Glendevon. Has been very good, but we've heard the quality hasn't kept up with the rising prices.

The Tower Hotel Gastro Pub on Perth Road, the main road through Crieff. Newly redesigned the pub has a bistro feel and service is very friendly, but the food is still just pub food.

Tullybannocher Farm Food Bar (cafeteria) just out of Comrie toward St Fillans. Funky cafeteria with some good food at reasonable prices.

St Fillans Golf Course Tearoom at the St Fillans Golf Course. A good bet for lunch or early dinner--simple fare, good quality.

Willows Coffee Shop and Restaurant on St John's Place in downtown Perth. Modern cafe with full breakfast and lunch menu and a more limited dinner menu. Busy.

Yann's (restaurant) on Perth Road just down from the main shopping area in Crieff. Award winning fine dining French and Scottish restaurant in Glenearn House B&B. Best restaurant in the area, reservations recommended.

LODGINGS

In this and subsequent chapters we will list the B&Bs and small guest houses we feel confident to recommend to our traveling friends. Owners change, situations change, but we've tried to check these details as close to publication as possible. Use websites listed or phone numbers to check more carefully for yourself.

Errolbank Guest House
9 Dalgleish Rd., Dundee DD4 7JN
01382-462118 www.errolbank-guesthouse.com £60
A pleasant B&B in the Dundee suburbs close to Broughty Ferry.

Fisherman's Tavern Hotel
10-16 Fort Street, Broughty Ferry DD5 2AD
01382-775941 www.fishermanstavern.co.uk Moderate price
Tavern and hotel often spells a sleepless night, but at Fisherman's Tavern that wasn't a problem. Comfortable accommodations and good food.

Five Gables House
Dundee Road, Arbroath DD11 2PE
01241-871632 www.arbroathbandb.com £60
Converted from the old (1877-1984) clubhouse of the Arbroath GC, Five Gables is a lovely B&B with great views of the golf course and the North Sea.

Merlindale B&B
Perth Road, Crieff PH7 3EQ
01764-655205 www.merlindale.co.uk £70

Our Scottish home and one of the best B&Bs we've ever stayed in. John and Jacky Clifford are golfers and Jacky is a Cordon Bleu trained chef. The 1860s house has been significantly remodeled and is constantly being upgraded. Rooms are large and beautifully appointed. A lovely, award winning, friendly place to stay in the heart of Scotland.

ATTRACTIONS

Scotland has much more than golf to offer the traveler. In each chapter we will try to highlight local tourist attractions, including ancient sites, castles, gardens, distilleries, and other tourist and shopping spots.

Branklyn Gardens (NTS), Perth. A lovely small (two acre) garden which always has   plenty in bloom.
Dewar's World of Whisky, Aberfeldy. The old Aberfeldy distillery, now home to Dewar's, has a high tech tour and the normal dram after the tour.
Famous Grouse Distillery, Crieff. The Glenturret distillery, now Famous Grouse, has an informative distillery tour in a lovely location.
Innerpeffray Library and Chapel, Crieff (about 4 miles east of town). The oldest lending library in Scotland is open limited hours, but is a bibliophile's treasure. Interesting history of the Drummond family.
Scone Palace, Perth (northwest of the city). Scone Palace, the home of the Stone of   Destiny used to install Scottish monarchs, is a fine grand house with lovely grounds and tons of history.
Stanley Mills (HS), Stanley (north of Perth on the A9). Newly opened (2008) cotton mill museum. Informative self-guided tour.
Stirling Castle (HS), Stirling. One of the two premier castles majestically over the city. Plan a couple of hours or more to see it all. Great views of the surrounding town and countryside.

Chapter 4: The Highland Road-- Up the A9 to Dornoch and North

Boat of Garten Golf Course

Scotland's Highlands are its prototypical landscape; a land of sweeping mountains of heather, fern, and rock. A rugged, imposing landscape full of adventure, intrigue, and romance.

A great way to experience the Highlands is to take a trip up the A9, Scotland's main motorway from Perth north. All along this route you'll find interesting golf courses, pleasing eateries, and wonderful tourist attractions.

Alphabetically the first golf course in this region is in the golf rich area just south of Inverness, the unofficial Capital of the Highlands.

ABERNETHY GOLF COURSE
Nethy Bridge, Inverness-shire PH25 3EB
www.abernethygolfclub.com   01479-821305
Heathland, 5052 yards, par 66, £20 day

AMENITIES: There's no golf shop, but the tearoom food is lovely and the staff is great. It's a popular spot with locals.

COURSE COMMENTS: The Abernethy course was built in 1893 and the new clubhouse in 1965.   This 9-hole track is slightly hilly, but not a difficult walk.   As one golfer noted, the course is "not particularly difficult, but easy to get into trouble and lose strokes around the greens."   The 2nd, a 115-yard par 3, crosses a small pond (shouldn't be in play) and a road.   The tiered green is protected on both sides by bunkers.   The 7th is the hardest hole on the course, a 414-yard par 4 which starts with a blind tee shot into a large hill. The second shot for most is still blind into a green fronted by numerous undulations. It's a beautiful hole with a stand of fine old Caledonian pine trees along the left.   A unique feature of the course is the World War I monument in play in the middle of the 8th fairway.   Local knowledge says to aim just left of the monument on your tee shot, but take care, the monument is in play.   A fun, challenging course and some good home cooking before or after; what could be better.

COMMENTS FROM THE FORWARD TEES: This 9-hole course was so much more than it seemed when we drove up.   The holes are quite unique one from the next.   The yardage for nine holes is 2420 yards which isn't too long and has a par of 36. On the second water can be difficult so "don't see the water." The 7th at 364 is a short par 5, but there are several other things to worry about on the hole including the sharp dogleg, woods and heather on left, and it's uphill to green. I especially liked the last two holes. Yes, you do have to shoot around the Monument on eight, but it isn't as much in play for women as men. The 9th goes back up hill and has a difficult approach shot that requires hitting up and over bunkers and landing on the green. Still it was straight and visible from the tee box.

BLAIR ATHOLL GOLF COURSE
Invertilt Road, Blair Atholl, Perthshire PH18 5TG
www.blairathollgolf.co.uk   01796-481407
Parkland, 5816 yards (18), par 68, £20

AMENITIES: Small clubhouse with bar and restaurant. No golf shop.

COURSE COMMENTS: The 9-hole Blair Atholl Golf Club was founded in 1896 and the present course was designed by James Braid. The club has continued to modernize with the addition of new stonework ponds. Bunkers, fairway and greenside, are in play on several holes, the ponds will play on two holes, and trees are always a concern. On one hole the River Garry plays all the way along the right side. The 3rd and 9th share a double green. Speaking of the 3rd (308-yard par 4) and the 9th (508-yard par 5), after the opening shot or shots you approach the double green which is raised about 20 feet. The 6th is a 245-yard par 3 (plays 195 yards from the members' tee) on which five bunkers protect a medium-sized green. There is room to run a ball up between the bunkers. While playing the 9th with my friend, Grady Morgan, he chipped in his fourth shot from about ten yards off the green for a birdie. Several members standing outside of the bar gave polite golf claps. Grady yelled up to them, "My first birdie in Scotland." One of the members yelled back to him, "Laddie, we have a tradition around here that whenever someone makes their first Scottish birdie they buy drinks for the clubhouse." Grady would have done it too if his wife Helen hadn't taken the credit cards. Blair Atholl is a small course in a great tourist area (Blair Castle, Pitlochry, House of Bruar, Edradour Distillery are all nearby) and is worth a go.

COMMENTS FROM THE FORWARD TEES: Blair Atholl is a pleasant 9-hole course set across the road from the castle and along the River Garry. It has many challenges which make it interesting to play. There are long par 5s, a short par three protected by bunkers all around, and a very long par 3 with two mounded bunkers which must be navigated through or over. The 7th and 8th both have water in play, as well as trees along the right. This small course will hold your attention and require some golfing skills.

BOAT OF GARTEN GOLF AND TENNIS CLUB
Nethybridge Road, Boat of Garten, Inverness-shire
    PH24 3BQ
www.boatgolf.com   01479-831282
Heathland, 5876 yards, par 70, £35

AMENITIES: The attractive clubhouse lounge which looks out to the first hole is a good spot for lunch. The new golf shop is fully equipped.

COURSE COMMENTS: This James Braid 1898 design sets the standard of excellence in heathland golf. The holes naturally follow the contours of the Highland hills and the scenery, including the Strathspey Steam Railway which runs beside the course, is breathtaking. The challenges at Boat are the elevation changes (not really strenuous walking), the heather and rough under the birches, and of course, the Braid bunkers, more than 30 of which are in play and many are fairly tough. The course needs no water hazards. The greens at Boat are moderate sized and, except for the 12th which is two-tiered, have subtle borrows. Fun to play anytime, the course can exact its toll if you're not on top of your game.

All holes are lovely and interesting, but the real character of the course is felt starting at the second, a 351-yard par 4 called *Park*. Drive downhill on this moderate dogleg right, then climb to an elevated green with bunkers on each side. Lovely, classic golf. The sixth, *Avenue* (named for the avenue of birch trees you drive through), a par 4 of 393-yards, was Braid's choice as a signature hole. Stay left on your drive down the avenue to have the best chance to go for the green protected by bunkers left and right. *Avenue* is followed by the 370-yard par 4 seventh, *Bell*. The fairway is generous but rises to a crest about 80 yards from the green. Your approach will be blind to a green with a tough bunker on the left. The 11th, *Braeriach*, a 352-yard par 4, is a very tight driving hole and a good drive is the key here. No other hazards are needed on this pretty hole. *Gully*, the 289-yard par 4 fifteenth, is the hole everyone will ask about in the clubhouse lounge. "How'd you play *Gully*?" is a real conversation starter. With a deep 40-yard gully starting about 120 yards from the green, you can play the hole three ways: try to drive over the gully, hit for the gully and wedge to the green, lay back short of the gully and leave a short to mid-iron in. There is no correct way to play it and the green is tricky to putt no matter how you get there. Last time I played I tried to hit for the gully and ended up missing right into the heather. As I approached my ball, I flushed a covey of ptarmigan and all I could do was point (Good dog, Bob!). The 18th, *Road*, can be a real score-wrecker. This 426-yard par 4 is downhill from the tee and then back up to a very elevated green. The large mound of green is a hard target to hold and bunkers left and right are definitely in play. In wind and weather the Boat can be brutal, but in any condition it's a great course.

COMMENTS FROM THE FORWARD TEES: This is one course I love to play every chance I get. There are still holes I want to try again because I have never met my own expectations. The course has so much variety hole to hole. It has some very long holes and scoring well here is a challenge, but a great fun challenge. Fairways are wide enough for most women golfers to stay in play, but off the fairway is real trouble on most holes. The setting, in birch forest and Highland hills, is absolutely stunning.

BRORA GOLF COURSE
43 Golf Road, Brora, Sutherland KW9 6QS
www.broragolf.co.uk   01408-621417
Links, 6156 yards, par 69, £40

AMENITIES: Beautiful clubhouse with views of the course and the North Sea. Bar serves high quality full meals. Complete golf shop in the clubhouse.

COURSE COMMENTS: Brora GC is one of James Braid's most northerly designs and is the headquarters of the James Braid Golfing Society, a group organized to honor Braid, his accomplishments, and ideals.   The Braid 1923 layout has hardly been altered. The course is a lovely 18-hole links gem where the front nine follows the contours of Kintradwell Bay. The inward nine runs alongside crofter lands with OB ever-present on the right. A quaint aspect to Brora is the electrified fencing around the greens to protect them from livestock which still graze on this "common land."   It also makes for an interesting local rule which plays cow pies as "casual water."   Gorse, whins, bunkers, a burn, and even a railway on ten affect play. As on most coastal links courses it is the wind which will most affect your game.   The course always affords great views of the North Sea and nearby Ben Bhraggie. The holes at Brora will attract your attention as well. On the 5th, *Burn*, a par 4 of 428 yards, the small burn which crosses the fairway about 250 yards out after your blind drive (to the right of the aiming post is the best line) flows down from the Clynelish Distillery. Try a dram of the local product in the clubhouse after your round, or visit the distillery (closed on Sundays) only a few miles away.   Your tee shot should stay short of the burn and will leave a fairly substantial shot to the small green.   The burn comes into play again at the 7th, a 350-yard par 4. The fairway drops a bit from the tee and then drops again, over a rough-covered slope, at about 200 yards out.   The burn, about 75 yards from the green, will be a problem for short hitters or mishit second shots.   The small green has a pot bunker left and another right to add interest. The 13th is called *Snake*, which is exactly what the burn does across the fairway on this short par 3. Even though all tee shots must carry the burn twice, the water is only a visual factor. The five dangerous bunkers surrounding the small green demand far more attention. Both times we've played the course we've had to wait for either sheep or cows to cross in front of the green at the 430-yard 15th--be on watch for the locals there. Brora GC doesn't have the elevation changes of Royal Dornoch, nor the royal pedigree, but it is a fine course worth a special trip.

COMMENTS FROM THE FORWARD TEES: A great links course with specular ocean views. This course always seem to have the upper hand when I play. The effects of any links course seem to be magnified here; it's like the rolls and bounces take over and I am at the mercy of the course. The linksland can also be a friend, giving me an extra yardage or a good lie. The greens seem fast to me so it takes a little adjustment to get the speed right. I do like this course and enjoy the challenges.

FORTROSE & ROSEMARKIE GOLF COURSE
Ness Road East, Fortrose, Black Isle IV10 8SE
www.fortrosegolfclub.co.uk   01281-620529
Links, 5890 yards, par 71, £36

AMENITIES: Private lounge/restaurant above the well-stocked golf shop, but playing a round qualifies you as a member for the day. The soups in the lounge have been especially good.

COURSE COMMENTS: Golf has been played on this spit of land, Chanonry Point, since 1793, but the current course was the design work of James Braid in 1924 when it was extended from nine to 18 holes. The course, named for the two nearby villages, has been called "a gem of a course" and "perhaps the brightest jewel in the Highland's golfing crown." Whether it's the brightest jewel or not, it is one of my favorite courses. All the holes play on a spit of land, Chanonry Point, jutting out in the Moray Firth. With eight holes playing beside the firth and the rest of the holes playing in the linksland between the shores, all the elements of traditional links golf come into play--wind, weather, bunkers, marram or fescue grasses, and gorse or whins. The beach is in play, and not impossible to hit out of, as I found out at the second hole one round. There are many interesting holes at Fortrose (pronounced FORT-ress), but the fourth and fifth stand out. Number four, *Lighthouse*, is a 455-yard par 5 from the medal tees and a 446-yard par 4 from the member's/visitor's tees. Unfair! This tough hole plays along the firth, but it is the tall hummocks and blind second and third shots to an undulating green that will give you fits. The Chanonry Lighthouse is just off the back of the green, but from anywhere near the fairway don't use it as an aiming point. I've parred the hole once in about six attempts. Bogey is definitely your friend on this hole. *Lighthouse* is followed by *Icehouse*, a tricky 132-yard par 3 which can require anything from a gentle wedge to a rescue club depending on the strength and direction of the wind. The hole is named for an old icehouse behind the green, which is OB if you hit too long. It was on the tee box at the 6th that a local we were playing with told us about the dolphins. Steve, an oncologist at the Inverness hospital, pointed out that a pod of dolphins is often seen cavorting in the firth about this area. Just as he said that we saw the dolphins break water--not a nine-iron shot off shore. It was hard to hit the next tee shot while watching the dolphins play. I did get to experience hitting out of a Braid bunker on the next shot, though. The last hole, *Fiery Hillock*, is a challenging 212-yard par 3 where whins line the fairway ready to grab a stray shot. The bunker fronting the green was at one time a mound upon which fires were lit to send disaster news along the Moray coast. In fact, one of the qualities I like best about Fortrose GC is how steeped in history it is. Besides the *Fiery Hillock*, a memorial stands near the 13th hole to mark the spot where Brahan Seer was burned for foretelling doom and despair which was to befall the House of Seaforth (the local laird). The seer's predictions came true. A marker also rests where you want to land your drive on the 355-yard 17th, and marks the spot on which the last witch in Scotland is reputed to have been burned. Fortrose and

Rosemarkie may be a short course, but at about $50 it's still a great bargain.

COMMENTS FROM THE FORWARD TEES: This wonderful links course is much harder to play than it seems. It is short and flat, or so it seems. As stated above it comes with all the challenges of links golf and added to that is the fantastic setting which can be highly distracting for those who are visual (me). The wind blows here often and the ground is always very hard. I usually hit short but straight down the middle, but when I get here I never know where the ball is going to end up. I enjoy the course but not always my score. As challenging as Fortrose is, it is still one of my favorite courses.

GOLSPIE GOLF COURSE
Ferry Road, Golspie, Sutherland KW10 6ST
www.golspie-golf-club.co.uk   01408-633266
Links, 6000 yards, par 69, £35

AMENITIES: Golspie has a lovely clubhouse which houses the Fairway Restaurant which boasts a new menu every week. No golf shop, but some supplies are available in the bar.

COURSE COMMENTS: The James Braid designed Golspie GC is a better course than it looks on first impression. We had passed it by several times as uninteresting. When we finally played it, we found that the four holes you can see from the parking lot are rather featureless, but that the rest of the course playing along the North Sea and though the dunes is an exciting challenge. Over 50 bunkers, many deep and troublesome, will add to the challenge provided by the almost constant wind. The second is *Kirk*, a 175-yard demanding par 3. The green is protected by four dangerous bunkers and is severely sloped. The 5th is definitely a Braid design. *Sahara* (a popular hole name for links courses) is a 292-yard par 4 which plays along the edge of the sea. It starts with a 150 yard carry to a mogulled fairway which has a large rough-covered hill on the right. An elevated green means the second shot is semi-blind. The hole is a typical example of Braid's work on short par 4s. On the back we enjoyed (although I didn't play it well) the 345-yard two-shot 11th named *Tinker's Camp* (probably a historical reference to a place where itinerant workers or gypsies camped). A narrow fairway is made more narrow close to the green by bunkers left and right. *Sahara Back* is the 217-yard par 3 seventeenth. The long tee shot is made tougher by a large rise in front of the green. Bunkers left mean you should stay right. Thankfully, there is a bailout area short for hitters who can't carry the 195 yards to clear the rise. Golspie GC is busy, and after playing it we know why. Don't be fooled like we were.

GRANTOWN-ON-SPEY GOLF COURSE
Golf Club Road, Grantown-on-Spey, Morayshire
    PH26 3HY
www.grantownonspeygc.co.uk 01479-872079
Parkland/heathland, 5710 yards, par 70, £29

AMENITIES: Very pleasant clubhouse with comfortable bar which serves good food. Separate golf shop is one of the best in the area.

COURSE COMMENTS: Built in 1890, this undulating heathland course with eye-popping views, several burn crossings, and plenty of bunkers has been termed "a challenge to all golfers." The original 9-hole course was expanded in 1911 by Willie Park of Musselburgh, and then in 1921 James Braid was asked to redesign and modernize the course. It is the Braid course golfers play today. Besides the course's trees, more than 70 bunkers will bother your shots, especially on the 16th, a par 3 with 9 traps in play. Seven holes at Grantown have water to contend with, mostly small ditches or burns. The greens here are moderate to small and mostly flat with mild slopes. It's difficult to pick out a couple of holes that will represent the "feel" for the entire course because all the holes are good. The course splits into three distinct areas: holes 1-6 play in the flat parkland, 7-12 play in moderate hilly heath, and 13-18 return to the flat parkland.

The 386-yard par 4 called The Dyke is typical of the parkland front. A small burn runs the length of the hole on the left and two crossing bunkers about 100 yards out from the green will test driving and approach accuracy. The green is distinctly sloped to the left and guarded by one bunker on the right. Next we liked the 5th, Larig Ghru, a 354-yard par 4. The crux of the hole is a nest of traps that cross the fairway just under a 100 yards out from the relatively flat green. The 9th, *Murphey's View*, is probably the most picturesque and finest short par 4 in the area. At only 275 downhill yards, it's easy to go for the green, but be warned: bunkers and heavy rough both right and left wait for any missed shot. This hole is also special for spring-fed water fountain at the tee box. It's some of the sweetest water you'll ever taste. Every time we play we fill extra bottles so we'll have plenty in the car. The 10th, *Caper Cailzie*, a 367-yard par 4, is lined by woods right and left requiring a precise tee shot. A burn crosses about 75 yards in front of the green, making the blind second shot even more demanding. The 16th is a fun one-shotter. *Wee Dunt* is 137 yards from an elevated tee to a green with five fronting bunkers and three more behind. Par is an excellent score here. Another special feature of the course used to be Shaw, the starter/golf shop manager. He was one of the friendliest golf staff we have ever met. On our visit to the course in 2008, Shaw was a week away from retiring. We hope the club has found an able replacement and that Shaw is enjoying his retirement.

COMMENTS FROM THE FORWARD TEES: This course can be hard for ladies because there are some very long holes and numerous hazards, but it is always fun--it is such a beautiful setting and the holes are very interesting and unique. I think 8th is one of the harder par 3s I've played in Scotland. It's only 150 yards but is steeply up hill with heather left and right and a narrow landing area if you're going to lay up. To reach the green you must carry 150 yards to the small saucer shaped green because there is a long deep bunker fronting the green. If you lay up your second shot is still difficult because you'll have a short shot over the bunker to the green. The uphill 184-yard par three 11th hole is also difficult because the area in front of the green is blind from the tee. Check out the 11th when you tee off over it on the 7th. The par 5s are long with the second at 436 yards and sixth at 450 yards. The 12th is only 367 yards but is a tester with fairway bunkers, heather, and a tricky approach. The rest of the back nine is a bit easier. This course is always a challenge, yet it's a course I like to play again and again

HELMSDALE GOLF COURSE
Golf Road, Helmsdale, Sutherland KW8 6JA
www.helmsdale.org/golf 01431-821372 or -821063
Moorland, 1860 yards, par 61 (for 18), £10 for 9

AMENITIES: The old clubhouse was a quaint shack with barely any facilities. The charm may be gone, but the new 2007 small clubhouse is a huge improvement. Open mostly on the weekends. No trolleys for hire.

COURSE COMMENTS: Built in the 1920s, the Helmsdale GC has recently gone through much improvement, mostly by consistent maintenance. Cut into the side of a hill, the holes make good use of the contours of the land. Plenty of gorse and whins can cause trouble, as well as grass-covered dykes on a couple of holes. The 2nd, *Saucer*, is an 82-yard par 3 where a delicate downhill shot is required. The green is protected by a small bunker front and OB five yards past the green. Much more difficult than it seems at first. *Plateau* is the 238-yard par 3 seventh. It's a long, slightly uphill par 3 with the green hidden by a rock wall about half way. A bunker left of the green adds more protection--as if a par 3 this long needs more protection. The one time we played gave us a couple of interesting stories. A young boy followed us up the second and third and then walked into the house just between the third green and the fourth tee. Lunch time, we guessed. In the same round we met an older gentleman walking the course with his dog--one of those dogs who collects balls. The man said that after a busy day, the dog would collect up to a dozen balls on a walk around. Not destination golf, Helmsdale is nonetheless an interesting venture in old-style Scottish golf.

ISLE OF HARRIS GOLF COURSE
Scarista, Isle of Harris, Outer Hebrides
www.harrisgolf.com 01859-550226
Links 9-holes, 2089 yards, par 34, £20 for 18

AMENITIES: Small unique clubhouse built into the hillside above the 1st tee available for club functions. Toilets open and available in the clubhouse. Honesty box where you pick up card. Trolleys are available as are clubs when someone's around.

COURSE COMMENTS: "Golf on the Edge" is the appropriate motto for the club. The course plays on the edge of the island with the Sound of Taransay down the west side of the course. The course was built in 1930 and closed because of the war in 1939. The course didn't reopen until 1985. Now it is a thriving small track worthy of all the difficulties you face getting to it (ferry trip from Isle of Skye or Ullapool, plenty of single track road driving, fierce weather). The course is one of the most beautiful settings for golf in the world. Scarista beach and the Atlantic are in view from most holes and those views can be quite distracting; they are that beautiful. Hall of Famer Sir Nick Faldo has said, "This course is one of the most beautiful settings for golf I have ever experienced." Every year there is a competition at the club for the Faldo Fiver, a five pound note signed by Faldo when he played the course. As beautiful as the course setting is, it is equally challenging. Winds here can be extreme—we were told by a local restaurant owner that the locals consider it just a breeze until the wind reaches 60 miles per hour. The day we played (we were the only ones on the course) the flags were down on eight of the nine greens—only the ninth was protected enough from the wind that flag had not blown out. Besides the ever-present winds, several fairways are sloped and there are several blind shot (both tee and approaches). The usual troubles are also on Isle of Harris GC. Each hole had one of two small bunkers (mostly greenside). the greens are small with some slopes. The greens also are in fairly rough condition, but we found them very puttable. There is a ditch on the left side of the fifth and the sea is in play on the tee shot of the second. After a rain (which is most of the time) there can also be spots of casual water.

With nobody around when we played and the wind howling between 20 to 30 mph, it just seemed right to take a few clubs and non-essentials out of my bag and carry my clubs (my doctor won't know if you don't tell him). It just felt like the right way to play. Despite the wind, the course is great fun to play. The 1st, *Borve*, a 215-yard par 4, starts downhill with a blind shot over a hill and into the wind. A very fitting start to your round at Isle of Harris. The 2nd, *Scarista*, is a 260-yard par 4 where you can bite off as much as you dare on a tee shot over the sea and rocks. Be prepared to have to re-tee. Near the green two chasms cut into the fairway on the left. A long drive into the prevailing wind but downhill starts the 5th, *Langavat*. Second shots on this 297-yard par 4 must find a green protected by one bunker left. The 7th, *Pabbay*, is a fine one-shotter where the green is surrounded on the three sides by dunes. The 162-yard hole is a downhill shot with crossing wind to a green with large traps on the right. The finishing hole is *Killegray*—at 480 yards it's the only par five on the course. The hole plays downhill then up with a small dogleg to the right. The green is surrounded on three sides by dunes. You can call it extreme golf or rustic golf, but after playing you'll definitely call Isle of Harris GC fun golf.

FROM THE FORWARD TEES: The beautiful setting for the course can be distracting and the wind will most of the time be a factor making the course play very interesting. A passing rain shower is possible any day as well. Lots of links bounces means the ball may end up in places you didn't intend. The course is a good walk with most of the hills on the first three holes. Most holes will be a challenge, but for me the aim and slopes on the 7th with the bunker menacing on the downhill right side of the green was most demanding. Harris

GC is a great course for getting a sense of golf from years ago.

KINGUSSIE GOLF COURSE
Gynack Road, Kingussie, Inverness-shire PH21 1LR
www.kingussie-golf.co.uk   01540-661600
Heathland, 5643 yards, par 67, £28

AMENITIES: Classy clubhouse built in 1911 is a hub in the village and one of the liveliest spots in town. Good food served all day. Small golf shop has everything you need for a round.

COURSE COMMENTS: The 9-hole Kingussie (King-YEW-see) golf course opened in 1891 and Harry Vardon designed the second nine in 1908. The picturesque course has only one par 5 and has six par 3s. Heavy rough can cost you a stroke or more, especially if you tangle with the gorse or heather, and the bunkering is more strategic than penal. The course plays over varied topography; several holes play through a meadow, several are on a hillside, and finally you play back down to the meadow. The course has many interesting holes including the 6th, a 325-yard par 4 called *Shepherd's Hut*. On this hole your first shot must be accurate because the hill encroaches on the left and heavy rough waits on the right. If your tee shot is decent the second is short but must negotiate a significant dip in front of the green. The views of the Monadhlieth Mountains from the sixth green and seventh tee are stunning. Speaking of the 7th tee, the first shot from this elevated tee box needs to carry the Gynack River and avoid a large bunker left. Pick the correct club here. After completing the shortest par 3 at 105 yards (the 15th), you must hit next to the longest par 3. The tee shot at 16 must carry fields of gorse and heather and climb to an elevated green. Heavy rough is all the protection the hole needs. Kingussie was a surprise to us. We hadn't heard much about it, but certainly enjoyed playing the course and visiting in the clubhouse lounge. The beauty of the course made its way onto television through the BBC's *Monarch of* *the Glen.* Anne and I were watching one episode where two main characters are shown out on a local golf course. Anne saw twenty or thirty-seconds of the course and said, "That's the clubhouse, first, and fourth hole at Kingussie." We couldn't confirm that Kingussie was the course they used on the show, but Anne has an almost photographic memory for every golf course she's played (which is great, because all I have to do is show her a photo of a hole and she can give me all the details, including how badly I played it).

COMMENTS FROM THE FORWARD TEES: Bob's comments about the topography are right on. This course has it all, flat, hills and side hills, water, trees, wide and narrow fairways, and tough rough. Often for me several of those hazards would come into play. The setting is beautiful especially on a cheerful autumn day. The overall yardage isn't really too long but there are five par 5's and only three par 3's with an overall par of 73. Seven and eight are great back to back par threes. The 7th has an elevated tee and you must hit down and over the burn. A precise shot is required. Then you move on to the 8th which is very difficult because the tee shot is totally blind over a hill. Hole four, *The Fort*, has been difficult for me both times I played this course. It is only 390 yards and a par 5 but the biggest challenge is placing your ball correctly for a tough approach shot to an elevated green. I have also found the 18th hole to be a tester because of the water. Generally, a course I will visit whenever I get the chance.

MUIR OF ORD GOLF COURSE
Great North Road, Muir of Ord IV6 7SX
www.muirofordgolfclub.com 01463-871311
Heathland/moorland, 5229 yards, par 67, £25

AMENITIES: The pleasant clubhouse lounge with views to the 18th green serves golfers meals all day. The small golf shop is well equipped.

COURSE COMMENTS: We had driven by Muir of Ord GC several times without stopping thinking it didn't look too interesting. What a surprise we got when we finally played it. Designed by James Braid in 1875, the course has been updated periodically. The course is quite busy, but still very accommodating to visitors. There's far more challenge to the course than we originally thought. More than 50 bunkers (a good mix of fairway and greenside) are in play. Thankfully, none are too penal and the sand is good. A small pond on the left at the 11th and a double burn crossing on the 12th are the only water hazards. The greens are small and smaller and at least one I'd call miniscule. Most are flat with subtle slopes and a couple have more significant slopes or are tiered. From the course are interesting views of adjacent farmland and the local distillery.

We found much to like while playing the course starting at the 4th, Bridge, a 291-yard par 4. A stone fence runs all the way down the right and is OB. Two fairway traps and three more around the green add difficulty to the short hole. After playing you cross the bridge over the rail tracks to the next hole. *Corrie*, the 154-yard par 3 fifth, is listed as the easiest hole but is still a challenge. Your tee shot needs to clear a grass fore-bunker and avoid traps on each side. Check the flag for wind direction. The 7th, *Braid's* (he often would indicate his favorite hole on the ones he designed), is a short testing 286-yard par 4. Drive up the large hill to the split-level green at the top with a bunker behind. The hill is the only defense the hole needs. *Thirsty*, the par 3 twelfth, is a tough one-shotter of 195 yards. Drive from an elevated tee box (take one or two less clubs) to a fairway split by a burn-- actually there is a second burn before the first part of the fairway but not really a concern. A tree is in the way of the left side of the green so stay to the right. Very entertaining hole. The 14th, *Railway*, is almost a mirror of *Bridge* (4th). Left is the railway line (OB) and there's a large hill right (where ladies tee from). The smallest green on the course is tucked left next to the rail line and is elevated. Next is *Long*, the 415-yard par 4. I think this is the best hole on the course--stroke index #1 and very classic golf. Drive down a fairway flanked by heather and trees and protected by fairway bunkers on each side.

Second (or third) shots must contend with a large fore-bunker in the middle of the fairway as you approach the green with two more guarding bunkers. The 18th, *Hame*, is a long finishing hole with a very elevated green. Left is the best approach on this 395-yard par 4. The hole is much like the 18th at Boat of Garten, another James Braid course. Muir of Ord GC is a fine course to play when in the area.

FROM THE FORWARD TEES: This course offers much more than you see as you drive by. It starts out on one side of the railway and then comes back across the tracks to finish. While being an easy walk, there are dramatic up and downhill shots requiring all your golfing skill. The course isn't too long at 5128 yards and a par of 70. there are three par 5s (the longest at 421 yards) and five par 3s (ranging from 98 to 193 yards). The 98-yard 13th is quite difficult with the hole on top of a hill and the green blind from the tee. The course has great variety in the holes.

ORKNEY GOLF COURSE
Grainbank, Kirkwall, Orkney KW15 1RD
www.orkneygolfclub.co.uk 01856-872457
Parkland (sort of), 5627 yards, par 70, £25 all day

AMENITIES: Clubhouse has lovely views, but is only open certain times. No golf shop; the course has an honesty box for when no one is about.

COURSE COMMENTS: Built in 1903 as a nine-hole course, Orkney GC was expanded to 18 twenty years later. The course had to be redesigned after World War II took its toll. Today, at first glance the course looks uninteresting and plain (parkland turf, some gorse, no trees, only light rough), but looks can be deceiving. If there is no wind, which would be highly unusual for this windswept island location, what you see is what you get; a fairly straight forward course with a few benign bunkers, some gorse here and there, and a few slopes. If there's no wind Orkney golf course is a pleasant practice track. If the wind is up, look out--the wind is the teeth of the course. Although none of the bunkers are too penal, there is a good mix of greenside and fairway traps to keep you honest. The greens are small to medium and fairly flat; a few though have interesting swales. The views from the course of Kirkwall, the hills, and the bay are grand. Cloud formations coming over the hills can be dramatic, but that also might mean rain. In the wet the course drains very well. In the middle of the course is a modern windmill (can be seen from about half the holes) which generates power and will give a good indication of the direction of the wind. Finally, I repeat, be ready for the wind--the wind is Orkney GC. The day I played the wind was a constant 30 miles per hour with some higher gusts around the showers. In the wind I thought the par 3s were especially challenging and interesting. The 4th, *Helliar Holm*, is 153-yards downhill to a green guarded in front by four bunkers. The wind makes club selection difficult. *Whins* is the 151-yard 7th. The tee shot is almost blind over a stand of gorse (the whins) to a small green protected on both sides by bunkers. The 13th, *The Cassie*, is a 145-yard one-shotter uphill to a well-bunkered green. Again, the swirling wind is a key factor on the hole. Next is *Craigfield*, the longest par 3 at 218-yards. The hole plays slightly downhill and the wind is often behind, but it's still a long par 3. The green is small with guarding bunkers. Lest you think that Orkney is just par 3s, I really like one of the three par 5s on the course, the 480-yard 12th called *Scargum*. Much of the time the hole plays into the wind and all the time uphill for the first shot. A couple of fairway traps and a ditch about 200 yards out complicates the hole. The green is relatively unprotected. While no one would call Orkney a golfing destination, if you're touring the island with your clubs Orkney GC is a worthwhile break from the ancient sites of the islands.

PITLOCHRY GOLF COURSE
Golf Course Road, Pitlochry, Perthshire PH16 5QY
www.pitlochrygolf.co.uk 01796-472792
Hilly parkland, 5695 yards, par 69, £30

AMENITIES: Brilliant new (2007) Victorian-style clubhouse serves some of the best food in the area. Large outdoor deck for good weather. Small, but complete golf shop hires pull trolleys and electric trolleys, but not buggies (carts) because the course is too steep.

COURSE COMMENTS: The 18-hole Pitlochry Golf Course, known locally as the Switzerland of Scottish golf, plays up the side of a mountain, or at least it seems that way. On this 1909 Willie Fernie of Troon design, hills become a major hazard (condition of play). Renting a power trolley (called a power caddie) is not a bad idea as the first three holes climb significantly to the top of the course. From there the course plays up and down (less dramatically) until the big drop at the 18th. Druid stones and the remnants of a Pictish fort can be found on the course. The 6th, called *Druid Stone*, is a 378-yard par 4 where you hit from an elevated tee (the ladies' tee is even higher than the gents) down to a wide fairway with a copse of trees left and a bunker further left in play for longer hitters. The second shot continues down to a green protected all around by five bunkers. Druid stones are just off the back of the green. Another short hole with plenty of trouble is *Tulloch*, the 284-yard par 4 fourteenth. The fairway is filled with hummocks and hillocks, with trees left and right, and a small burn further left (can be in play). The second shot must negotiate more swales to a green protected back and right by bunkers. Next is *Drumcroy*, a 300-yard par 4 which turns uphill toward a very elevated green. Tee shot should skirt to the left of a large copse of trees which acts as a ball magnet. If you've left yourself in good position, the second shot is to a green only guarded by the hill, oh yes, and bunkers left and right. The 18th is just plain fun. Downhill blind tee shot to a wide fairway leaves a mid to short-iron over a major burn to a green protected by large bunkers. Don't let the reputation as a hilly course deter you or stories about needing mountain goats to haul your golf bag scare you. You might huff -n-puff a little, but Pitlochry GC is a fun track.

COMMENTS FROM THE FORWARD TEES: This course is hilly and if you survive the climb on the first three holes enjoy the break on the 4th because the 5th takes you to the top of the knock. At the tee box of 5 enjoy the view and ponder the legend that says that Mary Queen of Scots rested by this tee. I found I needed to rest at all the tee boxes. I do recommend bringing or renting an electric trolley from the pro shop. The course is 5127 yards with a par 72 from the forward tees. There are three par 3s varying from 115 to 149 yards. Each has a unique challenge but the 16h is the most fun with a steep downhill shot to a green with trees on both sides. The three par 5s aren't very long but offer true golf tests of skill. Besides the ups and downs to deal with the course has plenty of bunkers and two of the three par 5s (the 1st and 13th) have water to add to the test. I love the views from the course and the history of the area. This is always a fun golf experience and there are several holes on this course I still want to "do better next time." Enjoy!

REAY GOLF COURSE
The Clubhouse, Reay, Caithness KW14 7RE
www.reaygolfclub.co.uk   01847-811288
Links, 5831 yards, par 69, £25

AMENITIES: Reay GC has a pleasant clubhouse with lounge built in 1963. Golfers' snacks are served most usual hours. An honesty box is in the entry way for when nobody is about--sign in, put your money in the box with half a ticket, and play away.

COURSE COMMENTS: The most northerly golf course on the Great Britain mainland, Reay is out-of-the-way, but still worth the effort to seek out. The course, a 1933 James Braid layout, plays in the linksland along Sandside Bay. While the numerous bunkers aren't too penal, the dune grasses will eat any wayward golf balls. Wind and weather are the course's most formidable defenses. When we played the course, the wind at the beginning of our round was only about 20 miles per hour, but by the end was blowing at a hefty 40. We still enjoyed the challenge and found several interesting holes to attract our attention. The 4th, *Sahara*, a

584-yard par 5, is a long reach into the prevailing wind or a quartering wind. A blind tee shot to a fairly generous fairway starts the hole. Play down the mounded fairway to a green tucked between two fronting bunkers. *Braid's Choice*, the 477-yard par 5 sixth is a dogleg left which will often play downwind. The green is protected by a bunker right and a burn left and behind. It's still a birdie opportunity. The back side is generally more interesting than the front, and we picked the 13th, *Spring Lochy*, as an interesting example. This 305-yard par 4 plays downhill and into the wind. Watch your ball carefully on the drive because there's not much fairway. The green is down in a hollow with two pot bunkers fronting left and right for added challenge. Reay is a course meant to be played in the wind. No one we talked to could remember playing in the calm.

ROYAL DORNOCH GOLF COURSE
Golf Road, Dornoch, Sutherland IV25 3LW
www.royaldornoch.com 01862-810219
Links, 6595 yards, par 70, £85

AMENITIES: Beautiful, historic clubhouse available to members, guests, and day ticketers. Food is excellent. Golf shop beneath the lounge is the best in the area. The second Dornoch course, Struie, is well worth a round (see *Hidden Gems II: Scotland and Wales*).

COURSE COMMENTS: The third oldest golf links in Scotland of which there are written records (1616, St Andrews 1552, Leith 1593), the Royal Dornoch course is one of the best in the world. It would be an Open venue if it weren't so far out of the way. The Dornoch club was founded in 1877 when the course was only nine holes. It was redesigned by Old Tom Morris shortly after it opened and three years later a second nine was added. In 1906 the course was granted a Royal Charter by King Edward VII. Dornoch's remoteness adds much to its mystique and charm. Here is a topnotch course, on par with the Turnberrys, Royal Troons, and Muirfields, that almost anyone can play (with a handicap certificate under 25 for men and under 32 for women). Although the course is on the list of many tour groups, it's still possible to walk-on many days. The course is on almost everyone's "to do" list and consistently rated in the top twenty in the world. It's desirability has increased because of the fine book by Lorne Rubenstein, *A Season in Dornoch: Golf and Life in the Scottish Highlands*, which tells of Rubenstein's three-month stay in the village, and his love affair with Royal Dornoch. When Anne and I first played in 2002, we played with a Canadian who had come to Dornoch just because of the book, and it was to be his only golf during his trip.

Royal Dornoch has a strong American connection because the famous Scottish-American golf architect Donald Ross (Pinehurst #2 and over 600 other courses) was born in Dornoch and played his formative years on the course. This is a great links course with six holes playing next to the Dornoch Firth, spectacular bunkering, plenty of gorse and whins, several elevated tees and greens, and a few blind shots. The course begins innocently enough with a 331-yard par 4 protected by nine bunkers, heavy rough left and right, and OB further left. As fearsome as this sounds, it is really an easy beginning--the trouble is abundant if you stray, but birdie is available to straight hitters like Anne (a 24 handicapper). The second hole, *Ord*, a 177-yard par 3, presents more of a challenge. The plateau green is the target, and to miss right or left puts you into deep, punishing bunkers, as Anne discovered after her birdie. Ah, the fickle fortunes of golf! In fact, Tom Watson, five time British Open winner, was asked to name the toughest shot at Dornoch. He answered, "The second to the second." These opening holes indicate that fair, tough golf is what is to come in the round. Not a bad hole can be found on the course, and no two are really the same. The 6th, *Whinny Brae*, meaning "hillside full of gorse" (figurative and literal definition), is a tricky 163-yard one-shotter. Tee shots contend with a plateau green, a steep hillside of gorse left, three bunkers left, a deep bunker front right, and steep drop-off back and right. On my first go, I found the middle left bunker and made what, for me, was a great bunker shot to keep the ball on the green. Bogey can be very good here. The 13th, *Bents* is a tremendous par 3 at 166 yards from the medal tees. From an elevated tee you hit down to a small green surrounded by seven bunkers. Get plenty of bunker practice before coming to Dornoch because you'll get plenty of opportunities from bunkers when you're here. *Valley*, Royal Dornoch's 405-yard par 4 seventeenth is a fun hole. The blind drive (aim a little left of the aiming pole) is to a lower tier fairway (40-foot drop) which turns sharply left. The second shot must clear a high bank and avoid three bunkers. The green is relatively benign after the first two shots. My only complaint about the 18th, *Home*, is that it comes far too soon in the round. Especially if you get to play in pleasant or reasonably nice weather, you don't want the round to end.

Professional golfers like Tom Watson, Ben Crenshaw, Nick Faldo, and Greg Norman have sung the praises of Royal Dornoch. Other golfers call their experience at Dornoch "remarkable." This is an out-of-the-way golfing experience that's out of this world and worth every effort it takes to make it possible.

COMMENTS FROM THE FORWARD TEES: We have been lucky to play Royal Dornoch in good weather each time we played in September. I have played many links courses but on this one I seem to have more trouble placing the ball anywhere near the spot I'm planning. The challenges are all here: gorse, wind, links rolls, slopes, bunkers, and bigger bunkers and it is still one of my all time favorite courses. Yardage is very fair for women, but sometimes the bunkers along the way make the hole seem much longer. Always a fun challenge to play Royal Dornoch.

TAIN GOLF COURSE
Chapel Road, Tain, Ross-shire IV19 1JE
www.tain-golfclub.co.uk 01862-893313
Links, 6404 yards, par 70, £45

AMENITIES: 1998 clubhouse has a convenient lounge serving good food most of the day (not that the rest of the day they serve bad food). Small golf shop is well-stocked.

COURSE COMMENTS: The 1890 Old Tom Morris designed Tain Golf Club joins Nairn, Royal Dornoch, Castle Stewart, and Brora as the premier links courses in this corner of Scotland. The links course is set along the Dornoch Firth and affords grand sea views--you can also see over to the Glenmorangie Distillery, an interesting stop in its own right. Fifty-eight bunkers are in play and most are deep or penal. Gorse, Scotch broom, and burns on several holes will affect play--water is a major problem on the 2nd, 16th, and 17th. Greens are moderate and some have distinct sloping. The wind, though, as on all links courses is the most compelling condition of play. At Tain all holes are good, but several stand out. The 3rd, *Knowe*, a 435-yard par 4, is listed as stroke index #1, hardest on the course. This long curving dogleg left has burns short right and left off the tee. The narrow green is protected by a trap right and a gully in front. The hole is deserving of its rating. The 9th, *Mafeking*, is a 355-yard dogleg right with bunkers and trees at the inside corner. Laying up short of a left side bunker (227 yards) sets up a good view of the green. According to almost everyone who plays it, the 11th, *Alps*, is "a great hole." On the 380-yard par 4 your drive must be good because the second shot over a large hill will be blind. Be careful short of the hill because a dangerous pot bunker will collect shots. A par here will feel like a birdie on almost any other hole. For a par 3 we really like *Black Bridge*, the 215-yard 17th. A daunting tee shot must cross the river twice (the river is also close to the right side of the green). A mound between the bends in the river can also deflect low tee shots. It's a fun challenge. Tain is a championship course at a reasonable price.

COMMENTS FROM THE FORWARD TEES: This is a links course that is a true test of your golf. The course requires strategy in ball placement and some lucky links bounces. There are only three par 3s for ladies on this course--two are reachable for most ladies but the 8th is long at

179 yards and makes par difficult for me. There are four par 5s with two very long. The 4th is 478 gorse-lined yards with mounds in the fairway. Number 13 is 486 yards but is more open off the tee and seemed easier. Two memorable holes are the par 3 sixteen and seventeen. The burn twists around these two greens and the challenge is terrific. I was thrilled to bogey both of these holes. There are many bunkers, tough rough, gorse bushes, water and some great views which all add to the enjoyable golf challenge at Tain.

TARBAT GOLF COURSE
Tarbatness Road, Portmahomack, Ross-shire IV20 1YJ
www.tarbatgolf.com   07849-177353
Inland links, 5298 yards, par 68, £20 all day

AMENITIES: The Tee Up Cafe is the main feature of the clubhouse.   Check in for golf at the cafe or use the honesty box in the changing rooms. No trolleys.
COURSE COMMENTS: The 9-hole links layout (not too far from the Dornoch Firth) was established in 1909. The Dornoch and Moray Firths are visible from most holes. The course is a fairly simple layout with no trick, but enough bunkering to give a challenge. The 5th, *Don's View*, is an interesting 177-yard par 3. The tee shot must thread its way between two large, deep, steep-faced bunkers to a moderate sized green. My favorite on the course is the 8th, *Jackie's Brawist*, a 302-yard par 4. From the tee you can see the flag (with a local church behind), but between you and the flag are 250 yards of hillocks, hummocks, and swales. Play the course a hundred times and you'll have a different lie every time. The lies won't be bad, just different. The second shot must negotiate the rest of the swales. The course, especially with the addition of the new cafe, is worth a round.

PUBS, RESTAURANTS, & TEAROOMS

Anchorage Restaurant on the pier at Leverburgh on the southwest coast of Isle of Harris. Seaside nautical restaurant with good views of the harbour. Serves mostly fish with numerous specials. Fish pie and whitebait were both delicious. Gets very crowded in season, best to book.

Anderson's Restaurant on Desher Road in Boat of Garten, just a few blocks away from the golf course. The best bistro-style fine dining in the area. Emphasis is on local products and seasonal items. Quality selection of malts and delicious meals. Try the homemade ice cream for dessert. Be sure to book ahead.

An Lanntair Cafe in the An Lanntair (cinema and art gallery) on South Beach Street (waterfront) in Stornaway, Isle of Lewis. Modern cafe and bar with several eating and drinking areas. Pub food is quite good. No real atmosphere, but they did have a music session the night we were there.

Basil Harbour Cafe on the harbour at Nairn. Small cafe with l unches and larger meals available. Recommended by the Harbour Master.

Birsay Bay Tearoom at the end of the road in Birsay Village, Orkney (follow the signs). Cottage tearoom serves local produce (from greenhouses next door) and home-made sweets.

Ben Mhor Hotel (pub) on the main street through Granton-on-Spey. Comfortable old pub with upscale pub food and reasonable prices.

Cafe Biba on the main street of Pitlochry. Part of a chain with eight locations in Scotland, not a bad stop for a quick bite or a sweet.

Cafelolz@21 (tearoom) on Albert Street, Kirkwall, Orkney, in the heart of the shopping district. Limited menu, but good food.

The Cairngorm Hotel Restaurant on the main road through Aviemore is a good place for breakfast, lunch, after-noon tea, dinner, or just a dram or a pint. Broad menus and quality food are features of the restaurant. Special themed menus on certain nights to attract tourists.

Coffee Corner on the main road through Aviemore. Typical tearoom is extremely busy most of the time. Table service and the lattes were good.

The Coffee Pot on the main road through Aviemore north of the main shops. Small shops with typical tearoom breakfast and lunch items, as well as specialty sweets.

The Cluanie Inn on A87 about 20 miles west of Eilean Donan Castle on the way to or from Isle of Skye. Hunting or mountain lodge-style hotel with a great selection of whiskies plus lunch and full dinner menus. Great mountain views and friendly staff.

Crianlarich Hotel on the main highway through town. This hunting/fishing lodge has a small bar and large dining room which serves a full menu. Good spot in a snow storm.

Cromdale Bar and Restaurant (pub) in the Haugh Hotel on the main road through Cromdale. Excellent pub food in the bar which mostly caters to locals. Recommended to us by local golf manager.

Digby Chick at 5 Bank Street in downtown Stornaway, Isle of Lewis (a block off the harbour). The name Digby Chick refers to the village of Digby in Nova Scotia which is famous for its scallops, called Digby chicks. The Stornaway restaurant serves several version of scallops, thus adopted the name. Fine dining restaurant with a small eclectic menu of seafood and steaks.

Dornoch Patisserie and Cafe on High Street in Dornoch, behind the cathedral. Tearoom where all the sweets are homemade. Good spot for a snack or light lunch before or after golf.

The Eagle Hotel (pub) on the main street of Dornoch ten minutes walk from Royal Dornoch GC. A noisy golfer's pub which serves good pub grub at good prices. Occasionally has music.

First Fruit Tearoom across from the Tourist Information Centre in Tarbert, Isle of Harris. Cottage-style tearoom with basics nicely done. Busy place where you share tables waiting for the ferries.

The Garden (tearoom) near the ferry terminal in Mallaig over looking the water.Complete lunch menu and both indoor and outdoor seating.

Garth Hotel and Restaurant on the main street through Grantown-on-Spey. Fine dining, excellent food, and prices to match. Reservations recommended.

The Glenmore Cafe on the main road up to the Cairngorm Funicular Train and across from the Glenmore Visitor's Centre. Alpine-style cafe with simple booths and tables serves good soups, sandwiches, and sweets-- especially known for its homemade apple strudel. Outside the cafe windows are feeding areas for birds, red squirrels, and the occasional pine marten.

The Granary on the town square in Portree, Isle of Skye. Large restaurant with several eating areas. Old hotel-style, but it's not a hotel. Large lunch and dinner menu. Very popular with locals and travelers. We keep going back.

The Harbour Restaurant on the main road through Broadford, Isle of Skye. Nicely decorated bistro-style restaurant with full bar, but can only serve drinks with meals. Of course, the menu is heavy on seafood, but also has good selection of meat and chicken dishes. Excellent food.

Househill Farm Shop Cafe on A936 near Nairn. Modern farm store and cafe. Shop has interesting food items. Food is well prepared and tasty. Quite busy.

Howie's Bistro on the main street of Dunked and on St James in Perth. A cafe/bistro which serves a full menu of soups and sandwiches and dinner items.

Inshraich Nursery & Tearoom on B970 about four miles south of Aviemore. Small tearoom specializing in cakes (by the slice or whole) in a lovely nursery setting.

Julia's Cafe across from the ferry terminal in Stromness, Orkney. Seaside tearoom serving breakfast and lunches. The fish pie is a specialty and the apple pie is very good.

The Keeper's Kitchen on the main road through Newtonmore. The gift shop and tearoom in the middle of the village has a garden in the back with a pond and small eating area. Nice selection of sweets.

Kirkwall Hotel (pub/restaurant) on the harbour in Kirkwall, Orkney. Highly recommended as the best in town. We had tasty lamb and chicken dishes. Try the crispy cheese as a starter.

Le Bistro (restaurant) on St George's Street in the heart of the shopping area of Thurso. Better than pub food in a cosy setting.

Loch Croistean Tearoom on the only road out to the beaches at Uig on the Isle of Lewis. House converted to a tearoom in the middle of nowhere. Lovely room with great tearoom fare and homemade sweets. Very friendly owner.

Loch Tummel Inn (pub/restaurant) on B8019 west of the Queen's View Visitor Centre. Out of the way, but worth seeking out. Known for its interesting menu and great food.

Lower Deck on the Portree harbour, Isle of Skye. The nautical themed restaurant has a limited menu (small but adequate) of mostly fish dishes. Decent food.

Lucano (restaurant) on Victoria Street in Kirkwall, Orkney. Very tasty Italian dishes, but a little light on the protein. Good service.

Maclean's Highland Bakery on the main road through Grantown-on-Spey. Modern bakery/tearoom with meat pies, filled rolls, and plenty of sweets. Very popular with locals.

McKay's Hotel (pub/bistro) on the main street in Pitlochry. Outside seating on the busy main street of a prime shopper's town. Typical pub food.

Moulin Inn (pub) in Moulin about two miles east of Pitlochry on the way to Edradour Distillery. The inn and its brewery are about the only things in the hamlet, but that's all that's needed. One of the best pubs in

Scotland. Great food, interesting menu, wonderful ambiance, and its own brewery.

Mountain Cafe on the main road through Aviemore above the mountain equipment shop across from the village parking lot. Large room with great photos and displays of old mountain equipment. Breakfast and lunch menus plus a wide selection of sweets. One of the best places to eat in town, therefore one of the busiest.

North Harbour Bistro and Tearoom on the main road through the village of Scalpay, Isle of Harris. Don't be fooled by the bland exterior (the village community shop). Quaint dining room with a nice view of the harbour. Restaurant serves from a broad lunch and dinner menu where the mains are unique (such as porkbelly with scallops and braised beef cheeks). Excellent chowder.

North Kessock Hotel (pub) off A9 just north of Inverness. With a convenient location near the Moray Firth and the Dolphin Centre, the pub serves good food at decent prices. So good we ate there two nights in a row.

Old Bakery (tearoom) in Carrbridge across from the photogenic Packhorse Bridge. Good sweets and coffees and teas. Good place to pick up local events. Be sure to have a good look at the locally made quilt on the wall.

Old Bridge Inn (pub) behind the train station in Aviemore. Good pub food in a pleasant setting.

Port-na-Craig Inn and Restaurant (pub/restaurant) near the Festival theatre in Pitlochry. Both pub dining and fine dining in a beautiful setting along the Garry River. Wonderful outdoor eating area if the weather allows.

Roos Leap (restaurant) in the heart of the village of Aviemore across from the Cairngorm Hotel. Modern cafe/ restaurant in a part of the old rail station serves burgers, sandwiches, steaks, and a few Aussie items.

The Rowan Tree Country Hotel and Restaurant between Aviemore and Kingussie. One of the best places to eat in Scotland, The Rowan Tree Restaurant in the 18th century coaching inn serves elegant large meals in a beautiful rustic setting. Must book ahead.

Speyside Heather Centre & Clootie Dumpling (tearoom) on the road between Aviemore and Grantown-on-Spey. The Heather Centre is worth a browse and the Clootie Dumpling (a specialty cake with custard sauce) Tearoom serves soups, sandwiches, and sweets including 21 kinds of dumplings. Always a pleasant stop.

Storehouse Restaurant and Farm Shop (tearoom/cafeteria) at Foulis Ferry on A9 between Inverness and Dornoch. Great food and interesting shopping in the middle of nowhere. Recognized as one of the Top Ten Breakfasts in Scotland.

Sutherland House (restaurant) five minutes walk from Royal Dornoch GC. As far as we're concerned it's the best food in Dornoch. Always top quality and fair prices.

Sutor Creek Cafe on Bank Street in Cromarty (Black Isle) near the harbour. Cafe/bistro serves lunch menu and specializes in delicious wood-fired pizzas. Small dinner menu with interesting items. Worth making the effort to get to.

Taybank Hotel (pub) next to the River Tay bridge in Dunkeld. Old-style pub serves traditional Scottish pub food including stovies. Music in the bar and upstairs many nights.

The Tipsy Laird on the main street through Kingussie. Traditional pub with front bar and two dining areas. Traditional fare, heavy on burgers and specials. Takes pride in serving haggis.

Trenabies Bistro (cafe) Albert Street, Kirkwall, Orkney, toward the harbour from the cathedral. Typical town cafe with good food.

Victoria's Restaurant and Coffee Shop on Atholl Road (the main street through town) in Pitlochry. Modern restaurant with seating inside and out. Large restaurant menu and a wide selection of specialty sandwiches.

The Water Mill (tearoom) across road and down a side street from the entrance to the castle in Blair Atholl. Historic working mill with in and outside eating areas. Good soups, sandwiches, special breads and sweets.

Waterside Cafe Bistro & Gallery on the main road in Dunvegan, Isle of Skye. Tearoom with a large menu in a converted petrol station. Great story of trying to do it all themselves—local sources, finish the breads, change the fish in the chowder based on local catch.

The Winking Owl on the main street through Aviemore. Gastro-pub under new ownership serving some upscale pub favorites and eight of their own brews. Good food, decent prices.

LODGINGS

1 Janet Street B&B
1 Janet Street, Thurso, Caithness KW14 7AR
01847-895906 www.1janetstreet.co.uk £60
Lovely listed building houses some large nicely appointed rooms. Easy walk to the downtown area. Catrione and Andrew Tait are excellent hosts.

Ballach Guest House
Viewfield Road, Portree, Isle of Skye IV51 9ES
01478-612093 www.ballach-skye.com £70
Barbara Campbell runs an excellent B&B directly across the street from our other favorite, Durinish. Nice rooms and good breakfast.

Craigiewood B&B
Black Isle, near Inverness IV1 3XG
01463-731628 www.craigiewood.co.uk £80
Lovely country home about four miles from Inverness, but fairly isolated in the country setting. Hosts Gavin (who organizes garden tours in the area) and Araminta (who cooks with famous chef Claire Macdonald) work hard to make your stay enjoyable.

Durinish B&B
Viewfield Road, Portree, Isle of Skye IV51 9ES
01478-613728 www.durinish-bandb-skye.com £80
Ruth and Allan Prior are great hosts and the B&B is top notch. Don't be alarmed to see an ambulance in the driveway as Allan is a driver. Easy access to town via main road and even walkable in good weather. Highly recommended.

Eagle Hotel
3 Castle Street, Dornoch IV25 3SR
01853-855558   www.eagledornoch.co.uk   £ moderate
A golfer's hotel with a good pub for drinks, food, and craic. Not high-style accommodations, but decent for the price. With touring golfers the hotel can be noisy, but the staff works hard to not let things get out of hand.

Harris Hotel
Tarbert, Isle of Harris HS3 3DL
01859-502154 www,harrishotel.com £90 room, £110 B&B
Built in 1865 by the 7th Earl of Dunmore, the hotel has been owned and run by the Cameron family since 1903. Nice room and a good breakfast. Not far from the ferry terminal.

Hildeval B&B
Easthill, Kirkwall, Orkney KW15 1LY
01856-878840 www.bedandbreakfast-orkney.com £68
Hildeval is a 4 Star B&B with lovely views especially from the large breakfast room lounge and convenient to the town. Very good breakfast options, including huge Orkney kippers.

Hillside B&B
Durness 1V27 4QA
01971-511737 www.hillside-durness.co.uk £70
Modern B&B near Smoo Cave and only a short distance from the village proper. Gets constant raves of "outstanding" and "wonderful." Jill, Tony, and Ellie Jackson are fine hosts.

Jannel B&B
5 Stewart Drive, Stornaway, Isle of Lewis H51 2TU
01851-705324 www.jannel-stornoway.co.uk £80
Run by a nice young family, the accommodations are modern
and spacious. Hosts are helpful and the location, even though
a little far to walk to town, is nicely situated near the main
auction of roads in this part of the island.

Macrae Guest House
24 Ness Bank, Inverness IV2 4SF £60
01463-243658 www.scotland-inverness.co.uk/macrae
Small pleasant Victorian house on the banks of the River Ness
only five minutes walk from city shops and restaurants.

ATTRACTIONS

Cawdor Castle, Cawdor by Inverness. Just a couple of miles
off the A9 south of Inverness, Cawdor owes much of its
fame to Shakespeare's play *MacBeth*. The real history
of the castle is much different from the Bard's,and the
castle is good for touring.
Clava Cairns (HS), near Cawdor. A field of cairns (burial
mounds) and standing stones from the late-Neolithic or
early Bronze Age period. The cairns are extremely
evocative and date from before the Great Pyramids.
Culloden Battlefield (NTS), near Cawdor. One of the most
important historical sites in Scotland, the Drummossie
Moor, where the Battle of Culloden took place in 1746,
is the site of the last battle on British soil. The battle
ended the dreams of Scottish independence and a
return of the Stuart family (Prince Charles Edward
Stuart, Bonnie Prince Charlie) to the throne. A new
Visitor's Centre does a very good job of making the
complex history understandable.
Distilleries, up the A9. Eduador by Pitlochry, Dalwhinnie,
Tomatin, and Glenmorangie by Tain are all good

distilleries to visit, with informative tours and a tasty dram after. They are all easily accessible from the A9.

Dunrobin Castle, between Dornoch and Brora. The ancestral home of the Earls and Dukes of Sutherland, Dunrobin is the most northerly of Scotland's great houses. Many rooms are open to visitors as well as a formal garden.

Chapter 5: The Northeast Coast

Moray New Golf Course

Up the eastern coast of Scotland from just south of Aberdeen to about Inverness are some of Scotland's best seaside golf courses. Royal Aberdeen, Cruden Bay, Castle Stuart, Nairn, and Old Moray are but a few of the famous courses along this stretch of coastline. Also along this route are fabulous courses less well known, but deserving of a visit.

We start this chapter's tour with one of the best of the Dee-side course (east from Aberdeen along the River Dee).

ABOYNE GOLF COURSE
Formaston Park, Aboyne, Aberdeenshire AB34 5HP
www.aboynegolfclub.co.uk   01339-886328
Parkland, 6009 yards, par 68, £30

AMENITIES: The new clubhouse opened in 1980 and the lounge/bar upstairs has good views of the 1st tee and the 18th green. Serves good food, but only to players and guests. A well-stocked golf shop is in the clubhouse, as well.

COURSE COMMENTS: The club started in 1883, but the Archie Simpson designed course was built in 1905 and later extended to 18. The lovely course plays through rolling hills along the River Dee Valley. The forested course has a wide variety of trees and affords views of Loch Aboyne and surrounding mountains. Forty-four bunkers dot the course, but only 9 and 17 have fairway bunkers, and four holes have no bunkers. Water will be in play (mostly on the right) with ponds or burns on 9, 15, and 16. Greens are mostly small and flat, but a few have slopes and the 5th is tiered. There are a few blind shots, but they are well marked. A bell on the second hole used to be in the clubhouse and was used to tell a local doctor down the road that there was a medical problem on the course.

Although we like all the courses we've played along the Dee-side, Aboyne is our favorite with no bad holes. At the 7th, *Auld Line*, a 483-yard par 5, stay right of the marker post as everything runs left. Best line to the green is the tallest tree behind. The small green is protected by two bunkers left and one right. At the 9th the loch on the right is OB, and while it shouldn't affect play, it will. Aim straight on this gentle dogleg right, but avoid the bunkers left at 220 yards out. The green is flat, but typically protected by bunkers right and left. A blind drive starts *Bonnyside*, the 499-yard par 5 tenth (from members' tees, 426-yard par 4). The fairway dramatically narrows the closer you get to the green which has interesting slopes and no bunkers. The 15th, *Ladywell*, is a sharp dogleg right around a large pond. Take less than a driver on this 377-yard par 4 since it's easy to run out of fairway with a good shot. Be careful when putting because the green has more slope than is evident. Supposedly, the well on the left side of the hole has healing powers. The day we played it could do nothing to heal my game. Next is another dogleg right with a blind drive. Play to the outside of the turn on this 431-yarder as the ball will run to the right. Anything on the right side is in danger of being blocked from the green by a large oak. The green has significant left-to-right break when facing the hole and is guarded by two bunkers. We enjoyed our round with local members, David and Muffie Monroe, who also gave us some useful recommendations for eateries in the area.

COMMENTS FROM THE FORWARD TEES: This pleasant course was harder than it looked. There are slopes, trees, some water, tiny greens, blind shots, and some long carries off the tee. The scenery is stunning when you get up on the side of the hill above the clubhouse and the loch. Par 3s on this course are reasonable lengths but that doesn't make them easy. The 8th hole is the shortest but feels like it is surrounded by trees (it isn't of course) and is visually intimidating. The par 3 twelfth hole requires a long shot to the green. There is no fairway and only a sloping approach for landing short. Par 5s are reasonable with the 7th being the only really long hole. Ladies should enjoy a round on this course, especially if the weather cooperates and is sunny and bright.

BANCHORY GOLF COURSE
Kinneskie Road, Banchory, Aberdeenshire AB31 3TA
www.banchorygolfclub.co.uk 01330-822365
Parkland, 5813 yards, par 68, £30

AMENITIES: The 1980 clubhouse looks out onto several holes and serves good food all day. The golf shop has all the supplies you'll need. There are toilets by 7 and 10, but ask at the golf shop about entry.

COURSE COMMENTS: Another Archie Simpson (of Royal Aberdeen) 1905 design, Banchory (BANK-or-ee) is a lovely parkland course set along the River Dee. Even though close, the town doesn't intrude except with one row of beautiful homes. A grand feature of the course is its absolutely spectacular trees--worth the price of admission. Seventy bunkers, a mix of fairway and greenside, are in play, and three holes have water, all of which is visible and in play. The small to moderate sized greens are mostly flat, but a few are swaled. The course can be wetter than some others in the area because of the proximity to the river. Professional Paul Lawrie (winner of the Open in 1999) started his professional career at Banchory.

One of the most interesting holes at Banchory is the 125-yard 3rd, *Hollow*. The downhill tee shot needs to carry a small burn backed by a stone fence to reach the green with eight bunkers (!) around it. The front is open. Take one or two less clubs and stay to the right side of the sloped green. Good luck! Next is *Fernbank*, a 444-yard par 4, with a long, narrow fairway. Bunkers at about 150 yards should be no problem, but the one left at 225 yards can be. Mounds and three traps about 60 yards in front of the green complicate the approach, as does the one bunker right of the puttable green. On *Firs*, the 353-yard par 4 eleventh, the bunker 190 yards from the tee isn't as much a concern as the OB right--the fairway is plenty wide. The trouble is the massive bunker completely crossing the fairway 50 yards from the otherwise unprotected green. *The Wood*, the 183-yard 12th, has a sloped green set at an angle to the approach and is protected by OB left and burn a few feet in front. Take plenty of club as all the trouble is short. *Doo Cot* (named for the historic dovecot or dove house on the right side of the green) is the short (88 yards) par 3 sixteenth. All uphill and completely blind--similar to the 2nd at Dollar or the 3rd at Shiskine. Hit and hope. One of the best courses to play in the area.

COMMENTS FROM THE FORWARD TEES: Banchory is a lovely course set in stands of evergreens and deciduous trees. The course is of reasonable length at 5357 yards with a par of 71 for ladies. I think this is a very good course for women, but there are plenty of challenges throughout the course. Water is in play for ladies on many holes. It starts with a pond on the left behind the first green. Then on tee shots on the 4th and 6th there is a wee burn that must be cleared. Water also invites your ball on the 7th to the right of the green, and on 8 you must fly at least 120 yards to avoid the next wee burn. On the 9th the pond in front of the green requires approach shots from the right side. The back nine has less water but does have several long holes. I especially liked the 16th which is totally blind from the tee box and the aiming point is just to the left of the copse of trees in the middle of the fairway (unless you can hit 230 yard and get over it). The second shot is down hill to a large green with three bunkers. I want to play this course again soon.

BUCKPOOL GOLF COURSE
Barhill Road, Buckie, AB56 1DU
www.buckpoolgolf.com 01542-832-236
Clifftop links, 5826 yards, par 70, £22

AMENITIES: Pleasant clubhouse lounge which opens onto the tenth and eighteenth greens. Good food and drinks. No golf shop, but trolleys are available.

COURSE COMMENTS: The Buckpool course was built from three farms by the Town Council as part of a national plan in the late 1930s to relieve some of the severe unemployment caused by the depressed herring fishing Industry. While there's no water in play, today's course has a mix of 72 fairway and greenside bunkers, most of which are riveted and penal. The greens are moderate to large and mostly flat; the 12th and 18th are two-tiered. All the greens putt very true, probably because they are some of the best conditioned greens we've seen and will be hard to hold in the dry. Neil, 2011 Club Captain, said the club takes great pride in having the finest greens in the area. Typical of a seaside course, the almost constant wind is a condition of play--and when there's no wind even the locals can be confused about how to play. The sea is in view on about half the holes with great shore views on a couple of holes. Playable all year--bad weather seems to go around the course--Buckpool can be very busy; be sure to call ahead so you're not disappointed.

Buckpool is filled with interesting holes, but one of the most interesting features is a bomb crater in front of the green at the 13th. Fairly recently a World War II bomb was found while making a new bunker on the hole. The course was closed and the Ministry of Defense detonated the munitions and the club left the crater in play. The good holes at Buckpool start with the first, a 358-yard par 4 called *Whitewash*. Both challenging and fair, your drive should avoid the nest of bunkers right about 190 yards from the tee. The approach is over a fronting bunker (50 yards out) to a green with more traps on each side. *Morven* is the dogleg right 421-yard par 4 fifth with three bunkers on the right and gorse on both sides. The green is protected by four more bunkers. The 9th, *Road*, is a drivable par 4 of 300-yards. When we played Neil drove the green and one-putted for an eagle, while I dodged tee shots of players mishitting off the first. The best approach (also the least in the line of fire) is from the right to a green with two fronting bunkers and five more around the green. Another good short hole (294 yards) is *Plateau*, the par 4 twelfth. The small two-tiered green protected by deep traps on each side is a tough target best approached from the left. The 15th, *Gollachy*, is a 212-yard par 3 which plays downhill and usually into the wind. The tee shot is visually intimidating as it looks like you have to carry all the way to the green over gorse--actually, the carry is only 135 yards. The green is a small target with two bunkers around it. *Long*, the 16th, is the only par 5 (514-yards) on the back (there's also only one on the front). The tee shot looks tight with gorse on each side and gorse in front which is unreachable and makes a good aiming point. The fairway is plenty wide and birdies are possible if you stay in the middle. In an area rich with fine golf courses, Buckpool is one of the best.

COMMENTS FROM THE FORWARD TEES: Buckpool is a wonderful links-type course and a sunny dry day with mild wind made scoring easier. The greens were particularly hard and fast the day we played and the fairways are wide and straight; as a result I was able to play the fairways well, but the fast greens were hard to adjust to. There are the usual bunkers, gorse, and some trees to avoid and fantastic views to distract. The course has a good variety hole to hole. The course is a par 71 for ladies with doable distances for par 3s. Hole six is a good example of the one-shotters at 115 yards down hill. The problem is landing on the green, because a ball that lands in front of the green will probably roll into one of the three bunkers that guard the green. The two par 5s are not unusually long. One of the most unusual holes is the 15th. The men's tees are elevated and they tee off over a valley of gorse. The ladies shoot from a slightly elevated tee surrounded by gorse and drive through a long narrow path in the gorse valley.

CULLEN GOLF COURSE
The Links, Cullen, Buckie AB56 4WB
www.cullengolfclub.co.uk 01542-840685
Links, 4597 yards, par 63, £18

AMENITIES: Small clubhouse lounge does serve the local specialty, "Cullen skink," a smoked haddock stew or chowder. There is also an outside service window which is much used by beach-goers as well as golfers. Check in for golf at the clubhouse window.

COURSE COMMENTS: Come to Cullen GC for the sea views and the par 3s. It's a great vacation course, called "quirky" by some. Leave your scoring expectations at home. This short Old Tom Morris 1896 design demands a strong short game. Dotted throughout the course are The Three Kings, beautiful rock outcroppings that come into play on several holes. Bunkers, a burn, and the wind will be the other tests, besides the rocks. The view as you walk up the second hole is breathtaking. This 130-yard par 3 called *Farskane* requires a delicate shot to hold the small green protected by a ditch and OB behind. Another fun one-shotter is the 172-yard

6th. Called *Bay View* for obvious reasons, this green is protected all around by high rough. To play the hole well you must hit a high shot which is then at the mercy of the wind. The 7th at 231 yards is an impressive par 3. The best views on the course are from this long one-shotter named *Firth View*. A ditch lurks only four yards behind the green, but I certainly didn't have to worry about hitting into it on my first shot. If you haven't guessed yet, we think the best holes on the course are the ten par 3s, and the 13th, *Red Crag*, is one of the best. On this 149-yard hole the green is hidden behind 80 foot tall Boar Crag. An arrow painted on the rock helps you find the way. The whole course is fun, but the par 3s and the views are what to come for.

DALMUNZIE GOLF COURSE
Dalmunzie Estate, Spittal of Glenshee, Blairgowrie, Perthshire PH10 7QE
www.dalmuziecottages.com   01250-885226
Moorland, 2099 yards, par 30, £14 all-day

AMENITIES: Hotel bar and restaurant where dinners are set price and reputed to be very good, if a tad expensive. Bar menu is available. No golf shop, check in at the bar for golf.

COURSE COMMENTS: It's taken us years to play this very out of the way course with an intriguing location, the Spittal of Glenshee (meaning either the head of Glenshee or referring to a "hospital" once at Glenshee Village). In the middle of nowhere on a beautiful, but minor road between Blairgowrie and Braemar in the Highlands, you wouldn't expect to find a 1920s Alistair McKenzie (Augusta National and Cypress Point) and James Braid designed 9-hole track. Most of the players are either locals or guests staying at the hotel. When we played on a lovely Saturday afternoon there were only two other players on the course. The hilly course is fairly easy to walk, but you do have to carry your clubs as no trolleys are available. Nestled in the valley between mountains, the course and views are drop-dead gorgeous on a good day, but mountain weather can change within minutes, so be prepared. Dalmunzie has no bunkers, but a river crossing (the Lochsie Burn) on the 7th, heavy rough off the fairways, and elevation changes make the course a challenge. The greens are mostly flat, small, and quite rough. The quality holes reflect the designer. The 3rd is a par 4 of 354 yards where you tee from an elevated box down a wide fairway--the fairway of six is on the left, but heavy rough is right. Second shots are semi-blind climbing steeply to an elevated green. The par 3 fourth at 162 yards is not long, but the green is a plateau with rough all around. A grass-covered stone fence (dyke) can present trouble for those short. Another challenging par 3 is the 116-yard 7th. Drive across the first fairway and the Lochsie Burn (quite wide for a burn) to reach a wide, shallow green backed by a protecting hill. Long is preferred to a watering landing. The all-day price is steep for nine holes, but a real bargain for all day--where else can you play all day on a McKenzie/Braid course for under $20?

COMMENTS FROM THE FORWARD TEES: Dalmunzie is a fun interesting short 9-hole course. Yardage for ladies is 1855 and a par of 33 for nine holes. The setting is pretty and made it hard sometimes to focus on the golf. Holes were either very long or very short. I especially liked the 1st because it has an elevated tee where you drive over trees and a burn. The 3rd was particularly hard because you have to lay up to get up the very steep hill in front of the green. The 5th is the shortest hole at 70 yards, but great accuracy is required to land on the very shallow green. My favorite hole is the 7th which requires a long accurate tee shot to hit a shallow green across a burn and over small trees. This small out-of-the-way course is well worth the time especially with the Highland setting and the castle hotel in the background.

DUFF HOUSE ROYAL GOLF COURSE
Barnyards, Banff AB45 3SX
www.duffhouseroyal.com 01261-812062
Parkland, 5849 yards, par 68, £30

AMENITIES: The modern clubhouse which looks out to the 1st tee and 18th green serves good food all day, including interesting dinner specials. Everyone watches players putting the two-tiered 18th green. The club has a well-stocked golf shop run by professional Gary Holland.

COURSE COMMENTS: The seaside parkland Duff House Royal Golf Course not only has its "Royal" designation awarded in 1925, but also has a pedigree of design by Alister MacKenzie (Augusta National and Cypress Point) who updated the course in 1923. The course is a lovely riverside parkland track sited just across the highway from the North Sea. The tree-lined course has more than 50 fairly penal bunkers--most are greenside or are fore bunkers affecting your approach shots. The greens come in two sizes: large and larger. Several of the greens are tiered and all have tricky borrows. The course has two double-greens--1/17 and 6/15. The River Deveron is in play on the side of 7, 16, and 17, and the sea is in view on a few holes but never in play. The course also has interesting views of Duff House (mansion) beside early holes and views of MacDuff Distillery across the river. The course is an easy walk, but the wind and weather will definitely affect play--when we played the wind seemed to be into us on every long hole. The key to scoring at Duff House Royal is to avoid the bunkers.

All the holes here are very good but a few stood out for us. The 3rd, *Gaveny*, is a dogleg right par 4 of 372 yards with three fairway bunkers on the inside of the turn. Two more bunkers (on each side) are a problem on the approach. The large green gives plenty of options for strategic pin placements. The next hole is a 348-yard par 4 called *Alexandra*. It's another moderate length two-shotter with loads of sand--seven bunkers, five fairway and two greenside. Stay out of the traps and birdies are possible, although the green is extra large. *Kirkside*, the 161-yard par 3 ninth, is a straight shot to a typically large green with two bunkers front left and right. The entry to the green between the bunkers is fairly narrow. Complicating the hole is a berm (OB) running the length of the hole. A tougher one-shotter, one of the toughest we've played especially into a 20 mile per hour wind, is *Venus*, the 235-yard sixteenth. The River Deveron is on the right the entire hole. A great drive left me short and right of the green by 20 yards. Three-jacking the large green killed my score. *Venus* is followed by the 17th, *Bridge*, which plays a very challenging 436 yards into the prevailing wind. Drive over the three cross-bunkers and stay out of the river which guards the right side of the entire hole. Two deep pot bunkers are left of the fairway and a very large bunker protects the green shared with the 1st. Into a 20 mile per hour wind three good shots left me 10 yards short of the green which is quite swaled. After this hole the 18th is a relief. Put Duff House Royal GC on your play list--it is both classic and classy.

FROM THE FORWARD TEES: Duff House Royal is in a beautiful setting for a golf course--along the River Deveron and the North Sea, among mature trees, and flanked by Duff House, a lovely mansion. At 5457 yards the course is lady friendly--the trouble is to the sides and straight shots are rewarded--with a par of 71. All four par 5s are over 400 yards, but even on the cold and wet day we played the good roll meant pars and birdies were possible. The par 3s have reasonable distances, but are well protected by bunkers which can be quite penal. The greens are large, larger, and huge and I couldn't seem to putt hard enough. Even in the extreme conditions in which we played--cold and windy--I'd love to go back again.

ELGIN GOLF COURSE
Hardhillock, Birnie Road, Elgin, Morayshire IV30 8SX
www.elgingolf.com   01343-542338
Parkland, 6449 yard, par 69, £37

AMENITIES: Lovely clubhouse with a lounge/bar which looks out onto the 18th green is open from 11:00AM daily. Golf essentials available.

COURSE COMMENTS: The Elgin (with a hard "g" as in "gun") Golf Club is a fairly flat parkland track which has hosted many professional tournaments. In contrast to courses like the short Cullen GC, Elgin is 6449 yards with eight par 4s of more than 400 yards. Trees, bunkers, and the coastal winds will be problems in addition to the length of the course. The course began as a 9-hole course in 1907 and was extended to 18 in 1924. Elgin has the distinction of having its first greenskeeper, John McPherson, serving the club from 1907 to his death in 1951. His pride in keeping the course in top quality condition is still with the club today. A nice par 3 at Elgin is the 4th, *The Birches*, at 155 yards. Your tee shot to the elevated green must clear the two bunkers fronting the green. The wind, which can swirl between the trees, makes this one-shotter even trickier. The 5th, *Hardhillock*, a 483-yard par 5, has an uphill fairway which snakes around six traps with trees encroaching into the fairway. It's unusual to have a par five be the second hardest hole on the course, but its rating is well deserved. The 10th green affords some fine views of the town below. After many long, difficult holes, the hardest comes at the last. The deep, slightly raised green on the 440-yard par 4 is protected on both sides by bunkers, just waiting for any slightly errant shots. The views of the town to the north and the Cairngorm Range to the south make Elgin a welcome break from the seaside courses in the area.

GARMOUTH & KINGSTON GOLF COURSE
Spey Street, Garmouth Moryshire IV32 7NJ
No web   01343-870388
Parkland & Links, 5903 yards, par 69, £20

AMENITIES: Small clubhouse lounge is only open at certain times. The office has a few golf essentials. Seniors (55 years) get on for half price.

COURSE COMMENTS: If you pick your time right this is stress free golf. Be on the course at the wrong time and you risk drowning. That's a slight exaggeration, but the course does flood at high tide. The first eight holes are pleasant parkland with nothing very tricky. At nine you head into the oceanside linksland along the River Spey. When we played, nobody had told us about the high tide flooding which was particularly important since we played at high tide during the autumnal tides, the highest of the year. As we played on the 9th we watched the path from the 9th green to the 10th tee submerge. Then we noticed the tide literally pouring in to cut us off--a few more minutes and we would have been stranded on the 9th fairway. From that point on we played parts of several holes while other parts were under water. When I asked a local about the flooding he said they avoid playing at high tide or they just play the dry holes repeating enough to make up an full round. A couple of the holes that weren't completely under water will give a feeling for the course. *Skeens*, the 6th is 389-yard par 4 which doglegs left around a copse of small trees, though the middle of the fairway is the safest route. The large, flat green is protected by three fronting bunkers. The 17th, *Whinnie Side*, a 531-yard par 5, plays along the River Spey on the left with trees and gorse on the right. Three traps front the small green. At high tide the ladies' tee was an island and the drive from the back tee had to carry 180 yards of tidal rush. Garmouth and Kingston GC is inexpensive stress free golf, if you avoid high tide.

HOPEMAN GOLF COURSE
Lodge Road, Hopeman, Morayshire IV30 5YA
www.hopemangc.co.uk   01343-830578
Links, 5624 yards, par 68, £23

AMENITIES: Modern clubhouse has a comfortable bar which serves good food and a small, but adequate, golf shop.

COURSE COMMENTS: The original 1909 9-hole course at Hopeman was extended to 18 holes in 1985. The greens are always in good condition and the gorse which lines many of the holes is healthy also. The coastal wind will always be a condition of play at Hopeman. The course is mostly flat, but that doesn't mean uninteresting. The 5th is a moderate length (337 yards) severe dogleg left with mounds on the outside of the corner and gorse on the inside. A drive of about 215 yards in the middle will give you a good look at the green protected by one bunker left and two dangerous pot bunkers right. *Warren*, the 348-yard par 4 eleventh, is a fairly straight hole, but the fairway is full of humps and bumps. Three bunkers guard the green. The green is the target on the most dramatic hole at Hopeman. The 12th, *Prieshach*, playing at Clashach Cove is a standout. The 135-yard par 3's first shot drops 150-feet to a green protected left and right by bunkers and rough all around. The prevailing wind is directly into the tee shot--25-35 mph the first time we played--so consider taking one or two more clubs than usual. Professional Paul Laurie, when he played a centenary round in 2009, called the 12th "one of the best par 3s" he's ever played. The 15th is a funky par 3 of only 91 yards, but it's not easy. The green is protected in front by a bunker and heavy rough all around. Prevailing wind is crossing which make the shot more difficult. Hopeman may look easy at the start, but fun challenges abound.

COMMENTS FROM THE FORWARD TEES: Hopeman is a fun course with plenty of variety in the layout and individual holes. It's a long course at 5288 yards with a par of 72. The par 3s are long, ranging from 166 to 193 yards. Only the 12th is short at 133 yards, but it's all drop from the headland down to the shore with gorse, rocks, and the sea to contend with. The par 5s are reasonable with the exception of of the 4th which is a 444-yarder. Hopeman is a fine, play-anytime headland links course.

INVERURIE GOLF COURSE
Davah Wood, Inverurie, AB51 5JB
www.inveruriegolfclub.co.uk 01467-624080
Parkland, 5430 yards, par 69, £30

AMENITIES: Comfortable clubhouse lounge with views of the course, particularly 18 and the village. Serves golfers usual hours. Small golf shop with equipment, clothes, and friendly staff.

COURSE COMMENTS: This lovely parkland track like many others began as a nine-hole course (1923) before expanding to 18. The tree-lined course (sometimes heavily tree-lined) has views of the village and the surrounding hills. The course plays along the hills and slopes, but is very walkable. The few blind drives on the course are well marked with aiming posts. Fifty-eight bunkers, a mix of fairway and greenside, are in play. I found the fairway bunkers to be very strategically placed (or at least my ball did). The greens are moderate to large with plenty of slope, but never too extreme. Several greens have steep runoffs behind. A small ditch or burn crosses two holes, but it's easily visible. One comment we heard several times about the members is how hospitable they are, and we definitely agree.

The course caught our attention right from the start. The 1st hole, *Firs T*, a 285-yard par 4, is a gentle two-shotter with two fairway bunkers left and two more at the green. Try to take advantage of the kind start. A nice par 5 is the 495-yard 5th called *Brigadoon*. The hole is a dogleg left around two fairway bunkers. The fairway drops about 150 yards from a large green protected by bunkers left. It's a very classic hole. A tough one-shotter is *Donview,* the 171-yard seventh. Visually intimidating, you begin by staring at two fore bunkers right and the green with more bunkers front and left. Carry the bunkers and a good score can be yours. On the back we liked the 13th with the classic name *Dinna Ditch It*. This par 4 of 254 yards is one of several good short holes on the course. A tight tee shot with trees on both sides, the hole doglegs left as the green tucks in behind the trees on the left. The ditch crosses the fairway just in front of the green—be aware of it if you try to drive the green. The last two holes make a good finish to your round. The 17th, *East Neuk*, a par 4 of 363 yards, is a slight dogleg right starting with a blind shot (aim for the marker pole). There's a bunker on the outside of the bend instead of the inside. The second shot is to a large green with a bunker right. The green is dramatically sloped back to front —try not to be above the hole. Eighteen, *Heiden Hame*, is a 334-yard par 4. This is a nice finishing hole with bunkers 150 and 120 yards from the green on the right. Two more bunkers guard the right side of the two-tiered green and one guards the left. In an area rich with good golf, Inverurie is a course not to be overlooked.

FROM THE FORWARD TEES: The course is a very nice, playable parkland course set in the hills just west of the village of Inverurie. Most of the course has tree-lined fairways and nice views. The overall yardage from the Forward Tees is 5167 yards with a par of 70, 35 on each side. Most holes are easy to see. I found the 7th difficult for a short hitter. It's 163 yards with two bunkers on the right and two more around the green which slopes left. It's easy to find a bunker and the opening to the green is quite narrow. This is a classic course —fun and challenging with friendly staff. It's a definite do again for me.

KINTORE GOLF COURSE
Kintore, Berdeenshire AB51 0UR
www.kintoregolfclub.net 01467-632631
Parkland, 5425 yards, par 70, £25

AMENITIES: There is no pro shop at the club, but a few golf essentials are available at the lounge bar where you check in. The clubhouse lounge, new in 1981 and extended in 1995, provides views over the River Don Valley and the first hole and serves food the usual hours.

COURSE COMMENTS: The first 9-hole course at Kintore was opened in 1911 and a second nine was added in 1991. With nice views over the River Don Valley, the town, and the Grampian Mountains, Kintore GC is a lovely setting for a stress-free round. Not that the round will be easy. Forty-eight greenside and fairway bunkers are in play and a burn will cause concern on five holes, particularly holes six and nine. The greens are moderate to small and mostly flat, though a couple are two-tiered and one, the 13th, is severely swaled. The course can be breezy and golfers will be challenged with a few blind shots (all well marked), some stone dykes in play, and few steep downhill sections--the course goes up gently but comes down more steeply. It is interesting to note that a large burial mound affects play on 15 and 16 and that the standing stone on the 18th tee was found on the course and moved to its present location.

The course itself has many interesting holes. *Woodside*, the 386-yard par 4 fifth captured our attention as the number one stroke index hole. The hole plays particularly tough if you are at all off line. The tee shot needs to avoid forest left, stone fence right, burn right, and a large tree encroaching on the fairway from the right. Three fairway bunkers and one on the right side of the large green add difficulty. Even if you don't play the hole well you are rewarded with good views from the green. The 6th, *Neuk* (Scots for nook or corner), is a 169-yard par 3 with a tee shot over a burn and rough to a green with bunkers left and back right. Accuracy in club selection is key to success here. The 7th, *Burnside*, completes what locals call their Amen Corner. Stay left with your drive on this short (267-yard) two-shotter, but not so far left that you catch the large bunker. On the right of the fairway are two smaller traps and the burn. Your approach must contend with the burn crossing in front of the green protected by one more bunker right. Coming in we liked the 12th, *Lone Pine*, a 277-yard par 4. This is a good short slight dogleg right hole where you have to avoid the large pine on the outside corner. Big hitters can try to drive the green, but the trees which line the hole are unforgiving. Played smartly the hole is a definite birdie opportunity. *Tuach*, the 181-yard 13th is a lovely hole--bring your camera. A burn at the left ends by a lightning-struck tree, but a large ditch runs all the way across the front of the green and directs missed shots into a troublesome bunker right. The small green, the most undulating on the course, is difficult to putt. On the short 235-yard par 4 sixteenth named *Kopje* the prudent play is to take an iron over the pole at the top of the burial mound. The finishing hole, *Don View*, is a 305-yard par 4. This short downhiller has great views of the River Don. Stay in the middle, avoid the three traps left and the one right, and you can finish strong. Kintore GC is quite popular with the locals for good reason; be sure to call ahead.

COMMENTS FROM THE FORWARD TEES: The Kintore clubhouse is in the River Don Valley, but the course climbs up and around a knock (hill). The views from the west side of the knock are stunning. There is quite a bit of altitude change and several holes play up or down hill, yet there aren't too many side hill lies. Water is in play on several holes and wind and weather can also make this course more challenging. It has big wide fairways on most holes. This is a good track--fun but demanding planning and thinking, too.

MAVERSTON GOLF COURSE
Garmouth Road, Urquhart, Moray IV30 8LR
www.mavertstongolf.com 01343-843863
Parkland, 6118 yards, par 70, £30

AMENITIES: Small, but very nice lounge which serves drinks, golfer's snacks, and light meals. Open to the public. No golf shop, but a few essentials are available at check in.

COURSE COMMENTS: The course opened in 2013, but it's more mature than its opening date would show. Euan McIntosh, a Scottish professional, did a fine job designing a course that will take its place among other fine courses in the area. Though the course would technically play as a parkland track, the feel especially on the front nine is very links-like. There are 43 mix greenside and fairway bunkers in play and some are fairly penal. Good sand to play out of (sorry to say from experience). The greens range from small to fairly large and most have some slope. Several of the greens are plateau green, but all putt true and are well-conditioned. A pond on the 11th and a loch on 13 are the only water hazards, but both will affect play. The fairways are plenty wide, but anything past the first cut will likely be lost. The course is very walkable, though an electric trolley could make it more fun. The course offers lovely views of the surrounding hills and farmland and the front nine is especially picturesque with dry grasses past the first cut in the fairway. It's nice that the track comes back to the clubhouse after nine.

I liked the front nine the best, but both sides have very good holes starting at the first. The 1st is a short (260-yard) par 4 where length isn't really the issue. This tough starting hole plays uphill to a raised green tucked around a copse of trees. One bunker right guards one of Maverston's smallest greens. The 6th is a 568-yarder known locally as the "Wee Monster"—this hole is not "wee." When we played the par 5 was into the wind and the last third plays uphill. Three fairway traps and one greenside add difficulty, as does OB all down the right. Into the wind take one or two extra clubs on the approach. A real test where bogey is good. Obviously, the hole is stroke index #1. Next is the 7th, a 168-yard par 3. This picturesque one-shotter plays down from the tee to a raised plateau green protected by one bunker front left. Trees on the right off the tee tighten the first shot. The 9th, a medium length (344 yards) dogleg right par 4 starts uphill and then goes down to a raised green with a bunker front left. Rough and trees on the right make it fairly risky to try to cut the corner. On the back I like the 11th, a 372-yard par 4, which begins with a downhill tee shot to a generous fairway. About 100 yards from the green the hole doglegs right around a pond and few trees. There's lots of room to miss the pond (of course, I didn't), but the small raised green is well guarded by slope and signature bunker front left. A scenic par 3 is the 188-yard 16th. Here the green is protected by three tough bunkers. Accuracy is key to the hole. A lovely visual tee shot begins the 338-yard par four 17th. Drive uphill to the right of a copse of trees where the hole doglegs left. Too far right (to avoid the trees) significantly lengthens the second shot to one of the few non-raised greens—there is one bunker on the right. A very classy hole. Even though young, the course is very playable now and has the potential to mature into a great course.

FROM THE FORWARD TEES: This is a good playable golf course. The fairways are wide and inviting, but the rough is difficult to play out of. The course is a long walk, but the front tee yardage is not too long at 5265 yards and the par 73. The front has three par 5s and the longest hole on the course is the 6th at 486 yards. The back side has two par 5s which aren't too long. There are two par 3s on each side. I found the twists and turns on the back more difficult than the more open front. The 16th was a hole where I wanted "do overs." It is a downhill par 3 of 147 yards with three fronting bunkers—I should have laid up. Maverston is a good new course which will only get better.

MORAY NEW GOLF COURSE
Stotfield Road, Lossiemouth IV31 6QS
www.moraygolf.co.uk 01343-812018
Links, 5863 yards, par 69, £25

AMENITIES: Moray New shares the fine clubhouse of Moray Old with its classic lounge overlooking the 18th green (Old) and the Moray Firth with the Lossiemouth Lighthouse in view. PGA Professional John Murray runs an excellent golf shop which serves both the Old and the New courses.

COURSE COMMENTS: Not a championship track on calibre with Moray Old (see *Hidden Gems II: Scotland and Wales*), the New though is, in the words of assistant pro Andrew Rollo, "a proper course." Easier to get on than the Old, the New is still a demanding course playing over the same linksland as the Old and facing the same vagaries of Scottish coastal wind and weather. The course extended to 18 holes in 1979 by famed British golf architect Sir Henry Cotton, has a mix of twenty-seven strategically placed fairway and greenside bunkers which demand player's attention, though not as penal as those on the Old. Six holes are bunkerless. Greens are small to moderate sized, three are tiered, and others are flat with subtle slopes. They are always in good condition. While the sea is in view on a few holes, five holes have ditches or small burns crossing the fairway (definitely in play). Views from the course are mostly gorse, the lighthouse, and the RAF base. By the way, on most weekdays jets from the RAF base will be practicing take-offs and landings. They are noisy, but dramatic as they land right over your head on some holes.

To reach the first tee at the New you must walk the length of the first hole on the Old. Then again when you come in, the 18th green is near the first green of the Old. Both ways it's best to walk down or back following golfers playing the Old. One more note about routing is that the 5th and 12th of the New connect with the Old course; make sure you're playing the right hole. The "proper course" that it is, Moray New has several interesting holes. The 2nd, *Pitgavery*, at 312 yards is a fun short par 4, drivable with the wind behind. Bunkers on the left can come into play at about 230 yards out. The small green has no bunkers making the hole an early birdie opportunity. It's a chip shot to the green at *JR Robertson*, the 92-yard par 3 sixth. The green is small, but you've got to clear a ditch immediately in front and be short of the mound of rough behind. Another ditch bisects the fairway at the 354-yard par 4 ninth called *Ca'Canny*. It's a 190-yard shot to clear the ditch at the extreme right (you'd still be in the rough) or 250 yards at the left. Laying up leaves a long second shot to a green guarded by two bunkers. The first shot makes or breaks the hole. You start the back at the 10th, *Bents*, a par 4 of 321 yards. Cross yet another ditch on your drive (this time only about 100 yards out) to a fairway with significant mounds right and unforgiving gorse left (the bents). The green has mounding all around, but no traps. At *Auld Dyke*, the 334-yard par 4 thirteenth, the old dyke (grass covered stone fence) bisects the fairway and can affect drives. The green is raised slightly but is not guarded by bunkers. This is one of the narrowest holes on the course. Next is *Dinna Top*, a par 5 of 504 yards. It's a fair par 5 for men, and very hard for ladies. The second shot is the crux of the hole with a burn (ditch) crossing the fairway about 110 yards from one of the larger greens on the course. It's a par or birdie hole for mid-handicap players who stay out of trouble. Moray Old would always be our first choice to play, but I'd never turn down a round at Moray New.

COMMENTS FROM THE FORWARD TEES: A links course that has fantastic views of the Moray Firth, lighthouse, and the ever present jets taking off and landing (which is interesting to watch). As usual the "links-ness" means you have to plan where you hit and hope the land cooperates. There is a burn that runs through the course, gorse that narrows the landing areas, and of course bunkers well placed to "trap" you. None of the par 3s are long, but on the 6th a burn in front of the green makes this shortest hole harder. The par 5s are all over 400 yards and the day we played it rained so we didn't get as much links roll which made the longer holes seem even longer. A good course to play when the Old Course is busy.

NAIRN DUNBAR GOLF COURSE
Lochloy Road, Nairn IV6 7SX
www.nairndunbar.com 01667-870825
Links, 6765 yards, par 72, £45

AMENITIES: Pleasant clubhouse has lounge which overlooks both the course and the Moray Firth. Although the lounge is open late, food is only served 9:00 to 4:00 on weekdays and later on weekends. The club also has a well-stocked golf shop.

COURSE COMMENTS: Across town from the famed and more expensive Nairn Golf Club (see *Hidden Gems II: Scotland and Wales*) is another fine links track, the Nairn Dunbar Golf Club (the Dunbar comes from Sir Alexander Dunbar who gave land to start the club in 1899). Thick gorse, woodlands, and large greens will keep players thinking their way around. Fifty bunkers will keep you honest and the greenside bunkers are particularly penal. A pond is in play on the 7th and several small burns create problems, especially on 13, 16, and 17. The 2nd, *Hilton*, a 333 yard par 4, has a narrow mounded fairway. Your approach shot is blind with only the top of the flag is visible. Two bunkers guard the back-to-front sloping green. Numerous bunkers left on the 419-yard par 4 sixth can grab big drives, but the approach to the green is the crux of the hole. The platform green, thus the name *Table*, is about ten feet above the fairway. No bunkers are needed to guard this green. The 10th, *Westward Ho!*, a 411-

yard par 4, is considered the toughest on the course. Trees, gorse, an undulating fairway, and water all come into play. Your tee shot must carry a burn (at over 200 yards), while avoiding the additional challenge of OB. If you've driven well you are left with a long iron or fairway metal to the green. A complex approach is the challenge at the long, 499-yard par 5, finishing hole. The green is offset left and raised about twenty feet. Plenty of slope around and on the green add to the difficulty. Nairn Dunbar is one of the few Scottish courses which provides USGA ratings, thus can be included for your handicap, although with a rating of 73.8 and a slope of 139 from the back (lower from the members' or visitors' tees) you may think twice about posting your score. While Nairn GC (the one a mile away) will be on all golf tours, Nairn Dunbar should not be passed by.

COMMENTS FROM THE FORWARD TEES: This links course looks like it will be easier than some other links course because the visual is of a course with less severe dips and slopes, but it has other hazards. The course is longer than many Scottish courses, has water on many holes, and of course has gorse, trees, bunkers, and bigger bunkers. I worked hard on this course and found I needed to really think about shots. Perhaps the hardest hole is 18th with a steep straight uphill shot required to get to the green. I definitely would like to play this course again. I always want to try again to play better, especially on a course that requires planned shots like Nairn Dunbar.

PETERCULTER GOLF COURSE
Old Town, Burnside Road, Peterculter AB14 0LN
www.petercultergolfclub.co.uk   01224-735245
Parkland, 6009 yards, par 71, £36

AMENITIES: The 1991 built clubhouse has views of the 18th green and the first fairway and serves food the usual hours. Not open to the public. The golf shop is well-stocked and has friendly staff.

COURSE COMMENTS: Situated on the River Dee, the Peterculter course is one of the newest in the region. The first nine opened in 1991 and the course was later expanded to 18. Peterculter is a lovely track with six holes playing to or along the river (OB). The course does have water in play on six holes, mostly burn crossings. More than 30 bunkers, greenside and fairway, are in play with a few penal, but most fairly playable. Greens are small to moderate in size and fairly flat and easy to putt. The views along the river are pleasant, but there are good views of the surrounding hillside and nearby village as well. Peterculter has a few long walks between holes, but nothing too dramatic. The course has some blind drives which are difficult (well marked), but several of the tees are elevated which is fun. An Osprey hunting along the river was an attractive addition.

Peterculter GC is characterized by good variety in its layout. *Kirkview*, the 290-yard 2nd is a short two-shotter where you drive over a knoll and downhill to a burn about 100 yards from the green. It's best to lay back. The green is long and narrow, but bunkerless. Next is *Peter's Pot*. This flat 152-yard par 3 has the river in play behind and to the left of the small green which is further protected by a bunker right. A double-dogleg with a blind tee shot--play to the left of the marker pole--is *Lang Trachle*, the 502-yard par 5 seventh. It's gradually up to the green which is tucked in to the right (the second dogleg) with protecting traps and trees behind. Near the 9th tee is a small halfway house with toilets and a coffee machine (an indicator of typical Scottish climate). Finishing the outward side is *Cloch Na Ben*, the 394-yard par 4 ninth. This hole is a sharp dogleg right from an elevated tee. The bunker at the inside corner of the dogleg is a good aiming point (if you miss it left). The moderately sized green has bunkers left and right. On the inward nine we liked the 14th, *Elders Brig*. This 372-yard par 4 is the number one stroke index hole for good reason. Tee off across a burn about 120 yards out--the gap between trees is fairly narrow. The green is steeply raised on top of a hill at the right side of the fairway. No bunkers are needed for protection. The 17th, named *Old Town* for the view from the tee, is a long (523 yards) downhill par 5. The fairway has two plateaus which means a blind tee shot and probably a blind second (both shots have aiming posts). Besides one fairway bunker on the right, the green is guarded by one large bunker right and two smaller bunkers left. The last 150 yards is fairly steep down and the green has trees close behind. Peterculter GC is a course we will definitely return to.

COMMENTS FROM THE FORWARD TEES: T h i s course was a surprise to play. When you are in the Clubhouse looking out over the part of the course you can see, it looks very plain and bare. But as you finish the first hole, which in downhill from the clubhouse, and cross over the hill you see the River Dee as it flows beside the course. Water is in play on several holes and there is some altitude change on this course. Many unique holes and grand views make Peterculter fun to play. Par 5s are long (over 400 yards) and par 3s are challenges but doable. The 14th was very difficult for me. It is divided by a burn and takes a well planned tee shot to set up the approach to the elevated green. Challenges await.

PORTLETHEN GOLF COURSE
Badentory Road, Badentory Industrial Estate, Portlethen AB12 4YA
www.portlethengolfclub.com 01224-782571
Parkland, 6443 yards, par 72, £35

AMENITIES: The club has a lovely clubhouse and lounge with great views out to the course. Serves good food all day and is open to the public. Muriel Thompson, the club professional, runs a fine shop with all a golfer's needs below the lounge. The club also has a good practice facility, including a short game practice area and a 15-bay driving range.

COURSE COMMENTS: This is one of the newer courses in the Dee-side area having been designed by Donald Steel in 1989. The layout fits so naturally into the countryside that you'd swear the course has always been there. The tree-lined course is a lovely walk, though the industrial complex surrounding the course does intrude on a few of the views. Thirty-eight bunkers, mostly greenside, are in play and some are quite deep. There is nice variety in the size of the greens which have subtle slopes, but are good to putt. Two ponds are in play as are several burn crossings, particularly troublesome at 9, 15, and 18. At only a mile and a half from the sea, the course can be quite windy. You will face several blind tee shots and a couple of blind approaches, but as usual in Scotland these are well-marked with aiming posts. A major road runs beside part of the course, and though you will hear the traffic in a couple of places, the road doesn't visually intrude. The course is built as two nine-hole loops, but the course doesn't list a nine-hole price (wouldn't hurt to ask though).

When you visit Portlethen GC you will want to play all 18--it's really very nice. We particularly liked the 4th, *The Doctor*, a 458-yard par 5. Drive from a very elevated tee down to a wide fairway. To reach the green on your second requires a long shot over a pond and between large trees. The smart shot is a layup short of the pond and to the right. One bunker right complicates the approach. The next hole is a fine 135-yard one-shotter called *Cockburn's Creek*. The pond between tee and green should not be a problem, but it will be for many. One bunker on the right also attracts numerous shots. It should be an easy hole, but it can bite. The 6th, *Will Donald*, is a 382-yard par 4 where the tee shot is the crux of the hole. It takes a good straight drive of at least 220 yards to clear the burn. A good drive leaves a mid-iron up to a green guarded by two bunkers. Stay left with your tee shot at *Findon Burn*, the 437-yard 9th, to have a clear shot through the gap in the trees and over the burn toward the green. After the burn it's up to the green with bunkers on both sides. You'll need a big tee shot at the 15th, *The Isle*, to go for the green which is fronted by a burn on this 384-yard par 4. If you can't reach the green with your second, lay back to a good yardage for a high approach. The last hole, *Hame*, is a 489-yard par 5 with a dry stone wall (OB) from tee to green on the left. A good drive on this short par 5 will give even moderate hitters a chance to reach in two. Watch out for the double bunkers right and the one left.   When we played with Ian Cruikshank, the club Captain, and member Gary Stevenson they told us about a nearby stone circle (about a half mile from the course) which had been surveyed, moved because of industrial development, and rebuilt--a unique way to preserve heritage.

COMMENTS FROM THE FORWARD TEES: This is a nice open parkland course on the side of a large hill.   The course is very lady friendly with appropriate yardages and well placed, well maintained forward tee boxes. As playable as it is there is trouble as well. The course has a burn that will often be in the way. There are two small ponds, but the pond on the 4th will cause the most trouble. Par 5s are long with the 13th being 500 yards. The hole slopes to the left and plays slightly down toward the green guarded by water on the left. Three of the par 3s are over 150 yards and number five is over water. Portlethen will be a fun testing round and windy weather can definitely change the course. Enjoy the challenge; I did.

ROYAL ABERDEEN GOLF CLUB, BALGOWNIE LINKS
Bridge of Don, Aberdeen AB2 8AT
www.roayalaberdeengolf.com 01224-702221
Links, 6530 yards, par 71, £100

AMENITIES: Venerable clubhouse with the main lounge requiring men to wear coat and tie.   The Old Bar, a very nice lounge, is accessible without coat and tie. Separate golf shop is well-stocked and befits a championship calibre course.   Visitors are allowed times between 10:00 and 11:30 AM and 2:00 to 3:30 PM weekdays, and after 3:00 PM weekends.   Must book ahead.   There is a shorter 18-hole course called the Silverburn with tariffs about half the Balgownie price.

COURSE COMMENTS: Royal Aberdeen is the 6th oldest golf club in the world, established in 1780. Architects of the course include Archie and Robert Simpson, James Braid

(1925), with modernization by Martin Hawtree and Donald Steel. With beautiful linksland and dunes, grand vistas of the North Sea and town, and the Aberdeen lighthouse which can be seen from several holes, Royal Aberdeen is a spectacular course. Rated #36 in Britain and Ireland in 2009 by *Golf World Magazine*, the course plays extremely tough even from the members' tees. Almost 100 bunkers, most riveted (steep-faced) and penal, are in play. Some holes have as many as nine bunkers, including the par 3 eighth. Burns or ditches will bother your shots on five holes, but only on the 10th and 14th is water a major concern. The moderate to very large greens are fast and have plenty of slopes--7 and 17 are distinctly tiered. Gorse and heavy rough will cause trouble for shots off-line, and with the wind a constant companion, there will be plenty of off-line shots.

The character of the course which most affected my game was the narrowness of the fairways, especially in the blustery winds the day we played. On the 4th, though, you drive out to a fairly wide fairway (for this course). At the 442-yard par 4 the fairway narrows significantly about 100 yards from the green. The approach is protected by three bunkers and the narrow green is about 40 yards deep. *Blackdog*, the 375-yard par 4 seventh, has two nasty bunkers on the right which need to be avoided on the drive. The fairway snakes up to the green guarded by five bunkers. If you avoid the traps, the green is still no picnic to putt with two distinct levels. The next hole is 147-yard par 3 which plays slightly down, but with four bunkers left and nest of five right you must be accurate. The green is narrow and deep. It takes about 250 yards to clear the burn which crosses the fairway at *Dyke*, the 390-yard par 4 fourteenth. If, like me, you can't fly that, then be sure to avoid the two bunkers left. Your approach must contend with a grass-covered dyke (stone wall) which crosses diagonally just in front of the green protected by three bunkers. The 15th, *Well*, begins with an absolutely blind drive over heavy rough. The lighthouse in the distance is a good aiming point. Still take less than a driver; with roll I hit a 3-wood about 250 yards (my usual would be 180-190). The "well" before the green is filled with a large bunker covering the front of the green--it's big enough to have a grass island in the middle. At 17, the 180-yard par 3 called *Pots*, if you can miss the five traps protecting the front of the green, you still must deal with a large green with three tiers. Try to stay below the hole. One golfer commented that "the front nine will stir your soul and the back nine will break your heart." All agree Royal Aberdeen is a stern, but lovely challenge.

COMMENTS FROM THE FORWARD TEES: Royal Aberdeen is a links course on the North Sea which means it can be beautiful, sunny, windy, and rainy; and probably all of those is one round. It is a difficult course for ladies, especially the higher handicapper like me. The course is long at 5975 yards from the red tee markers and has a par of 71. From the tee box on many holes one must carry 125 yards to find the fairway and avoid heavy rough. I switched to the green tees on the third hole. From these tees it is shorter (5166 yards) and has a par of 68. That changed the longer carries to 110 to 115 yards and in most cases didn't take the challenge out to the hole. This course has two basic challenges: the links bounces and bunkers, bunkers, bunkers everywhere. The par 5s from the green tees ranged from 390 to 409 yards. Par 3s from the green tees were 138 to 150 yards. Length was the least of the troubles on par 3s since bunkers often surrounded them. This course was difficult enough that on another visit I might try the ladies' 18-hole course which plays on the same land.

ROYAL TARLAIR GOLF CLUB
Buchan Street, Macduff, Banffshire AB44 1TA
www.royaltarlair.co.uk   01224-702571
Parkland/clifftop, 5866 yards, par 71, £20

AMENITIES: Small clubhouse with upstairs lounge.
COURSE COMMENTS: Called by many a clifftop parkland course, Royal Tarlair plays like a clifftop links course with gorse-lined fairways and tough marram grasses. The course plays along the sea with great views everywhere. The

Tarlair course was completed in 1923 and received a Royal Charter in 1926. Anne noted that Royal Tarlair doesn't have the canyons of Stonehaven, another clifftop course, nor does it have the railroad bridge separating part of the course, but then neither does it have the long walks of Stonehaven. Bunkering is moderate and none of the bunkers are very penal. Greens are moderate to small and have tricky slopes. Royal Tarlair does feature a good variety of holes. The 5th, *Plateau*, is a 292-yard par 4 with a straightforward uphill tee shot and a second shot which is blind to the plateau green. The 331-yard 12th, called *Marven*, is a strong dogleg left where you have to decide how much of the dogleg you're going to try to cut across, then let fire. Be warned: three bunkers sit waiting to catch any balls that don't travel about 235 yards, and anything shorter than 210 will be in the deep, deep rough. It is the 13th, *Clivet*, though which gets most of the accolades at Royal Tarlair, and deservedly so. This 152-yard one-shotter gets called "the best golf hole I have ever played" by many golfers. It is a simple hole--shoot straight downhill to a moderately sized green, naturally protected in front by a steep grass canyon, right and back by cliffs dropping down to the sea. With light wind the shot can be two clubs less than normal, or two clubs more into a gale. Simply divine. I do have another warning for you: be careful to stay away from the cliff edge. My shot landed ten feet past the green and I could see that it hadn't rolled over the edge. As I started toward my ball to chip it back onto the green, I saw that about five feet past my ball was a straight drop of about 100 feet to the crashing waves below. I stepped away from my ball and reached out with my club to tap the ball closer to the green. Remember this is vacation golf. What you came down at the 13th you have to go back up at the par 4 fourteenth. The fairway has several ridges and OB left and right before cresting about 20 yards from the green which is relatively benign once you're there. The set of 12, 13, and 14 at Royal Tarlair is a lovely and challenging set of holes. Royal Tarlair is fun, beautiful, and inexpensive. Give it a try.

COMMENTS FROM THE FORWARD TEES: This course is truly a hidden gem. It is built on a headland on the North Sea and the views are fantastic. Part of the time you're playing on wide open fairways, but there are bunkers, sea grasses, doglegs, hills, slopes, and blind shots to trip you up. Five par 5s are on this course and two of the three on the front nine are long at 409 and 476 yards; the other and the two par 5s on the back aren't as long but have other hazards to contend with. Of the three par 3s the 13th is the jewel of the course. It is a drop off where you hit to a small green on the cliff edge with the sea behind. A hilly walk, but well worth the time.

SPEY BAY GOLF COURSE
Kilravock, Rowan Close, Nether Dallachy IV32 7QY
www.speybay.co 07826-748071
Links, 6220 yards, par 70, £20

AMENITIES: Clubhouse serves food most usual hours. No golf shop, but trolleys and even buggies are available.
COURSE COMMENTS: Situated near the Wildlife Centre and historic Ice House, this Ben Sayers 1907 designed course plays along the shore of Spey Bay and the Firth of Moray. Holes eight, ten, eleven, fourteen, and sixteen play next to the beach, with the tee box at sixteen less than ten yards from the water. Typical of links golf, Spey Bay has plenty of gorse and heather, tight undulating fairways, and its fair share of bunkers. The 374-yard par 4 third begins with a tee shot which must avoid six bunkers on the right. The closest bunker is at 160 yards and it's 250 yards to clear the last. If you've found a safe landing area, the shot into the green needs to split two more traps protecting the green. The 6th is a fairly short, but demanding 312-yard par 4 dogleg left. This hole is more about accuracy than length. Your second shot is over a small burn about ten yards in front of the green; no run-up shot on this hole. The 8th, the signature hole on the course, is a tricky 138-yard par 3 with a tough to hold plateau green on top of a hillock. I really enjoyed the 351-yard 11th.

The hole begins with a blind tee shot--stay to the right for a better chance to hit the green. Ending up too far left of the aiming post could mean a blind second to the green. One couple, who we met on the tee of 8, were enjoying a picnic lunch as they invited us to play through. Even though we struggled through one hole of driving rain and three of mist, the round was still enjoyable and could have been more enjoyable with a little more attention to the course condition which we found a little rough compared to other courses in the area. New owners are trying to get it back in playing shape and recent reports from players have been good, but it would be best to check locally before booking.

STONEHAVEN GOLF COURSE
Cowie, Stonehaven, Aberdeenshire AB39 3RH
www.stonehavengolfclub.com   01569-762124
Seaside cliff top, 5103 yards, par 66, £30

AMENITIES: No real golf shop, but the clubhouse lounge is great for the drinks, the food, and the views. Check in at the bar for golf.

COURSE COMMENTS: The Stonehaven Golf Club was formed in 1888 with a ten hole course, which was reduced to nine a year later. The new 18-hole course opened in 1897 and James Braid made some planned improvements in 1906. The seaside course is not links, but like Royal Tarlair GC plays on a headland and affords great vistas of the North Sea, Stonehaven village, and Dunnottar Castle. Several fairways are severely sloped as is the second green, back to front. The 17th fairway is so sloped to the left that it borders on being unfair. Two holes play across other fairways--the 5th plays across the 2nd and the 16th. There is a long walk under the train trestle after teeing off on 13 and back after teeing off on 15. Your round starts with the easy 305, par 4 first hole called *Ruthery*. The downhill tee shot should easily clear the mounds or grass dyke in the center of fairway (180 yards), but must avoid the OB right, which cuts toward the fairway 210 yards out. Two-hundred thirty-one yards off the tee on the left is Hitler's Bunker, the remains of a crater caused by a German bomb dropped in August 1940. The green is protected by bunkers left and right. As you walk down the first fairway you can't miss the ruins of St Mary's Church on the right. All the holes at Stonehaven are interesting, though the parkland holes (9-12) aren't as distinguished as the seaside holes. Several holes have carries over chasms or sea inlets. The 2nd, a 203-yard par 3, tees up along the cliff edge with the OB (the cliff) running about half the length of the hole. At the 13th and again at 15 tee shots must carry a large chasm leading down to the sea. These aren't physically difficult shots, but they certainly are visually intimidating. To get across the chasm that comes into play on 13 and 15 you must walk down the canyon and under the commuter train tracks which separate the parkland holes from the rest of the course. Reverse the walk to come back across. This walk on a gravel path, easily a quarter of a mile, caused one member to complain, "It wears the hell out of soft spikes." Stonehaven is a fun course with challenging holes, friendly members, and great views of the North Sea, the town, and Dunnottar Castle. Well worth more than one round.

STRATHLENE BUCKIE GOLF COURSE
Buckie, Banffshire AB56 1DJ
www.strathlenegolfclub.co.uk 01542-831798
Cliff top links, 5977 yards, par 69, £20

AMENITIES: Small clubhouse open usual hours. While the course has a very small golf shop, it also has well-developed practice centre across the road.

COURSE COMMENTS: Built in 1877 and redesigned in 1931, Strathlene Buckie plays on the cliff tops above the Moray Firth. Views of the sea on a good day are spectacular. Trouble on the course comes from the coastal winds, a few strategic bunkers, some gorse and heather. Several holes are quite straight and featureless (9-12), but the last four holes across the road are quite interesting. An interesting feature of the course is that when you reach the green at eight, you've reached the next village and a war monument shared by the two villages. Playing from one village to the next is a feature we've seen at a couple of other courses in Scotland, notably Inverallochy GC near Fraserburgh. In the spring fairways are flush with violets, harebells, daisies, and bunnies. Interesting holes at Strathlene Buckie include the 3rd, *Ben Rinnes* (the name of a fine local whisky distillery), a 369-yard par 4. The dogleg right runs along the edge of the sea and the elevated green is protected by grass bunkers and gorse. *Plateau* is the 147-yard 13th with an extremely elevated green guarded by fronting bunkers left and right. Across the road from the sea holes is the 16th, *Cabin*, a 272-yard par 4. Big hitters might try to drive the green, but the green is protected by a large gully on the right and bunkers as well. *Gullies* is the 408-yard two-shot 17th. Your tee shot needs to carry a large chasm and gorse. Bite off as much as you can, but you're lost if you don't make it. Along the Morayshire coast are plenty of fine courses, and the first eight holes along the sea at Strathlene Buckie add this course to the list.

TORPHINS GOLF COURSE
Bog Road, Torphins, Aberdeenshire
www.torphinsgolfclub.co.uk 01339-882115
Parkland, 2338 yards, par 32, £10 for 9, £15 for 18

AMENITIES: Pleasant tearoom, but no golf shop. Trolleys are available.

COURSE COMMENTS: This 1896 track has steady elevation gain early, but is never drastic. The few bunkers on the course are easy to avoid. The course is very typical of Scottish village courses and there are a few memorable holes. On the 3rd, *Reservoir*, a 291-yard par 4, you hit up to the foot of a knock (hill) with the green on top. A dramatic dogleg left about 190 yards out starts the 306-yard 6th, *Craigrannoch*. The second shot is blind down the hill--walk up and take a look before you hit. The most interesting feature of the 359-yard 9th, *Beltie*, is the tee shot which is straight off a cliff top.

Tee it high and let it fly--then watch the wind coming at you stop the ball and drop it dead. The green is easily approached, but is protected by four traps. Not championship golf, Torphins GC is still worth a visit.

WESTHILL GOLF COURSE
Westhill Heights, Aberdeenshire AB32 6RY
www.westhillgolfclub.co.uk 01224-740159
Parkland undulating, 5482 yards, par 69, £25

AMENITIES: Nice spacious clubhouse with views of the 18th and several lower holes. Serves golfer's meals all day. Pro George Bruce runs a small shop with the essentials for play.

COURSE COMMENTS: Westhill GC is very welcoming to visitors and fairly easy to get on. Designed in 1977 (Peter Aliss and Dave Thompson advised), the course plays around Westhill. The hill affects play on most holes but the climbs are fairly gentle (except a couple between holes). Taking an electric trolley is really advised here. Twenty-one greenside bunkers and a few fairway traps are in play, especially the nest of three bunkers on the 12th. Greens range in size from tiny on 14 to large on 15 which is tiered as well. There is plenty of slope to all the greens making them tricky to putt—in a match, think twice about giving a putt of any length. On the 6th you tee over a pond and cross a burn on both 7 and 8. A characteristic of the course is its numerous blind drives often with no marker or aiming posts. On a couple of holes the green isn't visible until you get within 150 yards. Several drives are quite tight through trees as well. With no Stroke Saver to help, it's important to pay attention to the hole diagrams on the tees.

The 1st, *Brimmond's Brow*, a 259-yard par 4, gives a good indication of what you're in for at Westhill. This short opener is blind off the tee which makes it very tricky the first time around. Hit straight over the hill. The green is tucked left, guarded by a bunker left, is small and quite swaled. Tough start. Next is a fun par 3 called *Clinterty*. From the top of the knock tee dramatically down to a large green 193 yards away. Bunkers guard both sides of the green, but try not to be short because the rough is very wiry. An interesting par 5 is the 504-yard 5th named *Broadside Dyke*. After a long but downhill walk off the knock to the lower course, tee off slightly downhill with trees left and a pond right. About 200 yards from the green is a rather troublesome valley (no hazard) and then it's up to a large green with bunkers on both sides. *Fiddler's Elbow*, the 222-yard par 4 tenth, one of the funkiest holes we've played, is a tricky beginning to the back. It's a blind tee shot (not a bad idea to send a spotter up ahead) on a dogleg left around a hill. There is an aiming pole almost out of sight on the left from the tee for those trying for the green. Anything short aimed at the green risks getting hung up on a very steep side hill; therefore, the prudent play is to hit about 150 yards to the right of the post and wedge in. You'll also be able to see the two bunkers at the green. The final hole for us to mention is *Sonsie Skelp*, the 431-yard par 4 fourteenth. Stroke index #1 for men, this hole has a fairway which slopes slightly to the right and trees that close in as you near the green which drops down slightly. One bunker on the right complicates the approach. A classic-style hole. Although Westhill GC is hilly and won't be everyone's cup of tea, it is playable and has interesting holes and friendly members.

FROM THE FORWARD TEES: The course plays around the knock (hilltop) but most ups and downs are gradual —I'd advise using an electric trolley which are available for hire in the pro shop. The overall yardage is 5309 yards with a par of 73. the front has two par 5s and two par 3s, while the back has four par 5s and three par 3s. The par fives are more difficult on the back but not a lot longer. The longest par 5 is the 4th at 491 yards. With the numerous blind shots and tricky holes, the course will be more fun the second time around.

PUBS, RESTAURANTS & TEAROOMS

The Boat Inn (pub) on Charleston Road in Aboyne.
Traditional pub setting and menu which specializes in

local produce. Enough pub favorites and specials.
Always busy and always good.

The Bothy (tearoom) on the main street (A93) in Ballater.
Typical tearoom popular with the locals and usually
busy. Best choice in town.

The Bothy (tearoom) on Grant Street, Burghead. Newly
opened tea room with back patio for nice weather.
Breakfast items all day and delicious sweets.

The Broken Fiddle (tearoom) on Straith Path Street off the
main shopping street in Banff. Situated in a late 1700s
building, this little cafe serving typical tearoom fare is
popular with locals. Be sure to notice the "Broken
Fiddle" mural on the back wall.

Buchan Braes Hotel Grill Room in Boddam (near Peterhead) not far from the Buchan Ness Lighthouse. Fine
dining in a large room (although close to bar and hotel
lobby). The menu features fish and steaks and
interesting starters. Very formal, but prices are
reasonable.

Buffer Stop in a rail car in the train station in Dufftown. This
tearoom in an old dining car serves soups, sandwiches,
coffee and teas. Stop in for the setting as the food is
just average.

Covesea Cafe on the coastal tourist route a couple miles east
of Moray Golf Club, Lossiemouth, practically beneath
the Lossiemouth Lighthouse. A driving range, golf
shop, par 3 course, gift shop, and cafe, Covesea Cafe
has an unusual menu. The half-lobster salad was
outrageous for only £9. A better stop than it looks.

Cock and Bull Bar and Restaurant on Ellon Road,
Balmedie, near Cruden Bay. Over-the-top kitsch decor--
you could spend an hour browsing the lounge--
but good food. Worth a visit.

The Creel Inn (restaurant) in the historic fishing village of
Catterline just south of Stonehaven. One of Scotland's
premier seafood restaurants. Pricey, difficult to get to,
but well worth the effort. Specializes in fresh lobster
and crab caught in Catterline Bay. A Must Stop.

Crossroads Teahouse on High Street in Buckie. Very popular with locals. Tasty food, and inexpensive as well.

The Falls of Feugh Restaurant just past the falls bridge in Banchory. Lovely inside and out with pleasant views of the river. Used to be a fine tearoom, now just another upscale bistro.

Gordon Arms Hotel (pub) on the square in Huntly. Good pub fare, and an especially tasty Sticky Toffee Pudding.

Gordon's Tearoom and Restaurant at the edge of the village of Braemar. Good food when we visited, but we've heard negative comments recently. Check with locals before stopping here.

Kilmarnoch Arms Hotel and Falcon Restaurant (pub/restaurant) on the main road through Cruden Bay just down from the Cruden Bay GC (see *Hidden Gems II: Scotland and Wales*). Classy place with good food and fair prices.

Kimberley Inn (pub) on the bay in Findhorn. We have loved the fresh seafood here, but our last visit was definitely below par and locals say it 's only average. Check before making the drive.

La Mangiatoia Restaurant and Pizzeria on Bridge Square in Ballater near the River Dee Bridge. A slightly limited Italian menu, but the quality is excellent. Adequate wine list.

The Mains of Drum Garden Centre (tearoom) in Drumoak near Banchory. Cafeteria coffee shop with snacks and full meals.

Noah's Ark Wholefood Cafe on the main street of Dufftown, a half block from the tourist Centre. Funky decor and an interesting menu are the attractions here. One of the best fish soups I've ever had.

Pennan Inn (pub) in the small village of Pennan along the Morayshire coast. Recognizable from the movie *Local Hero*, the village of Pennan is nothing more than a row of buildings along the steep-sided shore. Most notable is the Pennen Inn, a small pub (reopened in 2009) serving interesting pub food in a spectacular setting. Visit for the experience as well as the food.

Prince of Wales Restaurant and Lounge Bar just off the main square in Ballater. The pub menu includes some very interesting sandwiches. Great for lunch.

Riverside Gelateria and Tearoom on A93 a few miles east of Ballater. Small tearoom, ice creamery with picnic tables outside for good weather. Specialty sandwiches, soups, and salads. Cute little place.

Scott's of Banff on High Street in Banff. Traditional tearoom upstairs from a chemist shop, postie, and gift shop. Soups, sandwiches, and sweets recommended by staff at Duff House Royal Golf Course

The Ship Inn (pub/restaurant) on the harbour in Stonehaven. Great view of the harbour with seating outside for good weather. We've always stopped for a drink, but the meals are highly rated as well.

Skerry Brae Pub in Lossiemouth overlooking the 18th hole at Moray Old. Pub/restaurant with several eating areas, including a great outside patio. Typical pub food, but good quality.

St Olaf Hotel (pub) on the main road through Cruden Bay. Along with the Kilmarnock, St Olaf's is a good bet for dining in Cruden Bay. Good menu selections.

Three Kings Inn (pub/restaurant) on North Castle Street in Cullen. Traditional low-ceiling pub with small bar and crowded tables. Larger dining room with interesting decor. Serves "good pub grub"—steaks, seafood, with a nice vibe. I didn't have the venison; it was too deer.

The Tolbooth Seafood Restaurant on the harbour at Stonehaven is one of Scotland's premier seafood restaurants. Restaurant has grand views across the harbour and seafood rich ala carte lunch and dinner menu. Pricey and you need to have reservations.

LODGINGS

45 Guest House
45 Braemar Road, Ballater AB35 5RQ
01339-755420 www.no45.co.uk £100
This converted Victorian home built in 1890 is only a five minute walk from the main village. Lovely rooms and a great breakfast in the conservatory.

Academy House
Schoolhouse Road, Fordyce, Moray AB45 2SJ
01261-842743 www.fordyceaccommodation.com £70
Dating from the early Victorian period, Academy House began life as a school and schoolhouse. The house was refurbished in 1977 by present owners Sandra and Richard Leith. Rooms are well-appointed and spacious, and the breakfast plentiful and tasty. Dinners can be arranged.

Buchan Braes Hotel
Buchan Braes, Boddam, Peterhead AB42 3AR
01779-871471 www.buchanbraes.co.uk £105
Modern hotel not far from the Buchan Braes Lighthouse and the sea. Comfortable even if a bit sterile.

Cedars Guest House
339 Great Western Road, Aberdeen AB10 6NW
01224-583225 www.cedarsaberdeen.co.uk £70
Small private hotel on a busy residential street has access to the heart of town, about a mile away, by local bus service. Rooms are comfortable and breakfast is good. Since Cedars mostly serves business people, weekend rates can be lower.

Cullen Bay Hotel
Cullen, Moray AB56 4XA
01542-840432 www.cullenbayhotel.com £105 for seaview
Hotel dates back to a 1677 residence which was converted to a hotel 1924. Pleasant modern rooms. Ask about golf packages.

Gleniffer B&B
Stonehaven AB39 2EH
01569-765272 www.gleniffer-stonehaven.co.uk £70
Four Star accommodation within easy walk to main town area and harbour. Very comfortable rooms and breakfast.

Greenmount Guest House
Huntly, Aberdeenshire AB54 8EQ
01466-792482 www.devonfishing.com £50
The welcoming Greenmount Guest House is a Georgian building providing lodging to anglers and other travelers (including golfers) since 1978. A good stop in whisky and castle country.

Milton of Grange Farmhouse B&B
Forres, Morayshire IV36 2TR
01309-676360 www.forres-accommodation.co.uk £70
The farmhouse B&B is on a working farm. Rooms are very comfortable and we had a great view out to the fertile fields as a storm swept through. Hilda Massie fixes a grand breakfast and the B&B is near the coastal village of Findhorn and the Kimberley Inn, usually an absolutely great spot for fresh seafood.

ATTRACTIONS

Castle Trail. The Grampian and Dee-side regions are home to numerous castles and great houses. Huntly Castle, Fyvie Castle, Kildrummy Castle, Drum Castle, Crathes Castle, Craigievar, and Braemar are all within easy reach. Each is distinct and worth a visit.

Dunnottar Castle (HS), Stonehaven. The ruins sit impressively on a promontory looking out to the North Sea. Present structures date back to the 1300s and were captured by both William Wallace ("Braveheart") and Cromwell. There's much history here, but it's quite a walk to reach (not recommended for small children). You might recognize the dramatic ruin as the setting for Zeffirelli's *Hamlet*.

Elgin Cathedral (HS), Elgin. A lovely 13C cathedral, which at one time rivaled St Andrews Cathedral in importance and power, is in the heart of the town. Rich in carvings Elgin is a must stop in the area. Only a couple of blocks away is Gordon MacPhail's Whisky Shop, another must stop.

Malt Whisky Trail. The area is the heart of Scotland's distillery business.   Glen Grant, Glenlivet, Glenfiddich, Glenfarclas, Cardhu, Straathisla, and Benromach are a few of the distilleries in the area. All offer informative tours. Dallas Dhu by Forres is a silent distillery now run by Historic Scotland. As a closed facility the tour is self-guided and unique--there's still a dram of spirit at the end of the tour.

Museum of Scottish Lighthouses, Fraserburgh. Home to an interesting collection of lenses and prisms, the museum has interesting exhibits relating to Robert Louis Stevenson's father and grandfather, builders of many UK lighthouses. While you're there tour the Kinnaird Head Lighthouse.

Chapter 6: The Kingdom of Fife

Crail Balcombie Links

If The Kingdom of Fife is anything it is the home of golf. Golf may not have been started here, and we know the oldest organized clubs weren't in Fife. Without question, though, the spiritual home of golf resides in St Andrews at the Old Course. Fees at the Old Course reflect its place golf history and if you want a guaranteed tee time you'll need to book well in advance. St Andrews Old Course is the Holy Grail, Mecca, and Shangri-La to golfers. What it is not is a "hidden gem." Even if the Old Course is taken out of the equation, Fife is still loaded with fine golfing opportunities.

The golf on Fife will be challenging, and at our first suggested course you'll find one of the most challenging par 3s in the world.

ANSTRUTHER GOLF COURSE
Marsfield, Shore Road, Anstruther, Fife KY10 3DZ
www.anstruthergolf.co.uk   01333-310956
Seaside links, 2345 yards, par 31, £15 for 9, £25 for 18

AMENITIES: Pleasant clubhouse pub with views of the course and the firth. The Rockies Restaurant serves lunch, high tea, and dinner. Check in at the bar for playing.

COURSE COMMENTS: Anstruther GC is a 9-hole seaside links course set along the Firth of Forth. The course starts simply enough with straight forward holes and some challenging bunkering. The fourth runs along the sea with the wind pushing your ball over the cliff. Five plays from the cliff down to a shelf green (more about this hole later). Six, from either the cliff top medals tee (dramatic climb to the tee box) or the members' tee near the fifth green, plays to an interesting shelf green with heavy rough all around. Now to describe the crux of Anstruther--the 5th, *Rockies*, a 235-yard par 3. This hole was voted the Most Difficult Par 3 in Britain by a 2007 *Today's Golfer* poll. From a cliff top tee box shoot down along the sea to a barely visible ocean-sloping green. The small ribbon of fairway has a gorse covered hill on the right and the firth on the left. Only the bravest (or the most foolish) go for the green from the tee. Most play the hole as a par 4 by laying up to the small fairway and chipping on. We've also heard that staying on the cliff top and chipping down near the green is a possible approach. It definitely is a hole which will challenge the best players. All of Anstruther is fun, but even getting a bogey on the fifth is worth the price of admission.

COMMENTS FROM THE FORWARD TEES: Anstruther is a delightful 9-hole course. It has all the advantages of links and has several holes that are straight ahead and not too tricky; however, holes 5, 6, & 7 are the exception. These three holes are the most demanding and require the most planning. Add to that the fantastic setting along the Firth of Forth and this small course is worth the time to play. Yardage is short at 2143 yards. The course only has par 3's and par 4's. None of the holes are long but there is enough challenge to keep you interested (see Bob's notes on the 5th).

BALBIRNIE PARK GOLF COURSE
Markinch, Glenrothes, Fife KY7 6NR
www.balbirniegolf.com   01592-752006
Parkland, 6300 yards, par 71, £40

AMENITIES: Pleasant, modern clubhouse which serves good food most usual hours. Very well equipped golf shop.

COURSE COMMENTS: One of Scotland's newer courses, Balbirnie Park was designed by Fraser Middleton and opened in 1984.   This undulating parkland track is set among stands of mature trees and looks much older than its 25 years. Plenty of bunkers are in play, some of them quite penal. There's a natural flow to the routing, even though there are some long walks between holes. All the holes at Balbirnie Park are interesting, we would highlight a few though.   The 2nd, called *The Mains*, is a 336-yard par 4 which begins with an uphill tee shot.   The hole then plays over the hill to an elevated green protected by bunkers right and left. A healthy challenge.   *Cadham Wood*, the 199-yard, one-shot 4th is a great visual challenge. The long par 3 has a mound on the right, a bunker downhill, and the green behind both. On the back we especially liked the 15th, *Kennels*. The dogleg right (with a name like *Kennels* you knew it had to be a dogleg) 412-yard par 4 plays uphill from the tee and then the fairway runs down towards the green which is guarded by four dangerous bunkers.   Next is *Fythkil*, the 16th at 395 yards. The hole is a dogleg left with OB on the inside crowded with trees.   Only one bunker on the left protects the flat green. Balbirnie Park GC is very popular, so be sure to call ahead.

BURNTISLAND GOLF HOUSE CLUB
Burntisland, near Kirkcaldy, Fife KY3 9LQ
www.burntislandgolfhouseclub.com   01592-872116

Parkland, 5513 yards, par 69, £28

AMENITIES: Pleasant lounge serves snacks all day, and breakfast and lunch many days. Well-stocked golf shop.

COURSE COMMENTS: Burntisland is the third oldest club on Fife, and the 10th oldest in the world. It is one of the clubs established before the 1800s. A course originally designed by Willie Park Jnr was redesigned in 1897 by James Braid. The course is an 18-hole parkland track that has a very links-like feel. It plays along Dodhead with several noticeable climbs--the elevation changes add greatly to the playing. Fifty-six bunkers are in play and many around the greens are penal and deep. The views on a clear day are spectacular--it's easy to see Edinburgh (castle, Scott monument, etc.) and the Forth Rail Bridge. The Firth of Forth is visible from most holes, but since it's along the firth, the wind is a major factor most days. Burntisland has no bad holes and many that are memorable. The first plays steeply up, but gets players out onto the course. The 5th, *The Pond*, is a 146-yard par 3 which plays from an elevated tee down and over trees to the right. The green is protected by two traps left, one behind, and a deep one right. The pond behind is OB. *Crow Wood*, the 347-yard 9th is all down hill, but trees and OB lurk right. The green is raised with the last 40 yards heavy rough. The hole needs no bunkers. Next is the 342-yard 10th called *Kingswood*. A blind tee shot up and over a hill starts this par 4 where you should stay left of the aiming pole. It's a steep drop down to the a green with bunkers behind. It's a quirky hole where you need to play it a few times to really know how to hit your first and second shots. Seventeen is a very demanding short hole; only 151 yards long, but the tee shot is semi-blind with only the top of the flag visible. Players driving on the 18th can be a distraction on your tee shot; best to wait until the tee is clear. You really need to carry up to a plateau where the green sits. A bunker from hell is left of the green--there are still golfers in it trying to get out and the staff comes out each night to feed them. The last, *Coronation '53*, is a 359-yard par 4 which is downhill all the way to the clubhouse. OB is left, trees right, four bunkers guard the green, and everyone in the clubhouse lounge watches you play the hole. The views and the golf will bring you back to Burntisland GC.

COMMENTS FROM THE FORWARD TEES: Burntisland is set on and plays around a knock (hill) on the Firth of Forth with grand views of Edinburgh and the Forth bridges. The course is hilly but well worth the effort to play. It is 5096 yards and par 70 for ladies. The course has only two par 5's, one at 502 yards and there are four par 3s. It isn't a links course, but the hills can create some of the same odd lies--balls aimed for the middle can end up near stone walls or bushes or...well you get the idea. Even after playing twice there are still several holes to be conquered on another visit. I really love the course, setting, and views.

CHARLETON GOLF AND COUNTRY CLUB
Colinsburgh, Fife KY9 1HG
www.charleton.co.uk   01333-340505
Parkland, 6446 yards, par 71, £27 and a 9-hole price

AMENITIES: The clubhouse, a lovely purpose-built building with stone floors, a comfortable bar, and beautiful ancient fireplace, has views out to the 10th tee and 18th green. Breakfasts are served from 7:30. No golf shop, but trollies and buggies are available, as well as a 9-hole beginner's course.

COURSE COMMENTS: Charleton Golf and Country Club is built on land owned by the St Clair family since 1713. The new course designed by John Salveson in 1994 and opened by President George H.W. Bush consists of two loops of nine, where the front is hilly and the back is flatter. The course is very natural with no dirt moved to create the holes, except for greens and tees. Fifty-four greenside and fairway bunkers range from tiny to quite large, most though are not very penal. Greens are large with interesting shapes. The 17th is only 17 yards deep but is over 50 yards wide. Greens have plenty of slope without being unfair, and a few have false fronts. Burns come into play on seven holes and ponds on two.   Vistas from the course include Bass Rock and North Berwick Law, and on a good day players can see Muirfield.

Not nearly as tough as some of the other area courses, Charleton is still challenging and fun. The 3rd, *Think & Thank*, a 430 yard par 4, is a long dogleg left around a couple of bunkers with another on the right.   Be sure to avoid the wee burn running for 200 yards on the left.   The second shot (or third) into the green must avoid a small trap left front.   The green is only 15 yards wide but is 40 yards deep and slopes back to front. A fine short par 4 is the 7th, *Limieside*, only 264 yards long.   This short slight dogleg right plays to another narrow long green and is a birdie opportunity with a good first shot.   Two fairway bunkers can be trouble for those short on either side. Next is *Feight* (meaning "fight," the family motto of the estate owner Baron St Clair Bonde), a 201-yard par 3. It's a super tough one-shotter. Drive over a series of trees and a burn to a diagonally placed narrow green. A saving bunker the length of the green on the right keeps balls from rolling off the green into the burn on tee shots or shots from behind the slippery green. Four is a good score anytime. For a long hole we like *Wellingtonia*, the 562-yard par 5 thirteenth. Your first shot faces a narrow fairway with trees and a burn on the left. The burn crosses the fairway about 270 yards out from the tee. Bunkers left and right complicate your second shot. The kidney-shaped green is protected by trees and one trap. The 16th, named *Smithy* for the old blacksmith shop near the green, is a par 4 of 415 yards. It takes a drive of 240 yards to clear the bunkers on the inside turn of the dogleg left, but it's downhill--I hit almost 250.   The large green has some protecting mounds but no traps. *Ha Ha* is another challenging short two-shotter.   At only 287-yards it's still a demanding second shot over a burn contained by a stone wall.   Three back bunkers create problems for those too strong on their approach to the wide shallow green. With its lovely big course and convenient small course,   comfortable clubhouse, and friendly attitude Charleton G&CC is one to put on your list to visit.

COMMENTS FROM THE FORWARD TEES: Charleton is a very pleasant surprise. If you judge the course by the two straight ahead holes you see from the clubhouse, you will miss a very interesting course. This course is a good length for women at 5477 yards and par 72. The tee boxes are adjusted to be reasonable but still maintain a good golf challenge. The par 5's are long at just over 450 yards. I was able to score well on them and as a short straight hitter par 5s are often too long for me. The three par 3's are very reasonable distances but they have plenty of challenge. This parkland course has great views of the Firth of Forth and the surrounding hills, and is visually appealing. It has hills, trees, and water as well as great views and old stone walls and buildings. A good straight ahead parkland course.

CRAIL BALCOMIE LINKS,
CRAIL GOLFING SOCIETY

Balcomie Clubhouse, Crail, Fife KY10 3XN
www.crailgolfingsociety.co.uk   01333-450686
Links, 5861 yards, par 69, £55

AMENITIES: A new clubhouse overlooks the Balcomie's 15th to 18th and serves excellent food most usual hours. The separate golf shop is fully equipped to take care of all your golfing needs.

COURSE COMMENTS: Crail Golf Links, with the older Balcomie course and the newer Craighead course, on the Neuk of Fife is a wonderful golfing venue. The club is one of the oldest, 1786, and the Balcomie course was developed in the late 1800s. This is a great course, short but definitely challenging to the best golfers.   The 18-hole links course affords a view of the North Sea from every hole, and beach views from most. Plenty of bunkers are in play, many fairly mild and a few downright terrifying. The rough can be thick, but the fairways are mostly generous. The wind will always be a major condition of play.

At Balcomie you will not find a weak hole, and many are well memorable. The 1st, *Boathouse*, is a good start from an elevated tee. The 328-yard par 4 plays down to a large green with a small dyke (grass-covered stone wall) in front and bunker on the right. The green that's closer and on the right from the tee is the 15th and is a free drop if you find it on the first. One of my favorite holes anyplace is Balcomie's 5th, a 459-yard par 4 called *Hell's Hole*. The hole stretches around the bay--bite off as much as you can on the tee shot, like at the first at Machrihanish. A good aiming point is the green of the 6th which is straight ahead without challenging too much of the water. A fore bunker left and a bunker right closer protect the green. A bogey here is a good score. If you continued north along the beach from the fifth green in a couple of miles you'd reach the 12th green at Kingsbarns. Great golf abounds in this corner of Fife. The 7th, *North Carr*, at 349 yards, is an interesting par 4 which begins with a blind tee shot over the crest of a hill. A well struck ball can run all the way to the green with a lucky bounce over a stone fence. The green is guarded by a couple of bunkers. Hit it at the aiming post and hope. The bunker at the 9th is a deep monster which runs the entire length of the long green. Both sides have some great par 3s. The 13th, *Craighead*, is the most demanding. This 208-yarder plays to an elevated green on top of a tall bluff. Some believe that this hole is the mystical hole referred to in Michael Murphy's *Golf in the Kingdom*. The *Cave* is the 150 yard 14th. The hole plays down from a teeing area near the first tee. The wind strength and direction will dictate which club--it can be a wedge one day or some kind of hybrid the next. The 16th, *Spion Kop*, is 163 severely uphill yards over gorse. There is a bunker near the green and a bailout area to the right.

The architect, Old Tom Morris, may have been prejudiced when he said of Balcomie Links, "There is not a better course in Scotland." We haven't played them all yet, but we keep returning to Crail Balcomie for the fun challenge.

COMMENTS FROM THE FORWARD TEES: This is a very challenging, interesting, and fun course to play. Course management is necessary at Crail Balcomie. I have played it several times and have changed my strategies on many holes which has been successful in some cases. There are still some holes that I haven't figured out, such as 13 and 16. They require lay ups to very elevated greens. Choosing the correct lay up position isn't easy. Then, of course, the weather and wind always add additional challenge. Visually the area is so beautiful it takes real concentration to keep your focus. I will always make time to play this course.

CRAIL CRAIGHEAD LINKS
Links, 6728 yards, par 71, £40

COURSE COMMENTS: The newer of the Crail courses, Craighead was designed by Gil House in 1998 to help relieve some of the pressure on the Balcomie course. From this course, too, most holes have ocean views. An interesting feature, particularly considering how important wind is to play is that no two consecutive holes face the same direction. For beauty it's hard to match Craighead's 166-yard par 3 seventh, *Kilmonan*. The first shot is a lovely downhill shot with the North Sea breaking just behind the green. Another beauty is the testing 346-yard, dogleg left 12th. Don't use the triangle target you see from the tee box as an aiming point; it's an aiming post for a different hole. The green is tucked right near the beach and is guarded by bunkers right. One Crail native said of the new course, "It's a must play course for someone looking for a challenge." Of course, he's probably also hoping if you play Craighead, he'll have a better chance of getting on Balcomie.

DUNFERMLINE GOLF CLUB, PITFIRRANE COURSE
Crossford, Dunfermline, Fife KY12 8QW
www.dunfermlinegolfclub.com 01383-729061
Parkland, 6121 yards, par 72, £35

AMENITIES: Beautiful 15th century tower house, the Pitfirrane House, acts as the clubhouse and serves food in the lounge most of the day during summer (more limited hours off season). Very well-stocked golf shop.

COURSE COMMENTS: The Dunfermline Pitfarrine Club was originally established in 1887, but the course you play today, the design work of J.R. Stutt, dates from 1953 and is the fourth course the club has played. The 18-hole course has five par 5s and 5 par 3s with plenty of bunkers, but no water hazards. The shot to have on the this course is a controlled fade. The course is very classic golf with lovely trees in play on most holes. We enjoyed the 7th, *Carlinthorn*, a 480-yard par 5. This dogleg right goes up and down with a blind tee shot. The green is guarded close by bunkers right and left, but it is the cross-bunker 30 yards in front of the green that will cause the most problem. *Myrend* is the par 3 sixteenth. At only 156-yards the hole ought to be easy, but even from the elevated tee the five bunkers front and right make this a frightening one-shotter. An interesting feature of the course is that on the 4th fairway (a 370-yard par 4) you can see traces of the old drovers' trail used to drive cattle between Stirling and Dunfermline in the 1400s. The pro at the course told us about two Dunfermline members, misters Reed and Lockhart, who emigrated to the US and created the first golf club in America. The Dunfermline GC still holds a yearly competition for the Lockhart Medal.

COMMENTS FROM THE FORWARD TEES: The setting here is excellent, with a castle for a clubhouse you can't help but feel special knowing you are playing golf on an old estate. Some holes on the course afford great views across the valley to the hills on the other side of the Firth of Forth. I was also taken with the old Abbey in the middle of the course, especially noticeable from holes five and six. This course is a good challenge at 5419 yards long with some short hills and a par 72. We played this course in 2002 and again in 2010. On the second visit many of the forward tees were not mowed. The par 3s are long for short hitters and are surrounded by fronting bunkers, but they are still fun. The fairways are open giving the hitter good landing areas. This course makes for a good golf experience.

KINGHORN GOLF CLUB
Macduff Crescent, Kinghorn, Fife
www.kinghorngolfclub.co.uk   01592-890345
Headland, 5166 yards, par 65, £15

AMENITIES: Limited. Small clubhouse has changing rooms, but no golf shop--no trolleys were available.

COURSE COMMENTS: Old Tom Morris designed the original 9-hole Kinghorn course in 1887. The course was expanded to 18 in 1947. The short Kinghorn course plays on a large hill above the village harbour. Even though the course is hilly, the views of the Firth of Forth are worth the effort. The course has some bunkers, but the elevation changes and the wind are the major problems. As short as Kinghorn is it still has interesting holes. The 3rd, *Loup Ower*, is a 205-yard par 3 which plays downhill.   The tee shot must carry a stone fence, yet avoid the bunker behind the green. Short, but tricky is the 281-yard par 4 ninth, *Inchkeith*. Your tee shot needs to negotiate a minefield of hummocks and rough. The back nine starts with *Linties Nest*, a 277-yard par 4 which is a narrow uphill hole with a serious amount of rough.   The most challenging hole on the course is *Lang Whang*. At 433 uphill into the wind yards this par 4 is tough. On the windy day we played, three good woods were still 20 yards short of the green. The 17th, *Road Hole* (what else?) is a 171-yard par 3 which is almost all carry over gorse with a bunker right. Anne, trooper that she is, lightened her bag and carried the whole round.   Don't be put off by the hills, the wind, or lack of a trolley--Kinghorn is a fun course.

LUNDIN LINKS GOLF COURSE
Golf Road, Lundin Links, Fife KY8 6BA
www.lungingolfclub.co.uk   01333-320051
Links, 6371 yards, par 71, £55

AMENITIES: An excellent old clubhouse which serves good food. The separate golf shop has all you will need and more.

COURSE COMMENTS: As old as 1868 when they separated from Leven Links, the current Lundin course was laid out by James Braid in 1909 when he added a new nine to the original. Lundin GC is an 18-hole mostly links course with some parkland features. Plenty of bunkers will give golfers fits, especially the Braid strategic fairway bunkers. The fairways are reasonably wide, but you can easily lose a ball in the rough. The greens all have subtle breaks that take some getting used to. One feature we find a little disconcerting (not limited to Lundin) is that tee boxes are often placed directly behind the previous green. It's hard to hit enough club because of the fear of hitting too much and into the players behind the green.

Lundin GC has been used as an Open qualifying course when the Open is held at St Andrews and has many great holes. The 3rd, *Bents*, is a 331-yard par 4. This nice two-shotter is one of five holes which play along the Firth of Forth. A good tee shot is one that avoids the five fairway bunkers. The next test is to avoid the four more bunkers fronting the green. *Silverburn* is the short, 141-yard par 3 fifth where correct club choice is critical because of the seven bunkers around the green--there is a clear shot at the green, though. On the back, the 13th, *Neil Shaw*, is an impressive hole. Two good shots on this 499-yard par 5 are needed to set up a third into a green hidden in a pocket of tall trees. Trees (and OB) right and a steep slope left make the shots harder. No bunkers are needed to protect the green. A long, blind tee shot makes the 343-yard par four 17th, *Station*, difficult. A bailout area is on the right, but don't be long to the green because of the three hidden traps there. As you can image, the course is very busy and hosts many golf tours. In season, call several days early.

LUNDIN LADIES GOLF COURSE
Woodielea, Lundin Links, Fife KY8 6AR
No Web, 01333-320832
Parkland, 4730 yards, par 68, £16 for 18

AMENITIES: A clubhouse for ladies (no bar or lounge), and an outside toilet for men. No trolleys available.

COURSE COMMENTS: The 9-hole Lundin Ladies course is often overlooked because of the other fine courses in the area, but the James Braid designed course is worth a stop. The club was formed in 1890, and at that time men could be associate members but could only play with an accompanying lady. In 1909 the present course was laid out by Braid to provide a greater challenge for ladies. In World War II the course was used as a Victory Garden, a community effort to grow food for the war effort, and soldiers were billetted in the clubhouse, the only time men have been allowed in. After the war the course was gradually returned to playable condition and is today much as it was then. There are some challenging holes at Lundin Ladies, but the 2nd, a 240-yard par 4, is most memorable. The tee shot on this short, straightforward hole must clear three dramatic 4000-year-old standing stones. The thirteen foot high stones, believed to be burial markers, standing in the middle of the fairway about 120-130 yards from the tee, have a tremendous affect the first shot. Bounce your ball off the stones or nestle a ball up against the base of one, and the impact is more than visual. Another quality hole is the 133-yard par 3 sixth. From an elevated tee, the hole plays down to a green protected left and right by bunkers and a two-foot tall dyke about ten feet in front. The hole plays longer because of the incessant, facing wind. Definitely a fun course, especially if you can link it with the nearby Anstruther GC.

COMMENTS FROM THE FORWARD TEES: This is the oldest Ladies golf course in Scotland. It is completely run by the ladies. It is a 9-hole course, but still a good test of your golf skills. The standing stones on the 2nd, the burn of 6, 7, and 9, and the rough around the 3rd and 4th holes all require some strategic play. There is even a hill or two to add to the interest. This is a good place to practice your skills, enjoy golf, enjoy the views of the Firth of Forth in the distance, and smile in pride knowing "the ladies" are in charge here.

SCOTSCRAIG GOLF COURSE
Golf Road, Tayport, Fife DD6 9DZ
www.scotscraiggolfclub.com   01382-552855
Heath-like links, 6550 yards, par 71, £56

AMENITIES: Beautiful clubhouse with lounge looking out to the tenth tee. Food is served all day to players and members (not open to the public). Golf shop is well-stocked and run by friendly staff.

COURSE COMMENTS: The club was begun in 1817 making it the thirteenth oldest club in the world. The course extended to 18 holes in 1905 and then was redesigned by James Braid in 1923. In its early days players had to wear uniforms to play and the penalty for playing without a uniform was two bottles of port. That Scotscraig was an Open Qualifying course for the 2010 Open at St Andrews attests to its quality. Sixty-two greenside and fairway bunkers, often in nests, will test accuracy of both long and short shots. Greens are mostly flat with subtle slopes and have a reputation for always being well conditioned. A little water will cause difficulty for players, particularly the burn crossing on 11,14, 15, and a pond on the 5th. Gorse and broom are beautiful in the spring, but will exact a toll any time of the year. The wind is always a concern and you would seldom play without it.

All the holes at Scotscraig are strong and the first is a fair, but tough start. Several of the other holes are the ones that really got our attention. The 4th, *Westward Ho*, a 366-yard par 4, has four fairway traps which complicate a drive that should stay short of the rough 260 yards out. Your second shot is down to a platform green with interesting slopes and is protected by a pot bunker front right. This is the number one stroke index hole on the course. A hole you'll want to play more than once is *Plateau*, the 401-yard par 4 seventh. A plateau of rough divides the fairway starting about 215 yards out. Lay up short of the rough-covered mound or chance hitting a small ribbon of fairway on the right. The green is protected by three small bunkers and can be difficult to find depending upon the lie of your first shot. Be satisfied with a five here. Six bunkers (five on the left) are in play on your first shot on the 8th, *High*, a 387-yard par 4. Finding the fairway is vital on this gorse-lined hole. Two more fairway bunkers and one greenside make the approach to the tiered green tricky. On the back we like the 11th. *Shanwell*, at 459 yards, it's a tough, long two-shot dogleg right around a bunker 260 yards from the tee. The next shot must contend with a burn hidden from view 90 yards from the flat green with one bunker front left. The 14th, *Garpit* (the land was once known as Garpit Links), is a fine par 5 of 523 yards. Gorse-lined fairways, burns on the left and right, two ponds, one burn crossing 150 yards from the green, two small dangerous traps, and OB right make this hole the local favorite. The pro says play the hole in steps and don't think of the results. *Road* (runs down the right and is a free drop unlike the *Road Hole* at St Andrews), the 380-yard par 4 seventeenth, is a straight ahead hole with some fairway mounds, two small fairway bunkers on the right, and gorse down the left. The kidney-shaped green is angled right and has a trap on the right. Classic golf. Friendly members, a routing that brings you back to the clubhouse at nine, and watered fairways help to make Scotscraig GC a true gem.

FROM THE FORWARD TEES: What a beautiful almost links course. It winds around at the top of the hill in the village of Tayport. The holes are close to each one another, but gorse, broom and trees make it seems as if you're on the course alone. The course is a good length and good accurate shot-making is necessary here to score well. There is only one par 5 on the front at just over 400 yards. The back has a two stroke differential and the three par 5s are very long, ranging from 440 to 475 yards. Three of the four par 3s are very short and the trouble isn't distance but gorse, water, and bunkers. Accuracy is vital on these par 3s. The par 3 third hole is 194 yards long. The trouble is not only that this hole is long, but you must stay straight to avoid bunkers and gorse. Scotscraig is a great golfing experience, especially if you're lucky enough to get great weather and friendly local folks as partners.

ST ANDREWS LINKS TRUST, EDEN COURSE
Pilmour House, St Andrews, Fife KY16 9SF
www.standrews.org.uk/golf   01334-466666
Links, 6200 yards, par 70, £40

AMENITIES: The Eden and Strathtyrum courses share a clubhouse just down the road from the clubhouse of the Old, New and Jubilee courses. Clubhouse has a pleasant lounge and small golf shop.

COMMENTS: The course was designed in 1914 by Harry Colt as a relief course for the Old, New, and Jubilee courses. The 18-hole links course is mostly flat with plenty of small swales, humps and hollows. Gorse, whins, heavy rough, and strategic use of bunkering create quite a fair challenge. It is the wind, though, which will determine how hard the course plays. Several holes have OB--a stone fence separates the Eden from the Old Course for several holes. One year while the Dunhill Cup was being played on the Old Course, we played the Eden and watched Ernie Els and a couple of professional groups playing fifty yards to the right on the Old Course. Unlike the Strathtyrum, the Eden offers enough variety and challenge to be a destination of its own. The 2nd, a 449-yard par 4, has 11 (Yes, eleven!) bunkers to be avoided. The series of five bunkers starting at about 200 yards out on the left means you need to stay right. After the tee shot, the second should seem easy with only one bunker protecting the green. A narrow fairway is the tee shot trouble at the par four 350-yard fourteenth. You must also be careful not to run your ball too far left or long (250 yards) because a large loch awaits. The approach must skirt the loch to reach the smallish green. At the 18th, a 351-yard par 4, your tee shot must avoid the two fairway bunkers on the left of the prime landing area. The green is protected by gorse right and a bunker left. With wind behind this makes a fun finishing hole.

The Links Trust manages seven courses, including the Old Course and the newly built Castle Course. Play the Old Course if that's your pleasure, but don't ignore the other fine links tracks [see information about the New, the Jubilee, and the Castle courses in *Golf in Scotland II: Scotland and Wales*]. All the courses are woman friendly as well.

COMMENTS FROM THE FORWARD TEES: This is a fun links course where I got great roll on the dry sunny day we played, although with links bounces the ball doesn't always go where you plan. The natural hazards on the course include gorse and water. Par 5s are long, all over 400 yards with the 9th being the longest. It also has five fairway bunkers and three deep bunkers on the left of the green to avoid. There are four par 3s, but none are extremely long, however the wind adds to the challenge. I especially like the 15th because of the pond on the left all the way to the green. The Stroke Saver advises, "The secret here is to over hit," and taking this advice lead to a par. Enjoy this great course right next to the Old Course--it will offer plenty of challenge at a fifth the price.

**ST ANDREWS LINKS TRUST,
STRATHTYRUM COURSE**
Links, 5620 yards, par 69, £25

AMENITIES: Same as Eden course.
COURSE COMMENTS: The easiest of the 18-hole courses run by the St Andrews Links Trust, the Strathtyrum course was designed by noted architect Donald Steel in 1993. The course plays on flat linksland with few hazards, except for some sticky rough and 15 bunkers. The wind will be the main condition of play here--fantastic carry and roll on the downwind holes, and tough play into the wind. Some of the fairways are fairly narrow. The 11th, a 447-yard is a short dogleg left par 5. A bunker right can worry your second shot and the green is protected by severe swales in front. It's tough to hold the green on the 148-yard par 3 thirteenth when it plays downwind, especially since you have to clear two bunkers fronting the green. Don't make a special trip just to play the Strathtyrum course, but don't pass up a quick round either.

THORNTON GOLF COURSE
Station Road, Thornton, Fife KY1 4DW
www.thorntongolfclub.co.uk   01592-771173
Parkland, 5859 yards, par 70, £25

AMENITIES: The pleasant 1995 clubhouse lounge has views to the tee at the 1st and the greens of the 2nd and 18th. Serves food most usual hours but only to members, guests, and paying players.   No golf shop, but a few essentials are available in the starter's office where you check in.

COURSE COMMENTS: Thornton Golf Club offers stress-free golf on a lovely tree-lined course.   The original 9-hole course was built in 1921 by a group of railway men, then moved to its present location in 1925, and finally the course was extended to 18 holes in 1970.   A mix of more than 60 greenside and fairway bunkers dot the course often in clusters.   None of the bunkers are too penal.   The greens are moderate to large with one double green (9 and 11).   Most are flat, except the 12th which is quite sloped and 17th which is swaled.   All the greens have well-conditioned putting surfaces. The River Ore runs beside 14, 15, 16, and 17 and can be in play for off-line shots.   Trees and bunkers present the biggest challenges at Thornton.   Most holes have markers about 150 yards from the green, but at 15 and 17 the same markers indicate about 80 yards to the green--can be confusing if you don't pay attention.

The course has several interesting holes like the 195-yard par 3 third called *Ore Mills*.   It's a straight ahead shot to a smallish green with two traps left and one right.   The trouble is the tree in the center of the line to the green.   The 120-yard long 9th, *Lochtyside*, is another fine par 3.   Hit over the mound to the large green shared by the 11th.   Four bunkers, two in front and one on each side, add difficulty to picking the correct club.   The 14th, *Burn*, is another challenging one-shotter.   It's a tricky 178-yard shot over a bend in the River Ore to the small green.   There's bailout room right, but there is also a large bunker on that side as well.   The next hole, *Hutton's Gap*, is a 348-yard par 4 which begins with a slight dogleg left to a fairway which slopes towards OB and the river. A good drive to the right will bounce down to the middle. Only one small bunker to the right protects the green. *Earlseat*, the 228-yard par 4 sixteenth, is a tricky hole. The green is easily reachable with a good tee shot, but six bunkers in front or to the sides should give pause for thought. The elevated green adds challenge. The 17th is a funky short two-shotter that should be easy after you've played it once. If you can, walk up part way and take a look. The last, a 381-yard par 4, is the narrowest true drive on the course with trees right and left--the trees left are OB. The green is guarded by six bunkers. The tightness is the key to the hole. Thornton GC is good value golf.

COMMENTS FROM THE FORWARD TEES: Thornton is an easy to walk parkland course with only slight ups and downs. The tree-lined fairways require accurate tee shots, and the front is wider than the back. The back, though, has more variety and includes some mounds, slight hills, and even a burn between 14 and 15. The course is only 5211 yards long and has a par of 70, with two par 5s and three par 3s. All the one-shotters are around 150 yards. Fourteen was the hardest for me because it is a dogleg left with water on the left.

PUBS, RESTAURANTS & TEAROOMS

1 Golf Place (pub) on the corner just down from the first tee at the Old Course in St Andrews. A golfer's pub with typical pub menu, but the food has always been good, especially the hamburgers.

Abbot's House Cafe next to the Cathedral in Dunfermline. Excellent spot for a coffee, scone, or hearty tearoom lunch, the cafe is located in the Abbot's House Museum. Open 7 days a week.

Anstruther Fish Bar (sit-in chippy) on the east end of the harbour in Anstruther. Reputed to be the Best Chippy (fish and chip shop) in Scotland and we won't dispute that. Good Scottish fast food. Be prepared to wait, especially on weekends the lines get long.

Berryfield Tearoom in Abernethy directly across from the Abernathy Round Tower. Open for only a couple of years, Berryfield Tearoom serves specialty teas, coffee, light lunches, and snacks. Friendly place.

Claret Jug Restaurant and Bar in the Dunvegan Hotel a block away from the Old Course in St Andrews. Eat in the bar if you can for the ambiance of being sur-rounded by photos of all golfing's greats. Food is good as well.

Crail Golf Hotel (pub) at the edge of town just before heading out to the Balcomie links. Always good food.

Dreel Inn (pub) on the main coastal road through Anstruther. Wonderful old (1600s) pub which serves good food. Fairly typical pub fare, but done well.

Drouthy Neebors (pub), meaning "thirsty friends," on the main shopping street in St Andrews. Decent pub food at good prices in a lively university town.

Golf Tavern or 19th Hole (pub) just off the fairways at Elie GC. Golfer's pub with decent food and good pizzas.

Kinneuchar Inn (pub) is a small village pub in Kinneuchar near Kilconquer Castle resort. A local village pub fun to visit to listen to locals and the food was good as well.

Red Lion Inn (pub) in the middle of the historic village of Culross. Large pub menu with some unusual items, such as fried cheese salad. Very popular with locals and tourists.

The Ship Inn (restaurant), owned by the same couple as Golf Tavern, on the shore in Earlsferry. Complete menu of good food and good prices.

Swilcan Restaurant in the Links, the clubhouse for the New and Jubilee courses in St Andrews. Golfers and non-golfers enjoy dining in the modern clubhouse lounge with views out to the Old and New courses. Extensive menu from soups to sandwiches and main courses. One of the best choices in town.

Weaver's Bar and Restaurant in City Hotel on bridge Street in Dunfermline. Large modern pub/restaurant in a building built in 1775. Typical pub menu. Numerous locals at midday.

LODGINGS

Ashbank Guest House
105 Main Street, Redding, Falkirk FK2 9UQ
01324-716649 www.bandbfalkirk.com £70
Ashbank retains many of its Victorian features and has views out to the Ochill Hills, the Wallace Monument, and Airth Castle. Rooms are lovely and Betty and Bede are friendly hosts. A good location for East Fife or to the west.

Errolbank Guest House, Dundee
Across the Tay from Fife.
See Chapter 3 Lodgings.

Fisherman's Tavern Hotel, Broughty Ferry
Across the Tay from Fife.
See Chapter 3 Lodgings.

Merlindale B&B, Crieff
We stay in this Central Scotland B&B which is only a little over an hour from St Andrews. See Chapter 3.

ATTRACTIONS

British Golf Museum, St Andrews. The museum, only a wedge shot from the first tee at the Old Course, houses 500 years of golf history, with photos, videos, and all manner of memorabilia.
Culross Village (NTS), west of Dunfermline along the Firth. A National Trust preserved 17C village with several building open including The Palace.

Dumfermline Abbey and Palace (HS), Dunfermline. The Abbey and ruined Palace dominate the town which was at one time the capital of Scotland. The Palace ruins are interesting, but it is the Abbey which draws the most attention. Dedicated in 1147, the old church is a large room supported by eleven 30-foot tall stone pillars. In the new church you can find where King Robert the Bruce is buried, except for his heart which is buried in Melrose Abbey in the Borders. Besides Bruce at least 22 other Royals are interred. Dating back to 1093.

Lochleven Castle (HS), Kinross. Ride a small 10-passenger ferry over to the island which houses the 14C castle. Mary Queen of Scots, William Wallace, and Robert the Bruce all have connections to the castle. The ruins are well-preserved and interesting to tour.

St Andrews Castle (HS), St Andrews. Built around 1190, the structure you can tour today dates from the 1400s. On a point of land overlooking St Andrews Bay, several rooms are open to the public.

St Andrews Cathedral and St Rule's Tower (HS), St Andrews. When intact, the cathedral was the largest in Scotland and would rival the largest in all the UK. Now, the ruins are an iconic image of Scotland. Wander the ruins, climb St Rule's 157 steps for a fabulous view, but be sure to find the memorial to and graves of Tommy Morris and Old Tom Morris (golfing royalty).

Chapter 7: The Borders and East Lothian around Peebles

Torwoodlee Golf Course and Border Hills

The Borders and East Lothian regions are full of great golf, much of it fairly old. Choosing Peebles as a central location for exploring this area makes good sense. It is close to Edinburgh and central to some of the best golf in the area. As a town, Peebles makes a great base for exploration with its pleasant B&Bs, guesthouses, hotels, restaurants, and shopping. It's a lovely town to walk the High Street shopping area--the town bustles with locals every day. This was the first place we stayed on our first trip to Scotland in 2000 and it's a town we love to go back to.

The first course for this chapter, though, isn't even in Scotland, but it has plenty of Scottish connections and it is just across the border.

BERWICK-UPON-TWEED GOLF CLUB, GOSWICK LINKS

Berwick-upon-Tweed, Northumberland, England
  TD15 2RW
www.goswicklinksgc.co.uk 01289-387256
Links, 6654 yards, par 72, £35 and has 9-hole price

AMENITIES: Pleasant clubhouse and lounge with separate dining room. Both look out onto the back nine. The award winning lounge serves food all day. Small but well-stocked golf shop and a full-size driving range complete the amenities.

COURSE COMMENTS: The Goswick Links course has flying geese as its logo since Goswick means area where geese are found. The first nine here was built in 1890 and extended to 18 by Scottish architect James Braid in 1894. The course existed little changed until it was modified and lengthened by Frank Pennick in 1964. Playing over rolling linksland the course exhibits the usual links difficulties of wind and tough seagrass or fescue rough. About 85 mixed fairway and greenside bunkers seem to come in clusters. Most are steep-faced and penal. Greens are moderate sized, except the 15th which is quite small. Most have typical links slopes with several being distinctly tiered. A small ditch or burn is in play on five holes on the back and a pond is a bother on the 8th. A couple of tee boxes are directly behind greens making it visually hard to approach the pin. Dunes, farmland, and the North Sea are visible on some holes with elevated tees or greens.

Several holes caught our attention, starting with the 1st, *Copse Corner*, a 394-yard par 4. The dogleg right around a copse of trees is a difficult opener with a two-tiered green protected by three fronting bunkers. The 5th, *Pennick's Way*, is a long uphill 418-yard two-shotter with three bunkers on the right. The approach to the swaled green is over a small valley which cuts across the fairway. The green is guarded by three small bunkers. Next is a 528-yard par 5 called *Cocklaw*. OB all the way down right and a fairway which slopes left makes finding the fairway difficult. Your second shot is to a very rumpled fairway with two bunkers left about 60 yards short of the tiered green. Again the green is guarded by a trifecta of bunkers, but there is also OB right and behind. A tough drive needs to stay right to have a view of the narrow green at *Cheswick* (named for the farm to the north), the 421-yard par 4 eighth. Stay right also because a nest of four tough traps encroach from the left. The green with bunkers on each side slopes right and has several tricky pin placements. On the back, *Pilgrim's Way*, the 367-yard par 4 twelfth, is a good hole. Drive uphill to the fairway which lies obliquely to the tee. Stay left to avoid the small burn on the right. Dunes and mounds hide and protect the narrow green which slopes back to front. An interesting short par 5 (491-yards) is the 17th, *Stonehenge* (I have no idea where the name came from). The center of three bunkers crossing the fairway is a good aiming point for your drive. Stay in the middle to avoid bunkers left and right. The green is well-protected by five bunkers and has a large depression across the middle making several tiers. A fine short finishing hole is *Westward Ho!*, a par 4 of only 269-yards. Drive over bushes towards a fairway with a bunker which crosses the fairway about 35 yards out from the green. Five bunkers surround the two-tiered green. While playing the fun Goswick Links be sure to note the World War II tank traps just off the course towards the sea.

BATHGATE GOLF COURSE
Edinburgh Road, Bathgate EH48 1BA
www.bathgategolfclub.com 01506-630505
Parkland, 5827 yards, par 70, £30

AMENITIES: Pleasant clubhouse lounge which serves light meals all day. The club has a good golf shop that is fully equipped.

COURSE COMMENTS: The fame of Bathgate GC may come from its Ryder Cup association (European Captains Eric Brown and Bernard Gallacher and 2014 player Stephen Gallacher have all come from the club), but its renown should start with its pedigree of designers. Willie Park Jnr designed the first 9-hole layout in 1892. Then Ben Sayers and Willie Fernie collaborated to extend the course to 18 holes in 1907. Finally, the course design was updated by James Braid in 1935. With this background the course is busy, but very accommodating to visitors. The few hills on the course add variety to the mostly flat parkland course--never a hard walk. You can expect, though, that there will be plenty of challenge at Bathgate. More than 40 bunkers (mixed fairway and greenside)--some very large and all playable--will give some challenge. Ditches or burns in play on six holes (all easy to see) will add more challenge. On the 6th the water to the right is blind from the tee. Greens are moderate to large and well conditioned. Most have subtle slopes, but at least one green is distinctly tiered. Despite the fact that there is some industrial noise and a commuter train runs frequently beside the course, the course itself is lovely and fun to play.

We had a difficult time selecting favorite holes since all the holes are interesting, but we start our course description with the 3rd, *Kirkton*, a 307-yard par 4. This is a short dogleg left around a bunker and over a burn. A good drive leaves a short approach to a large green guarded by bunkers. The next hole, *Quarry Knowe*, is a fine 177-yard one-shotter. It's a downhill tee shot to a slightly elevated green surrounded by four traps. From the tee is one of the better views of the village. The 5th, *Guildyhaugh*, is a long straight par 5 of 454 yards where you play up and down a hilly fairway. One fairway bunker adds challenge as do the three bunkers around the green. Stay straight and par or birdie can be yours. *The Knock*, the par three 131-yard 8th is an intimidating shot over two large traps to a mound green with more traps at the sides. Long is not bad on this hole. Another short testing hole is the 9th, *Rennie's Brig*. This 298-yard hole is a slight dogleg left with a bunker left on the drive. Cross bunkers in front bother the approach to a small green. On the back we like *Old Reekie*, the 483-yard par 5 twelfth. The burn which crosses just off the tee shouldn't be a concern on this straight, tree-lined hole. Of more concern is the OB all the way down the right. One fairway bunker right and two left of the green are the only other trouble. A classic hole. At the final hole, *Hame*, a 347-yard par 4, trees on both sides and traps around the green are the obvious problems. The fairway does cross the main road into the club about thirty yards in front of the large green. Bathgate GC is a fun challenge for any level of golfer.

FROM THE FORWARD TEES: Bathgate is a nice course in the middle of a village, yet there isn't much village noise. It is bordered on one side by rail lines and the station stop is beside holes 10, 11, and 12, but it's not much bother. Yardage from the forward tees is 5192 yards with a par of 72. The front, which has most of the hills, is 2644 yards and the flatter back nine is 2548--both are par 36. I liked the design of the front better, but could actually score better on the back. My favorite hole was the 3rd, a down and then up with a ninety degree dogleg left and bunker at the corner. The whole course is a fun challenge.

DUNBAR GOLF COURSE
East Links, Dunbar EH42 1LL
www.dunbar-golfclub.co.uk 01368-862086
Links, 6597 yards, par 71, £60

AMENITIES: Venerable clubhouse with pleasant lounge open to visitors. Food served all day. Dress smart casual. Fully stocked golf shop; one of the best in the area.

COURSE COMMENTS: Golf has been played on the linksland here since the early 1600s, although the Dunbar Club wasn't formed until 1856. The first course played on by the club was 15 holes, but it is the 1893 design work of Old Tom Morris with redesigns by Ben Sayers and James Braid that is played today. The course affords lovely views of the islands in the mouth of the Forth, the coastline of Fife, and Bass Rock. Those views are visible most of the time because some say that this portion of Scotland is the sunniest in the country. Wind, as on most links courses, will have a strong affect on your game as will the more than one hundred bunkers, some quite penal, in play. The sea can cause problems on wayward shots on eight holes, and a couple of others have small burns in play. While the course and the greens are mostly flat, there are subtle slopes to both fairways and greens.

As expected at a top calibre course, all the holes at Dunbar are excellent; some, though, attracted our attention more than others. It was the bunkers, all 13 of them, that grabbed my attention on *Broxmouth Wood*, the 474-yard par 5 first hole. Lining both sides of the snaking, narrow fairway, staying out of the bunkers is the crux of the hole. The first of the fine par 3s, the 173-yard 3rd called *Jackson's Pennies*, has six traps surrounding the large green and one more trap about 20 yards short. Obviously, a precise tee shot is require to score well--either that or a damned fine bunker game. The next hole, the 353-yard par 4 named *Shore*, is the first of the sea holes. With the sea running the length of the hole on the left and two fairway and two green side bunkers to bother you, length is not vital. Not a hole on which to be a hooker. The 9th has one of the few blind tee shots at Dunbar. The drive on the 506-yard par 5 *Longbanks* is over a rolling hill-- aim at the marker post and don't forget to ring the bell on the right when you've cleared the landing area. Your second shot must contend with the six bunkers on the hole. Another blind shot will be the second on the 457-yard par 4 twelfth. The sea on the right will form a major concern to all who have a tendency to slice. The green is protected by three bunkers and the sea right and back. The short 163-yard par 3 sixteenth is called *Narrows* for a good reason. OB left, the sea right, and four fronting bunkers close in this tricky one- shotter whose green slopes back to front. Dunbar GC is always in top condition and should be on everyone's play list.

GLENCORSE GOLF COURSE
Milton Bridge, Penicuik EH26 0RD

www.glencorsegolfclub.com   01968-677189
Parkland, 5217 yards, par 64, £25

AMENITIES: Guests are welcome at the course, but not in the clubhouse.   Go to the small golf shop north of the clubhouse to check in.

COURSE COMMENTS: The 1890 Willie Park designed Glencorse GC is a tight, undulating course which could be described as "mountain goat hilly."   It has some long walks between holes, and a few holes interesting enough to make the up and down worth the effort, at least once.   The walk is almost tougher than Pitlochry or Lamlash, but without their fine views.   Tight fairways, elevation changes, and 14 burn crossings characterize Glencorse.   The pro told us as we headed out on our round that we'd need to be particularly accurate with our long irons. The signature hole for the club is the 5th, *Forrester's Rest*, a 237-yard par 3.   It's a beautiful downhill hole with a burn running about 15 yards in front of the green.   The 11th is a 211-yard par 3 which doglegs around trees and over the burn.   Play for the left side of the green, and the wind and slope can help you.   Playing Glencorse will help you appreciate the openness of some of the East Lothian links courses.

HAWICK GOLF COURSE
Vertish Hill, Hawick TD9 0NY
www.hawickgolfclub.com   01450-372293
Undulating parkland, 5933 yards, par 68, £30

AMENITIES: Lovely clubhouse with comfortable lounge.   No golf shop, but trolleys, electric trolleys, and even buggies are available for hire at the bar.

COURSE COMMENTS: Hawick (pronounced "hoick") Golf Club, the oldest course in the Scottish Borders region, was formed 1877.   The course started as an 11-hole course with a full round being 22 holes (twice around). Changed to 18 in 1894 and the layout is the same today.   The course plays around Vertish Hill, but no uphill holes are very steep (you'll only huff and puff a little). There are plenty of sidehill lies, though, and the 15th and 18th play significantly downhill--both are adventures in club selection. Good tee shots are the key to scoring at Hawick, but placement is more important than length. Hawick has its share of interesting holes starting with the 5th, *Terrace*, a 338-yard par 4. The straight ahead tee shot should be toward the right middle of the left sloping fairway. The hole has a "stop board" at the left edge of the short rough from about 150 yards out which kindly (free drop) stops balls from rolling all the way down to the first fairway. The slope is all the protection the hole needs. The 9th hole called *Alcohol* (never did find out about that name) is a straight forward 430-yard par 4 with a rock wall right indicating OB. Spectacular views of the Border Hills are to the right. *Whitlaw*, the 382-yard par 4 tenth, is the only true dogleg (left) on the course. A generous landing area is protected by bunkers short and trees right and left. The green has two more traps to get in your way. A hole easily drivable with a fairway wood because of the 100 foot drop from tee to green is *Mclaren's Miracle* (aka *The Pit*), the 292-yard 16th. The green is protected by a trap and the pit (a deep grass bunker) on the right. The tee shot is everything on this hole. Hawick GC is well worth a visit as part of a Borders swing.

COMMENTS FROM THE FORWARD TEES: Hawick is a bit of a walking challenge with up and down hills. The views can be quite good especially from the top of the knock. The course yardage is not long and has a par of 69. Staying on the fairway is important because there are trees, gorse, and shrubs lining most fairways. The 6th is a long par 5 at 414 yards. The hole slopes to the right which narrows the fairway, but it is the only par 5 on the course. The par 3s on the back nine are long at 185 yards each, but both are downhill. Hawick is a good parkland course with plenty of hills and slopes to test your game.

INNERLEITHAN GOLF COURSE
Leithen Road (B709), Innerleithen EH44 6NL
www.innerleithengolf.co.uk   01896-830951

Moorland, 3033 yards, par 35, £10 for 9 holes, £20 for 18 or all day

AMENITIES: Small clubhouse with lounge that looks out to the first hole; open noon to 2:30, and evenings and weekends. Trolleys available, but no golf shop.

COURSE COMMENTS: Visitor attractions and eating places await in the village of Innerleithen, but on our first golf day in Scotland in 2000 it was golf we wanted to find. The 9-hole Innerleithen GC introduced us to Scottish golf, and our lives haven't been the same since. Innerleithen GC is a pleasing beginning to a Scottish golf experience--it's old (1886) and it has typical Scottish design features. From the very first hole we knew we "weren't in Kansas anymore." The 1st, *Bridge*, a 177-yard par 3, plays across the 2nd and 4th fairways, then over the 3rd green. A burn flows down the middle and fronts the green, and the main road stretches along the right side. A most interesting start to our Scottish golfing careers! The first hole may be the most convoluted, but there are other interesting holes here as well. One of the exciting holes at Innerleithen is *Pirn Craig*, the 433-yard par 4 third. For the tee shot you climb the side of *Pirn Craig* to a tee box about 25 feet above the fairway. Your drive must skirt the hillside on the right to a generous fairway below. Cut it too close on the right and the ball will hang up on the hillside rough; aim too far left and you may find your ball (if you're lucky) in the heavy rough defining the left edge of the hole. The second shot is easier, but the target is a small green that is just below the tee box of the 1st. Freedom of the Fairways, a discount golf promotion, labels this hole "one of the best par 4s in the Borders." The short 100-yard 5th repeats a theme we've found in several Scottish designs--the 3rd at Shiskine, the 2nd at Dollar, also at Lochgilphead and two at Braemar--a short hole, blind, straight up hill. Aptly named *Hill*, this one-shotter plays across the road and up to a plateau green about 30 feet above the tee. The shot is blind with only the top of the flag in view from the tee. Miss the green on any side and you're hunting in tall grass for your ball. It's a fun hole that I have special feeling for since it was my first par in Scotland. The 8th, *Dyke*, is the longest hole at 524 yards. This was the first time we saw stone fences (the dyke) in play on a golf course, a feature we have since found at many other courses. We've played Innerleithen a couple of times and always find the course in decent shape and the reception friendly.

COMMENTS FROM THE FORWARD TEES: In reflection, I think this is a typical small village course, nestled into a glen or valley (Leithen Valley), with sheep dotting the hillsides, and a small burn flowing through the course. This little course was the first course we played in Scotland. This course truly fits into the bit of land available to build this village course. The course also has a small country road running through and the 2nd and 5th cross the road. The par for ladies is 36 (72) and a yardage of 2706 (5412). There are three par 3s and three par 5s. The par 3s range from 89 to 170 yards. The 5th is the shortest par three but is elevated approximately 30 feet (a three story house) with rock, bushes, and rough and the green is small. Given the difficulties it is very parable because the distance is short. The par 5s are over 400 yards. The 3rd is only 412 yards long, but has a difficult elevated green which takes some planning for the approach. Eight is the longest of the 5s at 467 yards. Besides the length there is a dyke to get through but it doesn't encroach into the fairway very much. A wonderful unique experience, this course is not to be missed. You will better understand golf as it was played a century ago.

KILSPINDIE GOLF COURSE
The Clubhouse, Aberlady, East Lothian EH32 0QD
www.kilspindiegolfclub.com   01875-870695
Links, 5502 yards, par 69, £38

AMENITIES: Small friendly clubhouse bar and a small, but well stocked, golf shop.

COURSE COMMENTS: As the 35th oldest golf club in the world, Kilspindie is very popular with the locals in this golf rich area. Part of the charm of the course is that it is short, yet demanding to all levels of golfers. Kilspindie has six holes which play along Gosford Bay, numerous fairway and greenside bunkers, and mildly undulating greens. The wind, as always on these seaside links, will affect your game. Typical comments from players were: "I enjoyed every shot," "first class," and "an absolute gem." The 4th, *The Target*, is a good par 4. The fairway on this 365-yard hole is a gentle curve to the right, but is also sloped to the right toward the beach (OB). The green is a small target on the point and protected by several bunkers. It deserves its rating as the number one handicap hole. The signature hole is the dramatic 8th, *Gosford Bay*. A par 3 of 162 yards, the tee shot needs to carry 150 yards of the bay to a green guarded by several bunkers. The final hole is really unforgettable. For men it is 252 yards and plays as a par 4, but for ladies it is 240 yards and plays as a par 3! Anne really screamed about that, but then that's golf in Scotland. For both, tee shots must avoid the stone fence which bisects the fairway. Despite the 18th Anne shot her best score in Scotland on this day. Whether you score well or not, it never hurts that at Kilspindie the firth is in view from almost every hole.

COMMENTS FROM THE FORWARD TEES: A great links course along the Firth of Forth with views back to Edinburgh. The course isn't long at 5107 yards and has a par of 69. Here you will find all the challenges associated with links courses including bounces and rolls that put your ball in precarious places, bunkers, a burn, and water. Also, of course, are those beautiful views all around to capture attention and disrupt your concentration. The day we played we saw seals, heron, numerous other sea birds, and rabbits about. The course has one par 5 on each side and both are over 400 yards with the 2nd the longest at 490 yards. There are four par 3s, two on each side and the eighth is the signature hole. Kilspindie GC is worth your time to play.

MINTO GOLF COURSE
Minto, Hawick TD9 8SA
www.mintogolf.co.uk   01450-670220

Parkland, 5413 yards, par 69, £30

AMENITIES: No golf shop, but a pleasing clubhouse with good views of the hills and course. Good food served usual hours.

COURSE COMMENTS: The first 9-hole course at Minto opened in 1933. In 1977 ten new holes were added and one par 3 was dropped to make the current 18-hole Minto GC. The course has continued to update with some major modernization in 1999. With grand views of the surrounding hills and lovely trees throughout, Minto GC is a popular course (plan to book ahead in season). Although the course has some hills it really is an easy walk. The trees will be players' main concern because there are not too many bunkers, mostly greenside, and not very deep. Water does come into play when a drainage ditch crosses a couple of holes and runs beside a couple of others. A burn is a major concern on the approach to the 18th green. Most of the greens are moderate in size and many have significant back to front slope--it pays to be below the pin on most holes. The 8th is the only hole with a tiered green. Players need to be aware that several holes cross over others. Minto GC has its share of interesting holes. The 3rd, *Aintree*, a 414-yard par 4 is the #1 stroke index hole. The hole is a long uphill straight ahead hole where the line for your drive is to the left of the telephone pole in the middle of the fairway (hitting the lines requires playing the shot again). A ditch (hazard) runs the length of the hole left and the right has heavy rough. The green is not guarded by any bunkers, but it is quite sloped back to front. A fine par 3 on the front is *Benighn Bishop*, the 139-yard 8th. Hit to a multitiered green sited on a hill. Two fronting bunkers cause concern, but taking the correct club is a bigger concern. Four of us hit good shots, but all came up short. Even moderate hitters can try to drive the green downhill and tucked right behind a copse of large trees on the 10th, called *Hangin' Stane*. More often than not on this 245-yard par 4 those who try for the green get tangled in the trees or end up in the front left bunker. The prudent play is a 200-210 yard shot straight down so that you're left with an easy chip to the sloping green and a possible birdie. Next is *Dunion*, the 369-yard par 4 eleventh. The first hole on the hilly section of the course, the 11th is a fun hole. Tee off over the 13th green toward the aiming post-- the landing area is blind. The approach is steeply downhill to a flat green with a large bunker left. The signature hole of the course is next. *Everest*, a 255-yard par 4, is a hole you'll always remember. Drive between two large trees (shouldn't be in play, but I caught a branch) to a steeply rising fairway that gets steeper as you approach the platform green. One small bunker right complicates an already difficult blind approach. The 14th, *Teviotdale*, is a 393-yard two-shotter which is downhill with a slight dogleg right (crosses the 15th fairway before the green). A rise before the green means that most approach shots are blind or semi-blind. Beware of the hidden bunker on the right. Minto GC is one of the most enjoyable courses in the Scottish Borders and has a very friendly membership eager to show off their gem.

COMMENTS FROM THE FORWARD TEES: T h i s course is set on typically pleasant Borders land with hills, trees, and farmland. The course plays ten holes on one side of their private road, back to the clubhouse and then the final eight holes. There are hills on the course but nothing unreasonable especially on the first ten holes. The hardest hills are on the back with the 13th, *Everest*, being the steepest. Except for short stretches, the course is not difficult to walk. We played in the late summer after the wettest summer in a century. The weather the day we played started bright and sunny and ended cloudy with a very cool breeze. Lesley Moore, ladies' Vice Captain said, "We started our game in summer and ended in the fall." The overall course yardage is 5233 with a par of 71. The front side has two par 3s and the last nine has only one. The par 3s aren't unreasonably long with the 6th the longest at 184 yards, however it does play downhill. There are three par 5s; two on the front and only one of the back. They are all at or over 400 yards. The 13th seemed to catch me off guard. It is uphill with a slight dogleg left at the last. Since I couldn't see the green I found myself on the far right with a big pitch up to the green. The green is set into the hill so the best approach is from the left--a straight flat shot from that angle. This was a really enjoyable day of golf with some entertaining and unique golf shots. Definitely a course to plan to play when in the area.

NIDDRY CASTLE GOLF COURSE
Castle Road, Winchburgh, West Lothian EH52 6RQ
www.niddrycastle.co.uk 01506-891097
Parkland, 5914 yards, par 70, £19

AMENITIES: A small lounge is open most of the time (even early). Snack food served all day. No golf shop, but a few essentials are available at the clubhouse.

COURSE COMMENTS: Anne Leslie, the Ladies' Captain and the first lady Club Captain (not very common in Scotland), gave us a brief interesting history of a former club course. The earlier course was closed by the MOD (Ministry of Defense) during World War II because the local slate works was a target for enemy bombings. The course didn't reopen after the war and was left as pasture until 1982 when land for a nine hole course was leased from the local laird, Lord Hopetoun. The current parkland Niddry Castle course (named for the castle the course plays around) was expanded to 18 in 2003. The course has great views toward Edinburgh and the Pentland Hills and is nestled against slate tailing mounds 50 feet tall--plans are to remove the tailings when the new Firth of Forth Bridge gets built. The old holes (currently 1-7, 17, and 18) can still be used for a nine hole routing, as we did when the rain hit hard on the sixth hole the first day we played with locals Bill and Irene Watson. The well-bunkered course has water in play (burns and ponds) on about half the holes. Greens are small to moderate and several have strong slopes, most with tricky borrows. With a few hills on the course there are some blind shots, but it's still an easy walk. Your round starts with a nice bite, a 198-yard par 3. That is followed by *The Whins*, an interesting 248-yard par 4 which begins with a blind drive over a small knock. If your drive is short, the second will be blind as well. One of the largest greens on the course is protected by a trap on the right. The 6th, *Castle View*, a par 5 of 524 yards, has a downhill tee shot which leaves a tough decision: lay up short of the burn or go for it and risk the burn and/or a tough lie on the hillside. The third shot is blind over a hump to a green with a bunker left. We went back and played the whole course a year later. The newer back holes, 8-16, are broader and flatter, but still interesting. On eight, *Doon the Burn*, a par 4 of 295 yards, accuracy is the key to the hole with a burn and pond left and five bunkers fronting the tiered green. A chance for a birdie is the par five 450-yard 10th called *Auld Cathie*. With a narrow fairway without much trouble about except two traps by the green, there's a chance for a good score here. *Scott's Legacy* is the 13th, a short par 4 of only 288 yards. This strong dogleg right has three large bunkers on the outside of the turn, but a pond on the right near the green is a danger to those too bold. The green has the typical two bunkers left and right, but also has two behind. On the 17th, *Murray's Rest*, drive slightly downhill on the 352-yard two-shotter with rough left and trees right. Your approach is blind over a hill and trees to a green with a bunker left and a burn right. Niddry Castle GC is a good find--interesting holes, pleasant surroundings, and friendly members.

COMMENTS FROM THE FORWARD TEES: Niddry Castle is an entertaining mix of an old style course and a much newer layout. The old holes (1-7 and 17-18) are narrower with more obstacles to deal with and the newer holes are straight ahead with wide fairways. It makes for a interesting mix. Water is an issue on both sides and can cause problems on many holes. I found I had to really plan my second and third shots to be at the right distances for playing over water. The par 5s are all over 400 yards, but only the 6th caused much problem. There I crossed the burn on my third shot and still had a tough long up hill approach to the green.

NORTH BERWICK, WEST LINKS

New Clubhouse, Beach Road, North Berwick, East
Lothian EH39 4BB
www.northberwickgolfclub.com 01620-895040
Links, 6458 yards, par 71, £80

AMENITIES: Old established clubhouse where day
ticket holders are members for the day.   Very well-stocked golf
shop and starter's building.

COURSE COMMENTS: North Berwick West GC is
one of the oldest clubs in existence having been established in
1832.   The course is quite busy most of the time and requires
a handicap certificate (check well ahead).   The venerable links
course has eight holes which play along the sea and more
than 100 bunkers in play.   Wind and weather, though, are
often the course's toughest defense.   As one golfer
commented, "Every hole is memorable," but many have
special features.   The 1st, *Point Garry (Out)*, a par 4 of 328
yards, requires a layup to about 190 yards to set up a second
shot over a rough-covered hill.   The tee shot at the par 4
second skirts along the edge of the North Sea.   The 3rd is
very long (464-yard par 4) especially into the prevailing wind.
To add to the length a stone fence or dyke crosses the fairway
about 145 yards from the green.   The 6th is almost all carry
(162 yards) over an old quarry to a green with bunkers in front
and on both sides.   The 11th is a par 5 with an elevated tee on
the sea berm aiming at two imposing bunkers.   On the 13th, a
364-yard par 4, your second shot must clear a stone fence set
diagonally to the green.   Then comes a famous hole, the 15th,
Redan, a 192-yard par 3.   Bunkers and hillocks protect this
hard to hit green.   The hole is one of the most copied in golf.
Famed golf writer Bernard Darwin describes *Redan* this way:

"A beautiful one shot hole atop a plateau with a bunker
short of the green, to the   left,   and   another   further   on   the
right, and we must vary our mode of attack   according   to
the wind, playing a shot to come in from the right or making a
direct frontal assault."

He does make golf sound like war. On the 16th the green has a large valley cutting through the center--it's like two plateau greens separated by a valley green. Don't get caught on the wrong level on this hole. Like Royal Dornoch or Machrihanish, North Berwick West is how links golf should be.

COMMENTS FROM THE FORWARD TEES: I am such a strong visual person that the sheer beauty of the setting was a distraction from the first hole, but this is a testing course which demands your full attention. The course has many natural hazards including the North Sea, burns, mounds or dunes, stone walls, and often a quick shower. The course is long at 5751 yards with a ladies' par of 74. There are four par 3s and six par 5s, four on the front side. After playing I felt that I had "earned" a light lunch and a pint, but I would be first in the queue (line) to play again.

PEEBLES GOLF COURSE
Kirkland Street, Peebles EH45 8EU
www.peeblesgolfclub.co.uk   01721-720197
Undulating parkland, 6160 yards, par 70, £24

AMENITIES: The new clubhouse, opened in 1998 (dedicated by Prince Andrew) with views of the first three holes, serves a fairly complete menu. Golf shop is well equipped.

COURSE COMMENTS: The Peebles Golf Club, designed in 1892 by Harry Colt, climbs above the market town and affords great views of the town and surrounding Border hills. Wide fairways are complemented by strategic bunkering. Locals will say the course isn't very hilly, but even though it is no Pitlochry (the Switzerland of Scottish Golf) the elevation changes will affect your shot-making.

Peebles is a fairly classic track with some interesting holes. The course was one of the first big courses we ran into with a par 3 first hole. *Firknowe* is a 196-yard one-shotter up hill to a two-tiered green guarded by three bunkers. It's a challenging hole straight out of the car. The 5th, *Meiklehope* (big hope) is a par 4 of 342 yards which plays from a slightly elevated tee. Shoot out towards the fairway bunker. Your second shot must find the elongated green with bank on one side and traps on the downside. The tee at the 8th, *Peggy Lea's*, offers the best views of the town. The hole also is a good birdie opportunity as it usually plays downwind. The 13th is a 319-yard par 4 called *Ca'Canny*. The hole is a dogleg left over a small hill. Trees line both sides of the fairway leading to relatively flat green with a bunker left and drop-off behind. A good par 3 is the 194-yard 16th, *The Whaum*. The two-tiered green is surrounded by trees left and back and protected by three bunkers. The burn crossing the hole half way to the green is only a problem on a missed shot. The walk up and down the hills of Peebles GC will cause you to wheeze a little, but the quality course and the views will be worth the effort.

COMMENTS FROM THE FORWARD TEES: This is an excellent parkland golf course which plays up and around a hill. The views are terrific as is the setting. The ups and downs eventually wore me out so when I got finished with 16 and realized 17 went up I wondered if I wanted to finish, but of course I did. The longest hole on the course is the 18th, but with the down hill slope it's very playable. The course is not too long at 5195 yards and has a par of 70, however there is more than enough about this course to hold your attention. There are four par 3s at Peebles ranging in distance from 119 to 195 yards. See Bob's notes above about the first par three. The seventh hole is very short, but requires precision or get out your sand wedge. The two par 5s are well over 400 yards but both go down hill to the clubhouse. A great course to play anytime.

ST BOSWELLS GOLF COURSE
Braeheads, St Boswells, TD6 0DE
www.stboswellsgolfclub.co.uk 01835-823527
Parkland, 2637 yards, par 34, £14

AMENITIES: Small lounge bar open evenings and weekends in the 1999 clubhouse. No golf shop or trolleys for rent; plan to carry. We got a scorecard from the secretary and then paid the greenskeeper as he came around.

COURSE COMMENTS: Designed by Willie Park Jnr in 1899, the course closed down during World War II between 1944 and 1947. A year after it reopened the course was flooded out by the River Tweed and wasn't rebuilt until 1958. The 9-hole parkland track is set along the Tweed and only a mile away from Dryburgh Abbey. The 2nd hole, a 161-yard par 3, is the only non-flat hole on the course. The large green provides a good target for your shot from the elevated tee. Take about one club less for the distance, but be accurate because the green is well-guarded by bunkers. The 9th is a short demanding test. The hole is a 256-yard par 4 where the tee shot must skirt a large beech tree to reach a shelf-fairway and green. It's prudent to lay back on the first shot (150 to 190 yards), but that means the second shot is half-blind, with only the top of the flag visible. It might be tempting to try a long sweeping hook to reach the green, or at least the raised part of the fairway, but that would bring into play heavy rough on the left. A fun hole! Besides pleasurable golf, the course has much to offer. Grand views of the River Tweed, with fly fishers trying their luck, are plentiful. Rabbits, ducks, and a profusion of wildflowers (even in September) brighten the whole course. The course even presents an enigma to take your mind off golf. Between the 6th green and the 7th tee lurks a small, innocent looking pond with a bridge to cross over. On this bridge a sign warns, "THIS POND IS DANGEROUS." No information why the pond was dangerous. It didn't look particularly deep or as if it had poisonous water. The rest of the round I kept conjuring up images of miniature Nessies lurking beneath the lily pads. St Boswells GC makes a short, enjoyable stop while wandering through the Border's abbey country.

TORWOODLEE GOLF COURSE
Edinburgh Road, Galashiels TD1 2NE
www.torwoodleegolfclub.co.uk 01896-772260
Hilly parkland, 6021 yards, par 69, £32

AMENITIES: No golf shop, but the club has a lounge which looks out to the course and serves good food usual hours.

COURSE COMMENTS: The parkland Torwoodlee GC is more than hundred-years-old and plays over and around typical Scottish Borders hills similar to Peebles GC. Besides the tree-lined fairways, more than 25 mostly greenside bunkers will affect play, although none are very penal. The only water on the course is the River Gala which runs beside 15 and 18 (OB). The greens are moderately sized (a few are large) and fairly flat. Several of the greens are a gun-turret style, set into a side hill. Other problems presented by the course are a couple of internal OBs (at the 11th to keep players from dangerously cutting the dogleg and at the 16th to protect clubhouse windows) and several blind approaches. Surrounded by the forested hills and flanked by the river, Torwoodlee is a lovely, though hilly track where taking a buggy (powered cart) might be a good idea. Besides being a lovely parkland track, Torwoodlee has some interesting holes as well. The 4th, *Torwood*, is a 265-yard par 4 where you drive uphill towards the marker. Big hitters can hit through the fairway into unplayable rough. The green is tucked right behind a tree and is guarded by three bunkers. Should be easy, but can be tricky. *Bowland View* is the 337-yard par 4 sixth which begins with a steep downhill drive between tall trees with heavy rough and OB left. Here the green is tucked left behind trees with no guarding bunkers. A fun shot. The 9th called *Sunset* is a tricky 361-yard par 4. A large tree on the left is where you naturally want to go because the right side is lined with trees. A smooth draw is best (a shot I don't have). One fairway bunker on the left and two greenside bunkers complete the hole. On the back we liked *Buckholm View*, a 416-yard par 4 dogleg left where you have to be careful of players on the 11th green. The approach is down to the double green (with the 8th) protected by two bunkers. In the dry it's easy to run off the back of this green. A dramatic downhill drive begins *Ryehaugh*, the 521-yard par 5 fourteenth. Your drive must clear the steep drop you came over on the 2nd or risk getting hung up in nasty rough--only about 200 yards. The green is tucked a little to the right and is protected by one trap. On the 16th, *William Law*, a par 4 of 410 yards, you drive to the bottom of the law (hill) by the clubhouse while avoiding the fairway bunker left. Everyone on the clubhouse patio (good weather) will watch you hit your steeply uphill approach to the green hidden behind two bunkers. Torwoodlee can be a fun course with a buggy or an electric trolley.

FROM THE FORWARD TEES: Set in the Border hills and valleys this course is a hard walk, especially if you're pulling or pushing a non-motorized trolley. The course has many elevated gun turret greens surrounded by bunkers. It is a long course to walk, but ladies' tees are 5366 yards with a par of 72. The front has two long par 5s and two short par 3s. The backside has fewer hills, but when the 16th went back up I wasn't sure I cared about finishing, especially with the inviting clubhouse next to the fairway. The backside has two par 5s and two par 3s. Overall the par 3s are short and the par 5s ranged from 346 yards (steep uphill) to 493 yards (downhill, finally). An interesting feature of the course is off the tee of the 2nd you must go up over a steep area of heavy rough (at least 130-yard carry) and off the tee of the 14th you go down over the same steep rough (again 130-yard carry). I probably wouldn't play this course again without a motorized trolley, but the challenges here are a strong pull.

WEST LINTON GOLF COURSE
Medwyn Road, West Linton EH46 7HN
www.wlgc.co.uk   01968-660256
Moorland, 6161 yards, par 69, £30

AMENITIES: Catering available most usual hours in season in the pleasant clubhouse lounge. The golf shop, run by pro Ian Wright, is one of the best stocked shops in the area. Wright also has a great email newsletter.

COURSE COMMENTS: West Linton is a lovely moorland track which plays through Slipperfield Moor and affords wonderful views of the Pentland Hills. The original 1890 design was updated in 1926 by famed James Braid and is now recognized as part of the James Braid Trail of courses. It wasn't until 1972 that land became available to extend the course to 18 holes. Long holes, wind, strategic bunkering, and tough rough will be the major problems faced at West Linton.

The West Linton course is filled with classic golf holes. Among our favorites is the 6th, *Mendick*, a 360-yard par 4. The slightly downhill tee shot is to a bunkered fairway which narrows near the green. The deep green is guarded by one bunker right and falls off behind. *Wolfe's Wood*, is the 447-yard par 4 eighth and is the number one handicap hole at West Linton. The hole begins with a blind tee shot to a fairway which falls away. The long second shot is through the dogleg right to a green with rough and OB right and bunkers left. The hole deserves its reputation. Next is the 9th, *Kittley Knowe*, a 162-yard par 3 at the farthest reach of the course. Hit to an elevated sloping green with a bunker left and drop-offs on all other sides. On the back we really like *Westwater*, the 376-yard par 4 fourteenth. Shoot from an elevated tee to a valley fairway with a moor on the right. Be careful of the curlews who nest in the marsh during the season. Two pot bunkers left and one right guard the deep green. West Linton is an easy walk, but not an easy course. One of our favorites in the area.

COMMENTS FROM THE FORWARD TEES: T h i s pleasant moorland course is more testing than one would expect. It is one of those courses you want to play repeatedly. You know you can improve your scores. The course has hills, slopes, numerous bunkers, difficult rough, and views of the area to distract you. West Linton has a par 72 and is 5402 yards from the forward tees. There are four par 5s and four par 3s. The par 3s range in distance from 113 yards on the front to 179 on the back. The par 5s are from 439 to 458 yards. This moorland course is fun and a good golf test.

PUBS, RESTAURANTS & TEAROOMS

The 4 Mary's Pub in Linlithgow across the street from the
Palace. Named for the four Marys who were attendants
to Mary Queen of Scots, the pub serves good quality
pub grub and especially delicious soups.

Bass Rock Bistro (restaurant) just off the main shopping
street in North Berwick. Upscale restaurant menu at fair
prices in a lovely setting. Always a good stop.

Bella Italia (restaurant) on the main street in North Berwick.
Good Italian menu and the food was well prepared.

Beancross Hotel Restaurants (family restaurant) just off the
M9 near Falkirk. Highly recommended by a local B&B.
Three eating areas, from fancy to more family
oriented. Food was good quality off a broad menu. Look
for the special writing on the walls.

The Brasserie at the Townhouse Hotel on the main square
in Melrose. Known for excellent food (not pub fare),
this classy restaurant is a good choice when in the
area--busy, be sure to book ahead.

Corner House Hotel (pub) on the main street through
Innerleithen near Peebles. A typical hotel pub, but
special to us as the first Scottish pub we ate in. Food
was good for pub fare and the locals we super friendly.

Crown Hotel (pub/restaurant) on the High Street in Peebles.
Several dining areas including a conservatory. Good
quality pub food off a broad menu.

Deacon Brodie's Tavern on the Royal Mile in Edinburgh not
far down from the Castle. Famously celebrating the
notorious Deacon Brodie who was the real-life model
for Stevenson's *Jekyll and Hyde*. The pub serves
decent food, but is best for a relaxing drink while
shopping on the Royal Mile. Stop for a brew and the
history.

Golden Arms (pub) in the village of West Linton just a little
ways from the golf course. Lovely old pub with
overstuffed chairs and a piano in the corner with a sign

which says, "Play Me." Pub food was decent and the dogs were very friendly.

The Grange (restaurant) on the main street of North Berwick. Food was good, but the local art on the walls wasn't the best. Okay, but there are better choices in town.

Horseshoe Inn (bistro/restaurant) in Eddleston By Peebles. Award winning restaurant and bistro in a small village. Both the bistro/bar and fine dining restaurant have interesting menus and dear prices. Food is top quality. Great for a special night out.

Kailzie Garden Restaurant (tearoom) about four miles out of Peebles on the road to Traquair House. Serves snacks, lunches, and special Saturday evening dinners. Rustic decor and great food, including special "*Smorrebrod*" (open-face sandwich originating in Denmark). We had one of the best soups we've ever had here.

Monte Cassino Restaurante Italiano up the hill from the town square in Melrose. Top quality Italian for excellent prices means the restaurant will be busy and   noisy-- still, well worth it.

Mussel Inn on Rose Street in the shopping area behind Princes Street in Edinburgh (also in Glasgow). Top fresh   local seafood at affordable prices. Large portions. We always stop before heading home.

Neidpath Inn (pub) on the main road through Peebles on the west end of town. Neidpath, named after the local castle, has been a drinking pub for a long time and only recently added dining. We were there soon after they opened for dinners and the food was good and reasonably priced.

Park Hotel Bar in Peebles on the east end of the High Street shopping district. The Park Hotel has a fancy restaurant with fancy prices. The bar has a good menu and better prices.

Old Aberlady Inn (pub) on the main coastal road through Aberlady. A historic golfer's pub with a good menu and tasty food. A good place to stop in the area.

The Old Clubhouse Bar and Restaurant just off the main square in the village of Gullane. Golfer's pub with interesting memorabilia and history (in 1890 it was the original Gullane Golf Club clubhouse). Upscale pub menu, good food, and all the golf conversation you want.

Osteria (restaurant) on the main street of North Berwick. Italian fine dining by a renowned chef. The food is not cheap, but worth every pence. Reservations are necessary.

Ship Inn (pub) just down from the abbey in Melrose. The only public house in Melrose, the Ship Inn serves quality homemade pub food.

Traquair Arms Hotel (pub/restaurant) on the main road through the village of Innerleithen. Specializing in up-scale pub and unusual Italian fare, Traquair Arms is always a good bet.

Wheelhouse Restaurant (tourist restaurant) at the famous Falkirk Wheel. One of the premier attractions in Scotland, the engineering marvel Falkirk Wheel attracts plenty of visitors. The large Wheelhouse Restaurant is a good place to eat after a visit. The extensive menu isn't overpriced considering it's at a major tourist attraction.

LODGINGS

Allerton House
Oxnam Road, Jedburgh TD8 6QQ
01835-869633 www.allertonhouse.co.uk £95
A Four Star B&B just five minutes walk from town centre, Allerton House has won several "Best Breakfast" awards. Beautiful rooms and great hosts, Christopher and Carol Longden, make a stay at Allerton pleasurable.

Braidwood B&B
Buccleuch Street, Melrose TD6 9LD
01896-822488 www.braidwoodmelrose.co.uk £65

In the heart of the village literally across the road from Melrose Abbey, Braidwood is in an excellent location for a visit to the town. Five minutes to the best restaurants and well appointed rooms make it a good place to stay.

Eildon B&B
109 Newbigging, Musselburgh EH21 7AS
01316-653981 www.stayinscotland.net £80
Georgian townhouse built in 1802 and restored in 1993. Pleasant well-appointed rooms.

The Glebe House
Law Road, North Berwick EH39 4PL
01620-892608 www.glebehouse-nb.co.uk £100
The Glebe House is a listed Georgian Manse built in 1780 and now converted to a fine guest house. Convenient to town and golf.

Glede Knowe Guest House
16 St Ronan's Terrace, Innerleithen EH44 6RB
01896-831295 www.gledeknowe.co.uk £80
Pleasant modern B&B with well appointed rooms and good views. Hosts Bill and Alison Mason will make your stay enjoyable. A favorite of bicyclists and convenient to the village.

Glentruim B&B
53 Dirleton Ave., North Berwick EH39 4BL
01620-890064 www.glentruim.co.uk £90
Traditional 1895 sandstone design within easy walking distance to shopping, restaurants, and golf. Serves tasty breakfasts as well.

Lindores Guest House
60 Old Town, Peebles EH45 8JE
01721-7220272 www.lindorespeebles.co.uk
The B&B, when run by Carl and Kathryn Lane before they retired, was one of our favorite stays. The historic house, a

former home and surgery built in 1895 by Dr. Clement Gunn, has a great location on the main road through town and is only a short walk from shopping and eating. Beautiful bedrooms are one of the fine features of Lindores. New owners, Janice and Nigel Henderson, have reopened Lindores House--check current reviews.

Neidpath Inn
27-29 Old Town, Peebles EH45 8JF
01721-724306 www.neidpathinn.co.uk £90
The newly refurbished rooms are separated from the bar/ restaurant so there is no noise problem as in some inns. Easy walk to town. Excellent breakfast and friendly owners.

St Germains B&B
2 St. Germains House, Longniddry EH32 0PQ
01875-853034 www.st-germains.co.uk £50
Located on four acres of woodlands and gardens, St Germains has a long history including a stint in WW2 as a convalescent home for injured airmen. Dinners served by arrangement.

The Wing
13 Marine Parade, North Berwick EH39 4LD
01620-893162 www.thewing.co.uk £60
On the beach only about three blocks from the downtown area and only two blocks from The Glen GC, the Wing is a great place to stay in North Berwick. The Wing is a portion of a holiday home built in 1861 and was used in the past as a boys' boarding school and hotel before being separated off as an individual home in the 1950s. Owners James and Angie Sadison have turned the Wing into a lovely B&B with an upstairs lounge with views out to Bass Rock, the North Sea, and across to Fife. The rooms are comfortable and breakfast in the front parlour is delicious.

St Albans B&B
Clouds, Duns, Berwickshire TD11 3BB

01361-883285
www.bnbchoices.com/scotland/borders/ st-albans.bnb £70
There has been a house on this site since 1694, although the present structure was built in 1789 and remodeled in 1980. As a listed historic building the Kenworthys haven't been able to add ensuite facilities, but there are two bathrooms and no more than four guests. Rooms are lovingly furnished with period decorations. Breakfast is hearty and can be very entertaining if you ask about the history of Duns. By the way, Clouds Lane doesn't refer to the sky, but to *Clud*, an early Scottish material which was made in the area.

Traquair House
Innerleithen, Peeblesshire EH44 6PW
01896-830323   www.traquair.co.uk £180
Traquair House is one of Scotland's premier lodgings. Imagine staying in the oldest continuously inhabited house in Scotland, where Mary Queen of Scots and her son, James IV, stayed. Obviously, it's not an inexpensive stay, but to stay for one night can give you lifetime of stories. Only three bedrooms are for let, each with antique furnishings, canopied beds, and private (modern) bathrooms. Take your sumptuous breakfast in the Still Room surrounded by cupboards of antique china. During your stay wander through the museum rooms open to the public. If weather permits, roam the garden areas including the full maze. Be sure to visit the Traquair House Brewery (in the wing opposite the lodgings) which was founded in 1965 on the site of an original 18C brewery. Traquair House may be a once in a lifetime experience or you may find, as we have, it's a real "do again" stay.

ATTRACTIONS

Abbeys (HS). Jedburgh, Dryburgh, and Melrose Abbeys are prime attractions in the Borders area. At Jedburgh take in the great herb garden; at Dryburgh be sure to see Sir Walter Scott's memorial; and at Melrose see if you can spot the bagpipe playing pig (you can by looking up) and the burial place of King Robert the Bruce's heart.

Abbortsford House, Melrose. The wonderful stone fantasy home of Sir Walter Scott. was built in 1812, the "Conundrum Castle...this romance of a house," as Scott called it, was his dream castle. The rooms open to the public are stuffed with historic antiquities, including a lock of Admiral Nelson's hair and a comb lost during the battle of Culloden. One of the best things about touring Abbotsford is that interior photography is allowed. Outside a splendid garden completes the experience.

Robert Smail's Printing Works (NTS), Innerleithen. This print shop was started in 1866 by Robert Smail to take care of the printing needs of the Peebles-Innerleithen-Walkerburn area. Taken over by the National Trust for Scotland in 1986, the shop is now open for tours of the office, the composing room, and the printing room. A fascinating tour and history of small village life.

Rosslyn Chapel, Roslin. Built in 1446, the chapel has been described as a "Tapestry in Stone." Thousands of some of the most impressive stone carvings in Scotland, if not Europe, adorn practically every inch of chapel walls, ceilings, and pillars. Made more famous by Dan Brown's *The Da Vinci Code*, Rosslyn has been linked to the Knights Templar and is home to numerous myths, legends, and ghosts.

Traquair House, near Innerleithen. The oldest inhabited house in Scotland, Traquair has several rooms open for touring including the library with its clever cataloging system. The Priest's Room is where the family secretly practiced Catholicism when it was banned by Protestant reformers--be sure to see the hidden staircase in the room which allowed the priest to escape if raided. The brewery in one wing provides pleasurable tastings of the local brew.

Chapter 8: Southern Scotland along the Solway Firth

Colvend Golf Course

Visitors to Scotland seek out the Highlands with their lonely, haunting glens, Whisky and Castle Trails. They head to the islands filled with history and myth. Also they relish the Borders, Lothians, and Fife especially for the golf. One region often neglected is rich with historical sites and filled with wonderful golfing adventures for those willing to explore. This is southern Scotland, especially the Dumfries and Galloway area along the shores of the Solway Firth. The area hosts numerous links and seaside courses that are as good as the famous links in Fife and along the Moray Firth, but which aren't nearly as crowded.

This chapter's selections begin with a course we should not have passed by several times on earlier trips.

COLVEND GOLF COURSE

Sandyhills, Dalbeattie, Kirkcudbright DG5 4PY
www.colvendgolfclub.co.uk 01556-630398
Undulating parkland, 5036 yards, par 69, £30

AMENITIES: Modern clubhouse with a lounge which looks out onto the lovely 18th green. Excellent snacks and meals available usual hours. No golf shop, but a few essentials are available in the clubhouse.

COURSE COMMENTS: We by-passed Colvend GC on our previous trips to the south because the view of the very steep uphill 1st hole was so off-putting. What a mistake! An electric trolley makes the course quite an enjoyable walk. If you really want to play vacation golf, consider taking one of the club's numerous buggies (riding carts). The course has a fine pedigree with the original nine designed by Willie Fernie in 1905. It was extended to 18 holes in 1985 by Peter Aliss and Dave Thomas. With great views of the surrounding hills and the Solway Firth (the views alone are worth the price of admission) the lovely tree-lined Colvend GC (rowan, oaks, hawthorns) is a fun course to play in the south. Fun, but not without its challenges. Twenty-four bunkers, mostly greenside, will demand some precise short shots, while four holes have burns or ponds in play (8, 12, 13, and 18). The small to moderate greens are interesting to putt--subtle slopes, significant back to front slopes, and some with definite tiers. You must cross a road (A710) to play 9-17 and cross back to play the 18th. One tricky spot in the routing is that from the 15th green you must cross over the 13th tee to get to the tee of 16.

As club secretary Roger Bailey told us, "Don't be put off by the first hole; think of it as a door to the rest of the fun." After finally playing the course we wholeheartedly agree. One of the fun holes is *Solway View*, the 341-yard par 4 third. A blind tee shot starts this straight two-shotter. Aim at the post. A good shot can roll down into the dip in the fairway (not a hazard). Second shot is also blind into a sloping green with no bunkers to bother your approach. Aim straight over the rowan tree (195 yards from the tee) at *The Rowan*, the 303-yard par 4 fifth. Second shot is downhill to a narrow green tucked slightly right. Again, no bunkers. A dramatic one-shotter is the 178-yard 8th called *The Burn*. A large burn (Duh!) in front of the green, one bunker right, and OB behind make the hole a serious challenge. On the back we liked the 11th, *The Ruin*, a 283-yard par 4. The hole is a serious dogleg left with a stone wall, trees, and wild rough for 180 yards down the left--oh, yes, it's all OB. Find the middle of the fairway past the corner (200-220 yards) and you can have a simple approach only bothered by one bunker on the right. I had an easy par....on my second ball. The 13th, *Fairgirth*, has a burn and pond on the left and small ponds middle and right to complicate the 417-yard par 4. The fairway rises to the green protected by two bunkers left and OB behind. The drive is the crux. The finishing hole is a beauty. *The Oaks*, a 266-yard par 4, starts with an uphill tee shot. The drive is not the problem unless you stray too far right and are blocked from the green by tall trees. Local big hitters will often drive over a row of trees which runs down the left to have a better approach to the green tucked right. The real problem is the burn which surrounds the green on three sides. From the clubhouse lounge we watched a woman in a competition put three into the burn--she was really ready for a drink in the clubhouse lounge after that. The course is great, the membership super friendly, and we're sorry we waited so long to play.

FROM THE FORWARD TEES: This is a beautiful course with some amazing views of the Solway Firth. The first hole is very off putting in that it does go fairly straight up. The 10th also goes up but not as steeply. Colvend is not hard to walk, but a powered trolley is a big advantage here. Though there are differences between the two sides, both a quite lovely. The course is 4774 yards for ladies with a par of 70. There are no par 5s on the first nine but two on the back nine. The front has 3 par 5s and the back has only one. You will have to contend with water on four holes (8-12-13-18). Trees, and bunkers are the other main conditions of play. There are many very good golf challenges on the this course, but I especially liked the 18th. The hole begins with a tee shot up onto a plateau. The hole then climbs through the trees to the green which is a dogleg right around a large old tree and over a burn. Not an easy hole but one that makes one want to come back and try again soon.

GIRVAN MUNICIPAL GOLF COURSE
Golf Course Road, Girvan, Strathclyde KA26 9HW
No web 01465-714272
Links and Parkland, 5095 yards, par 64, £22

AMENITIES: The clubhouse is up the hill from the starter and the first tee.   Clubhouse has a very pleasant lounge. No golf shop, but the starter has a few golf items.

COURSE COMMENTS: Girvan is an 18-hole muni where the first eight holes are links and play along the Irish Sea.   Bunkers can be quite penal.   Links holes tend to be narrow while the parkland holes, 9-18, play wide. Some good holes on both sides. The 5th, *Ailsa Craig*, is a 171-yard par 3, with a tee shot straight out towards the famous rock to a green protected by three traps.   *Whales Back*, the 299-yard 6th, plays along the edge of the beach for its length.   The last of the links holes, the 243-yard par 3 eighth called *Right Scunner*, has a large grass-covered dune along the left of a green guarded by a deep bunker. The 18th is an entertaining 187-yard par 3. From the elevated tee at *Ower at Last* your shot needs to get up quickly to clear the large trees that rise in front of the tee box--unique. The green has a deep trap on the right. With Turnberry and Troon not far away Girvan GC may seem like a very weak sister, but at only about £22 a round it's bargain golf.

LOCHMABEN GOLF COURSE
Castlehill Gate, Lochmaben, Lockerbie DG11 1NT
www.lochmabengolf.co.uk 01387-810552
Parkland, 5933 yards, par 70, £32

AMENITIES: The clubhouse has a pleasant lounge with plenty of room and views of the 18th green, 1st tee, and out to the loch. There is no golf shop; check in at the bar where some golf essentials are available and trolleys can be rented. We had a lovely dinner after our round and can attest that the clubhouse food is very good.

COURSE COMMENTS: The club's motto, *E Nobis Liberator Rex* ("From us is born the liberator King") is reference to the local birthplace (the castle near the 2nd green) of King Robert I of Scotland (Robert the Bruce). The 1927 James Braid designed course, expanded to 18 holes in 1995, is worthy of a King's stature. Besides the castle, an ancient Roman settlement, Skelvieland, is to the left of the 9th fairway. The moderate length parkland track can be quite busy, but the local members are very friendly and accommodating to visitors. As was true of most Scottish golf courses the club did its part in the war efforts. The course was taken over by the Royal Engineers and was closed for five years--it reopened in 1947.

The course you play today is parkland with a nice variety of trees, but you wouldn't term the course tree-lined. There are more than 70 bunkers in play; a mix of greenside and fairway. The bunkers, even on the newer holes, are Braid-style and can be fairly penal. There are several grass bunkers also which will cause concern. A burn crosses the 9th in front of the green and the 8th is a total carry over the loch. Greens are mostly moderate to small and flat, except for the 15th which is quite sloped. We noted that the greens were well-conditioned and easy to read. Besides the wind which can add difficulty to any Scottish course, sloping fairways (up, down, and side) and three blind shots with marker posts give the course a few more teeth. The views of the loch and surrounding village, though, can make up for extra challenges.

Anne and I both enjoyed the play at Lochmaben and had a difficult time selecting our favorite holes. The two par threes early in the round are particular favorites of mine (Anne will definitely have a different perspective). The 2nd, *Bruce's Motte* (on the site of an ancient Bruce castle), is a 188-yard one-shotter worthy of its stroke index of 4. The hole is all uphill with trouble left and bailout area right--although it will leave a tough chip. The green is small and two-tiered. A four is a good score here. Next is an even longer par 3 called *The Moats*. This 190-yarder plays over two old moats (ditches) which must be carried to reach the smallish green guarded by three bunkers. Almost any miss leaves a tricky chip, although I found that birdies are possible by hitting the green. Next of note is the 6th, *The Beeches*, a 404-yard par 4. Drive uphill between two large trees (the beeches) on this slight dogleg right. A good drive leaves a downhill second shot to a sloping green guarded right and behind by bunkers. Deserving of its rating as the hardest hole on the front. A picture postcard hole, probably the signature hole on the course, is *Kirk Loch*, the 120-yard par 3 eighth. Hit directly over a corner of the loch to a raised green surrounded by four bunkers. A fun test of your short game skills. On the back we liked the 13th, *Lark's Rise*, a brilliant 425-yard par 4 with a tight uphill blind drive with a copse of trees left (and a real toilet in the trees, be sure to get the code at check-in) and OB right. Second shots (or thirds) are down to a green with traps on both sides making a narrow entrance to the green. The green is small for such a long hole. The final hole is another gem. *Cormorant's Rest*, is a 328-yard par four. The loch is OB left, trees right, and the green is raised and protected by four bunkers. The green is directly in front of the clubhouse windows. A fairway bunker 100 yards from the green adds challenge.

The course is a fun track and for the most part an easy walk. There's even a sense of humor to the course. Near the tee on one hole there is a sign which reads: "Blind tee shot. Ring bell on passing." The sign is also right next to the local cemetery.

FROM THE FORWARD TEES: The course actually plays around and over the Kirk Loch and is an interesting course with a good variety of challenges, yet it's very fair. Fairways are wide enough and yardages are reasonable for ladies. The overall yardage from the forward tees (red) is 5164 yards with the front at 2137 yards and the back at 3027 yards. There are no par 5s on the front and two on the back. The front has three par 3s and only one on the back.

The par 3s on the front were testing for me. The 2nd hole goes steeply uphill to a blind green and the 3rd goes over a large dip which fortunately isn't all rough. The 8th is all carry across the loch to the green. The back nine is longer and has more hills which add interest. The two finishing holes are played beside the beautiful, busy loch. This is a course that invites one to come back and try again.

POWFOOT GOLF COURSE
Commertrees, Annan, Dumfries-shire DG12 5QE
www.powfootgolfclub.com   01461-204100
Links, 6458 yards, par 71, £38

AMENITIES: Pleasant clubhouse serves good food most usual hours. Well-stocked golf shop. If you want to stay in the area, check out the nearby Powfoot Golf Hotel which has golfer specials and serves hearty meals.

COURSE COMMENTS: "The Powfoot Links are a fine natural course with springy turf and excellent greens." This 1922 Powfoot Golf Club guide description could have been written yesterday. Powfoot is a predominately links course with most holes offering views of the Solway Firth, the Irish Sea, and the English Cumbrian Fells (mountains). An early James Braid design (1903 for the original nine holes), the course plays out and back with fairly open fairways, strategic bunkering, and the ever-present wind which always seems against your shot. The 3rd, *Shore*, is a 265-yard par 3 which often plays into the wind--a daunting hole which most of us mortals will play as a two-shotter. The 9th, a 402-yard par 4 called *Crater*, has as a hazard a huge German bomb crater short of the green. This isn't the only remnant of World War II on the course; the last four holes are relatively flat and more parkland in design as a result of use as Victory Gardens during the war. *Sahara*, the 313-yard par 4 eleventh, begins with a blind tee shot with ample bailout room to the right, the direction the wind will push your ball. Climb the tee platform to check for golfers in the landing area before teeing off. The green is protected by hummocks as well as a large bunker. One player commented after a round at Powfoot that the course "is a hidden delight for any golfer seeking an enjoyable day's golf and an easy test on your legs."

COMMENTS FROM THE FORWARD TEES: This is an interesting links course. The views of the Solway Firth, the Irish sea, and the English mountains to the south can distract the more visual of us. Add the wind and you have a good golfing experience. Powfoot has several holes that look straight ahead but have challenges you can't see from the tee box. Examples are the 4th, a par 5 with a road in the fairway and a narrow approach to the green, or the 14th, the longest par 5 for ladies which has an elevated green where your approach shot must stay on the green or you will be chipping and chipping. Another example is the 17th which goes up to a rounded green and has six greenside bunkers. This is a course that will not be the same from day to day as the wind will change and so will your golfing decisions.

SANQUHAR GOLF COURSE
Euchan Course, Blackaddie Road, Sanquhar DG4 6JZ
No web   01659-50577
Parkland, 5646 yards, par 70, £15 day

AMENITIES: Small clubhouse open some evenings and on weekends. Honesty box. No trolleys.

COURSE COMMENTS: Sanquhar (SAN-ker) is a 1894 parkland 9-hole undulating course, typical of village courses. There is slight bunkering and a few blind shot, otherwise it's straight ahead golf. The first hole, a 259-yard par 4, starts your round with a blind shot over a hill, but the rest of the hole is straight ahead. The 6th, *Wull's Cairn*, is a simple hole with one bunker left of the green. What makes the hole interesting is that the whole thing is visible from the clubhouse with the green just off the clubhouse windows. Everyone can watch you play the hole--of course, the day I played there was nobody about and I muffed it anyway. *Road Hame*, the 9th, is the only par 5 on the course. At only 465 yards the hole isn't long, but the blind second shot over a steep drop-off about 75 yards in front of the green makes the hole tricky. Don't plan your trip around stopping at Sanquhar GC, but then don't be afraid to stop if in the area.

SILLOTH ON SOLWAY GOLF COURSE
Station Road, Silloth, Wigtown, England CA7 4BL
www.sillothgolfclub.co.uk
Links, 6641 yards, par 72, £32

AMENITIES: The lovely venerable clubhouse was built in 1903 and extended in 1908, and has been significantly modernized inside. The 19th hole lounge has good views of the 1st tee and the 18th green. A golfers' menu is served all day, and a more formal menu is presented in the evenings. The club also has a well-stocked, small golf shop.

COURSE COMMENTS: Aided in design by Willie Fernie and Willie Park Jnr in 1892 and retouched later by Alistair Mackenzie, the Silloth on Solway links course plays with four holes along the Solway Firth which is visible from all holes. A mix of narrow and generous fairways and plenty of gorse and heather characterize the course. The bunkers at Silloth are tough, but thankfully not very numerous. *Criffel*, the 371-yard par 4 third is a good example of the holes at Silloth. A blind tee shot between two traps and hills starts the hole. The second shot is to a plateau green. There's plenty of gorse to grab any off-line shots. A seemingly easy shot starts the 9th, a 144-yard par 3, but you have to avoid seven traps to have a chance at this hole. The next hole, *Blooming Heather*, the 308-yard par 4 tenth, is a challenging short dogleg left. Big hitters can try to cut the corner but two traps on the inside will keep you honest. The green is protected by bunkers on both sides. A good par 5 is *Hogs Back*, the 511-yard 13th. The tee shot is a long carry over gorse to a typically generous fairway. The hole tightens as you get closer to the small elevated green. This hole is followed by another par 5 and both play into the prevailing wind. The course has recently upgraded several holes. You might ask why is an English course in a book about Scotland golf? The answer is that Silloth on Solway GC is both Scottish in design and reception, besides both Scotland and England share the Solway Firth.

COMMENTS FROM THE FORWARD TEES: Silloth is a very strong links course set along the Solway Firth. Sometimes it was hard to focus on golf and not just enjoy the views of the Firth and mountains in Scotland. To me many of the fairways seemed narrow and set between gorse and heather, which in the spring is very colorful. The par 5s are long with the 17th being the longest at 464 yards. Even the par 3s are long with the 12th at 185 yards. Planning your shot placement doesn't always work on links courses, but fairway placement is paramount. This is one of my favorite courses in the area.

SOUTHERNESS GOLF COURSE
Southerness, Kirkbean, Dumfries DG2 8AZ
www.southernessgolfclub.com   01387-880677
Links, 6110 yards, par 69, £50

AMENITIES: The 1975 clubhouse has a golfer's lounge which overlooks the 18th green and a separate dining room. Both have good menus and are open to members, guests, and players. Small starter office has most golf essentials.

COURSE COMMENTS: The 18-hole links course, with views of the Solway Firth and the English Cumberland Fells, was designed in 1947 by Mackenzie Ross. The course is fair, but will be challenging to all levels of golfers. Many players rank this as one of the tougher tests in Scotland. When first we played, on a cloudy day with only light wind, I thought the course was very playable (don't read that as easy) for a mid-handicap player. The second time we played the wind was whipping and the course was brutal. The views of the Solway Firth and Cumbrian Mountains in England across the firth alone would be worth the trip, but it is really the golf that people should come for. Sixty-four bunkers in play, heather and gorse, and the weather add to the difficulties of the interesting links holes at Southerness. Fairway and greenside bunkers, most steep-faced, are in play on all but the 17th. Water is in play on several holes and will be of particular concern on 5, 6, and 11. Greens are fairly flat and easy to putt, but they are quick enough that the wind can affect the ball. Among the interesting holes at Southerness is the par five 479-yard 5th. Tee off avoiding the burn at the sides about 120 yards out on this dogleg left hole. The aiming cross (found on most holes) is a good line. The one bunker on the left is only a problem with the drive. The green is distinctly tiered. Next is the 6th, a par 4 of 367-yards, which is straight ahead with a burn crossing the fairway about 250 yards from the tee. If the hole is playing downwind (not the prevailing wind) be sure to stay short of the burn. One bunker left guards the relatively flat green. The 342-yard par 4 eighth has one of the best guarded greens I've played. Five bunkers near or around the green provide trouble, and mounding around the green adds to the challenge. A precise shot is needed to thread your way safely onto the green. The 12th is another fun hole. This 387-yard par 4 is a dogleg right where your tee shot must find its way past two bunkers on the right and one on the left. More bunkers protect the green on this long two-shotter. The par 3s at Southerness are outstanding as well. For example, the 15th at 217-yards plays into the prevailing wind, and a fore bunker and five surrounding bunkers make the green a difficult target. It's easy to understand why Southerness GC is consistently rated in the top twenty in Scotland.

COMMENTS FROM THE FORWARD TEES: T h i s great links course will definitely test your golfing skills. As with most links courses staying in the fairway is the key to success. Aiming for the middle however doesn't always result in landing and staying in the middle. Strategy and planning for slopes and bounces will help. But, you will probably get some chances to hit from the heather, sand, water, or the edge of the gorse. All these consideration didn't discourage me and I really enjoyed Southerness. I do want to visit again and plan to enjoy the course and score better. The par 3s are not too long for the higher handicapped golfer except for the 15th which is 187 yards long with bunkers all around. The par 5s are all just over 400 yards. The 5th hole is typical of the planning required for playing a links course. There is a bunker left at about 150 yards from the tee and a burn 90 yards further on. These require some shot planning. This course is great golfing fun and the views are amazing.

ST MEDAN GOLF COURSE
Monreith, Port Williams, Newtown Stewart DG8 8NJ
www.stmedangolfclub.com   01988-700358
Links, 4454 yards, par 63, £12 for 9, £18 for 18 holes

AMENITIES: Small clubhouse, rebuilt after a fire in 1920 and extended in 1980, with lounge open limited hours (April-October) and honesty box for when no one is around. No golf shop, but a few trolleys available for hire.

COURSE COMMENTS: The 9-hole St Medan course, built in 1905 by members and regularly updated, plays along Monreith Bay. A few bunkers will cause concern, but more problems will come from the five blind shots (more if you're off-line). Distinctly separate tee boxes on several holes makes playing 18 more interesting. The course itself is one of the finest small courses you'll find anywhere--although, it didn't hurt that we played in absolutely gorgeous weather. The 4th, *Well*, is a downhill par 4 (274 yards) reachable with a fairway wood (I hit the green two for two when we played), but there is trouble all around. The 6th, *Port Arthur*, a 276-yard par 4, plays along the beach with a blind tee shot which should cross the road through the course. The second shot looks like you are hitting straight into the bay. The first shot at the 273-yard par 4 seventh is a layup because the second is blind over a knock to a sunken green. Use the aiming pole for your second shot. Even though there is a nine hole price, plan to play at least twice. A true Hidden Gem.

COMMENTS FROM THE FORWARD TEES: This is a pleasant 9-hole course that plays up and around a small headland on the west side of the Machars peninsula right on the bay of Monreith. While St Medans is short, it isn't easy.

There are bunkers, blind shots, drops, and gorse to contend with. The red tees are often in the same spot as the men's tees making the distance only 191 yards shorter at 2086 for nine holes. There are three par 3s and six par 4s, but there are some different tee boxes for a second nine (there is not a second golf card, though). Probably the hardest hole, at least the first time around, was the 7th which required a blind high approach shot over the knock to the green. An aiming pole is a guide, but precision is required. It was a bit easier the second time around, but those are alway hard shots for me. Definitely a fun course to play with beautiful scenery to distract you and interesting challenging holes to force you to concentrate on shot choices.

WIGTOWN & BLADNOCH GOLF CLUB
Lightlands Terrace, Wigtown DG8 9DY
No web 01988-403354
Parkland, 5462 yards, par 67, £10 for 9, £15 for 18 holes

AMENITIES: Changing rooms and honesty box, but no golf shop.
COURSE COMMENTS: The 9-hole Wigtown course plays on a hill with holes 2 and 5 playing uphill and 4 and 6 playing down. Trees, a few bunkers, and small greens are the problems on the course. The course is pleasant as a diversion from sightseeing and has some interesting holes. The downhill 4th at 275 yards has a wide landing area protected by large trees on either side. Strong prevailing winds make the hole more difficult. The other major downhill hole is the 362-yard par 4 sixth. The hole doglegs left off a dramatically downhill tee shot. A large tree on the inner corner of the dogleg adds challenge. The green at the par 3 severely uphill 5th is a good example of a gun-turret green, so named because of its resemblance to a military gun turret platform.

WIGTOWNSHIRE COUNTY GOLF COURSE
(aka GLENLUCE)
Mains of Park, Glenluce, Newton Stewart DG8 0NN
www.wigtownshirecountygolfclub.com 01581-300420
Links, 5829 yards, par 70, £29

AMENITIES: Pleasant rustic lounge with sun room view of the tee of the 1st and the green of the 18th. Serves food usual hours. No golf shop, but a few essentials available where you check-in at the lounge bar.

COURSE COMMENTS: Wigtownshire County GC (known locally as Glenluce GC) is a flat links course playing along Luce Bay. The original 9-hole course was designed in 1894 by golf professional C. Hunter (Prestwick) and then extended to 18 holes in 1986. The course is well bunkered with a mix of fairway and greenside traps. None are too penal, but the fairway bunkers tend to be right in the way of tee shots. Greens are small to moderate with a few slopes, but nothing extreme. Even after a wet season they were easy to putt. There is no water on the course, except at spring tides when some flooding occurs on some of the furthest holes. The biggest hazard would be the wind, but some trees and gorse come into play as well. A few times there are long walks between green and the next tee, but the course is so flat it's never a problem. The day we played we caught a break between storms so played a shortened route before the next storm hit--we played 1-5 and 13-18, so that's what we'll describe. The 3rd, *Bowl* (the green was originally bowl shaped), is a 402-yard par 4. Play up the left short of the two bunkers and avoiding trees on the right. On the approach to the flat green avoid heavy rough on the left. *Wee Dunt* (small shot), is the 162-yard par 3 fifth. This is the first hole of the nine built in the 1980s (5-13). The green slopes right to left toward the one bunker. The moderately sloped green makes for some tricky putting. The 13th named *The Target* (for the RAF bombing target you can see in Luce Bay) is a 152-yard par 3. It's a short hole with danger all around. The drive is mostly blind with OB and heavy rough right and whins left.

Two bunkers on the right at the green add more trouble. Bogey can be a good score here. The 16th, *Pees'weep* (a kind of bird found in the area), is a 314-yard two-shotter which is a severe dogleg right. On your drive you will want to be between the two bunkers left and the trees on the right. A good tee shot should leave an approach of about 100 yards to a green with bunkers on both sides. On the finishing hole, *The Crook* (a local farm--not the farmer), a 397-yard par 4, drive between a wide avenue of trees. A good shot leaves a moderate approach to a flat green with a bunker left and hollows right. Strong finishing hole. The course is really fun in the calm, but even with wind the course is wide enough to be enjoyable.

FROM THE FORWARD TEES: As we found out one rainy September day, the Glenluce area can be dry even when the rest of the area is wet. The Wigtownshire & County Golf Course was very playable when other courses in the area weren't after several days of rain. This links course is very open with enough open area for good shots even with wind and links bounces. There are bunkers, copse (stands) of trees, gorse, and some heather to add difficulty to the course. Some tee boxes are behind and to the left or right of the previous green, so there is a bit of zig zagging. The yardage from the ladies' tees is 5414 yards with a par of 72. The front nine is 2789 yards and par 37 with the back being a bit shorter and par 35. Two of the three par 3s are short enough to be easy but have other hazards to avoid. The 17th is long at 180 yards, but it's flat and straight ahead with a green sloping towards the bay. The par 5s are long with two over 400 yards. The 6th is a long dogleg right, and the 15th is even longer and will often be into the wind. Glenluce is a delightful course in a great location with views of both Luce Bay and the Mull of Galloway.

PUBS, RESTAURANTS & TEAROOM

Abbey Cottage (tearoom) in New Abbey next door to
Sweetheart Abbey   (HS). A tearoom and gift shop
serving soups, sandwiches and sweets.

Cavens Arms Pub on Buccleuch Street down from town
square in Dumfries. A Victorian-style pub with a large
menu and a large page of specials. Pub of the Year for
the area at least seven years running. Excellent food
and good prices--deserving of its awards.

The Bistro Bar in the Selkirk Arms Hotel just off the main
street through Kirkcudbright. Recommended by our
B&B, the hotel has several bistro rooms and the
Artistas Restaurant (same menu throughout). Good
food, good service in a busy place.

Bladnoch Inn (pub/restaurant) in Bladnoch by Wigtown and
across from the distillery.   Great place for lunch or
dinner after a visit to Bladnoch distillery, Scotland's
most southern facility. Good pub menu with specials.

Crown Hotel on the harbour front in Portpatrick. Pub in the
front, a more formal restaurant in the back (with a
slightly different menu than the pub), and a front patio
for good weather. Scotland's Seafood Pub of the Year
for 2011, the Crown Hotel pub has great local seafood
specials. Food lived up to the awards.

Harbour House Hotel (pub) on Main Street in Portpatrick
near the lighthouse. A comfortable pub with a slightly
upscale menu.

Highland Laddie in Glasson, the **Hope and Anchor** in Port
Carlisle, and the **Kings Arms** in Bowness-on-Solway
are all wee village pubs on the England side of the
Solway Firth near Silloth-on-Solway GC. Each is a
good example of an English village pub and each
serves decent pub food. Frequented by plenty of
Hadrian's Wall walkers, the pubs are lively and friendly.

Huntingdon Hotel (pub) on St Mary's Street in Dumfries near
city center. Newly   refurbished in 2005, the small bar

serves high quality food off a limited menu to residents and nonresidents.

L'Aperitif (restaurant) on the edge of the downtown section on London Road in Stranraer. The name may sound French, but the restaurant serves a full Italian m e n u. Excellent food and service in a building which was originally the postmaster's home.

Powfoot Golf Hotel (pub/restaurant) next to the Powfoot Golf Course in Annan. Three eating rooms means you'll find the type of food your looking for, from pub fare to full restaurant menu, at Powfoot Hotel. Good food, fair prices.

Readingglasses Cafe on the main street in Wigtown. A bookstore with tearoom/cafe tables in each room. Eat among the books. Interesting menu items and a motto of "Read, Eat, Dream."

The Royal Hotel (pub) in the center of Kirkcudbright (kerk-COO-bree). Set in the middle of the artist town of Kirkcudbright, the hotel bar serves lunches and dinners from a typical pub menu.

Steamboat Inn (pub) in Carsethorn near Dumfries on the firth. Historic inn, 1813, was the emigrant embarkation point for many heading for a new life. Now it is an inn with an extensive menu for today's travelers.

Waterfront Hotel and Bistro (restaurant) near the harbour in Portpatrick. Interesting menu and well-prepared food in a lovely setting. Good choice when in the area.

LODGINGS

Ferintosh B&B
30 Lovers Walk, Dumfries DG1 1LX
01387-252262 www.ferintosh.net £60
Emma and Robertson, your hosts, do an excellent job of making guests comfortable. The rooms are comfortable and the B&B is an easy walk from the centre of town and good

restaurants. Breakfast is lovely and the *craic* (conversation) a joy. Definitely a top notch stay.

Glenaldor House B&B
5 Victorian Terrace, Dumfries DG1 1NL
01387-264248 www.glenaldorhouse.co.uk £56
Once you find Glenaldor House it's worth the effort. The lovely, centrally located home has spacious comfortable bedrooms and serves great breakfasts. On the same terrace next to Glenaldor is a house where J.M. Barrie (author of "Peter Pan") lived while attending Dumfries Academy. Several good restaurants are within easy walking distance of Glenaldor House.

Harbour Lights Guest House
7 Agnew Crescent, Stranraer DG9 7JY
01776-706261 www.harbourlightsguesthouse.co.uk £50
Conveniently located on the harbour road and a short walk (10 minutes) from the downtown area, Harbour Lights is a good place to stay in the area.   Rooms are comfortable and breakfast is good, and Rhone and Colin are wonderful hosts.

Hillcrest House
Wigtown, Newton, Wigtownshire DG8 9EU
01988-402018 www.hillcrest-wigtown.co.uk £70
The house, at the corner of Midland Place and Station Road, is a short walk from the main shopping area.   Built in 1875, hosts Deborah and Andrew Firth have retained much of the house's Victorian character.   The ensuite bedrooms are comfortable as is the lounge and large dining room. Breakfast is top notch and evening meals can be arranged.   Wigtown, with its numerous bookstores, is a great town to wander and the little village golf course is worth a round.

Linthorpe B&B
14 Arden Road, Twynholm by Kirkcudbright DG6 4PB
01557-860662 www.linthorpebandb.co.uk £75

Simon and Sue make Linthrope an accommodation with a difference. Linthrope has lovely rooms and a large guest lounge. The location, about four miles from the artist town Kirkcudbright is only slightly inconvenient, but the quiet situation in Twynholm and the fantastic breakfast makes up for it--be sure to have the fresh smoked trout if available (Sue teaches fly fishing).

Wallsend Guest House
The Old Rectory, Bowness on Solway, Wigtown, Cumbria, England CA7 5AF
01697-357055 www.wallsend.net £70
Yes, we know it's in England and this book is about Scotland golf, but Wallsend Guest House at the west end of Hadrian's Wall is excellently located for exploring the Wall, the golf in the Dumfries-Gallway area, and visiting the very Scottish-like course Silloth-on-Solway. Accommodations are lovely and breakfasts are great. There are some pleasant village pubs in the area for meals as well.

ATTRACTIONS

Caerlaverock Castle (HS), near Dumfries. The substantial ruins of this 13C Maxwell family castle has a complete moat around it. The grounds of the castle also host a locally run tearoom known for its homemade baked goods.

Castle Kennedy Gardens, near Stranraer. The more than 200-acre estate offers gardens, lochans, sweeping lawns, and tree-lined avenues for visitors. Particularly lovely in the spring.

Dumfries has numerous attractions connected with Scottish poet Robert Burns, including The Globe Tavern and Burns Museum.

Logan Botanic Garden, part of the Royal Botanic Garden of Edinburgh, is located south of Stranraer on the peninsula of the Mull of Galloway. Considered the most exotic of all the gardens in Scotland.

Mull of Galloway Lighthouse on the southern tip of the mull is a spectacular site with a nice tearoom.

Sweetheart Abbey (HS), New Abbey. The 13C Cistercian abbey gets its name from founder Dervorgilla who had the abbey built in remembrance of her husband, John Balliol, hence the name Sweetheart. The ruins are spectacular with great striding arches, semicircular arches, and the stout tower.

Threave Castle (HS), near Castle Douglas. Three-quarters of a mile walk from the parking area is well rewarded by the impressive ruins of the 14C former home of the Black Douglasses. Ring the bell at the small dock and the Historic Scotland Visitors' Centre on an island in the river will send a boat over for you. Definitely worth going out of the way to visit.

Wigtown. Modeled after Hay-on-Wye, the Welsh border Booktown, Wigtown is a small   village which hosts more than 20 bookstores and book related companies. For bibliophiles this is a dangerous place.

Chapter 9: Ayr, Isle of Arran, and Kintyre

Shiskine Golf and Tennis Club

Forty minutes south from Glasgow International Airport is Ayrshire, a region steeped in the history of Scotland and the history of golf. It's here that tourists find magnificent castles and abbeys. It's here too that one can trace the footsteps of the great Scottish poet Robert Burns. Golfers seek the links at the Open Championship courses of Royal Troon and Turnberry and Prestwick. From Ayrshire one can jump off the mainland to explore Scotland in Miniature, the Isle of Arran. From there it's an easy hop to the lovely Kintyre Peninsula.

Along this route golfers will discover some world famous as well as fun, lesser known golf courses, if they look.

The chapter's catalog starts with a fine parkland gem in the heart of Ayrshire.

BELLEISLE GOLF COURSE

Belleisle Park, Doonfoot Road, Ayr, Ayrshire KA7 4DU
www.golfsouthayrshire.com/courses-belleisle.asp
01292-616255
Parkland, 6446 yards, par 71, £27

AMENITIES: Pleasant clubhouse shared by the Seafield course, and the Tam o'Shanter Pub is next to the clubhouse. Large, fully stocked golf shop.

COURSE COMMENTS: This course has been called the best public parkland course in Scotland. It could be--on some days. While the championship course is good enough to host a Scottish PGA tournament and the prestigious Senior Scottish PGA Championship, there are days when it is rather scruffy (litter about, markers akimbo). The course is relatively unknown to outsiders because it's overshadowed by the links golf in the area at Royal Troon, Turnberry, and Prestwick. If you're looking for a fun, tough course, you shouldn't overlook Belleisle (bell-isle). Designed in 1927 by James Braid, the course starts at the impressive Belleisle Hotel, where the large golf shop and starter's office is on the lower floor. The course plays out through beech tree lined fairways with the Curtecan Burn cutting across and alongside several holes. Typical Braid bunkering adds to the challenge. The course may look relatively easy, but don't be fooled, it plays tougher than it looks. The 471-yard par 5 first is not a difficult start and it's followed by a second par 5 of 470 yards, made tougher by very strategic bunkering. After the unusual back-to-back par 5s, the course offers up other interesting holes. The 6th, *The Lang Drop*, a 429-yard par 4, affords the best views of the Firth of Clyde and Isle of Arran, and is also rated as the most difficult on the course. Even though downhill from the tee, the fairway is guarded by traps located in the landing area and the green is protected by more traps front and back. The greens, by the way, are always in great condition. *Summerfield*, the 431-yard par 4 thirteenth is another challenging hole. The drive plays uphill, but the green is hidden from the second shot and again is protected by heavy bunkering. Belleisle is a wonderful example of Braid's work--challenging, inexpensive, and fun to play. Both the Belleisle course and Seafield course have started major revision projects in November of 2012 to upgrade the courses. That will make either course a better stop.

BRODICK GOLF COURSE
Brodick, Isle of Arran KA27 8DL
www.brodickgolf.com 01770-302349
Seaside parkland, 4540 yards, par 64, £22

AMENITIES: The clubhouse lounge looks out onto the first tee and the 18th green and serves snacks and light meals usual hours. The club has a nicely equipped golf shop with a friendly staff.

COURSE COMMENTS: The quirky Brodick GC can be very busy in high season with many vacationers (playing and just walking through). Being a seaside parkland course, rather than a links course, Brodick can be very wet--try to play after an extended dry period, if you can get one in Scotland. There are less than two dozen rather benign bunkers mostly around the greens, but a small burn is in play on several holes and you cross the larger Cnocan Burn twice (both times on par 3s). Most of the trouble is easy to see, except on the 5th and 18th. Greens are small, flat, and fairly bumpy, but we played after a very harsh spring. You do have to tee off over greens a couple of times and there are some long walks back from greens to get to the next tee. Another problem, not the fault of the course, is that plenty of walkers use paths to and along the beach throughout the course, and for the most part they are oblivious to golfers and golf balls until they get hit. And hitting innocent vacationers always ruins my day. The course does have some interesting holes and some quite quirky. The 5th,

Ben Nuis, is a 463-yard par 5. Drive toward the opening between trees--the biggest tree at the right is a good aiming point, but there is a small hazard on each side of the opening. The hole doglegs left from that point. One bunker guards the green. This is the best hole on the course. Seven is a par 3 of 155 yards called *Shortcut.* Your shot is straight ahead over a large bunker with OB all down the left. At *Ormidale*, the 363-yard par 4 eleventh, you need to drive out to the right to avoid the gorse encroaching from the left. No bunkers bother the approach, but you still must avoid gorse left. Then walk half the hole back to the 12th tee. *Lagoon*, a 241-yard par 4, is one of the quirkiest holes anywhere. The flag is barely visible over gorse and the lagoon. All but the biggest hitters need to lay out to the right over the gorse. Again it's only gorse which guards the green. You hit over the Cnocan Burn on *Smacks*, the 121-yard par 3 fifteenth, to a small green backed by heavy rough and bushes. If the river (tidal) is up, the shot is almost all carry. The last is a very tough par 3 at 220-yards. *Memorial* has a blind tee shot over gorse. Big hitters can try for the raised green, but the prudent play is to lay up at about 180 yards to stay short of the small burn you crossed on your tee shot at the 1st. Again, the hole needs no bunkers. If the weather is right, the course is worth at least one visit to say you've played it.

CARRADALE GOLF COURSE
Carradale, Argyll PA28 6QT
www.carradalegolfclub.co.uk 01583-431321
Seaside links, 4740 yards, par 64, £15 all day

AMENITIES: The small clubhouse has changing rooms, but no lounge or golf shop (honesty box in the changing rooms). The Carradale Hotel next door is great for a drink, meal or lodging.

COURSE COMMENTS: The lovely 9-hole Carradale GC, built in 1906, plays along the shore of the Kilbrannan Sound with grand views of Arran, Ailsa Craig and Ayrshire. The course is short, but it has some steep up and downs as you play back and forth across a small dunes valley. Elevated tee boxes make for some interesting shots on entertaining holes. On *Hillocks*, the 287-yard par 4 fourth, you play from a raised tee to a broad fairway. If you try for the green, trouble such as heavy rough and uneven lies lay ahead. Another elevated tee starts the 6th, *Pudding Bowl,* which is a 289-yard par 4. Your drive should stay right because of heavy rough on the left. Second shot is up to a deep green with more rough all around. An interesting par 3 is the 7th at 175 yards. Again hitting from a raised tee your drive must clear several sections of deep rough. The view of the bay you're hitting toward is spectacular. Carradale GC is a fun stop on the way to the big courses of Machrihanish or Machrihanish Dunes.

CORRIE GOLF COURSE
Sannox, Isle of Arran KA27 8JD
www.corriegolf.com 01770-810606, -810223
Heathland, 3896, par 62, £15 day

AMENITIES: The small clubhouse is complemented by a homey tearoom which serves good food breakfast to dinner in season. Honesty box available for when no one is around.

COURSE COMMENTS: At Corrie GC you play the original 1892 9-hole layout which includes several holes which cross over other holes. The play is uphill (never too severe) for the first five holes, then level across the top at the sixth, and finally the last three are downhill. Besides the quaintness of an old Scottish course, the mountain scenery with the course located at the foot of Glen Sannox is spectacular. For a small course there is great variety in the holes, with only the 1st and 9th being straight forward. The most unusual hole is the second, a par 3 of 138 yards (plays as 200 yards for the 10th). The green is sited behind a large tree and over a slight mound. Locals may know how to reach the green, but it's a guessing game for visitors. When the course was young the tree was much smaller and probably not a problem. Another interesting par 3 is the 5th which is 128 yards blind uphill to a hidden green. The course is not as funky as I may make it seem, instead it is a fun natural example of what early golf was in Scotland. Along with Shiskine, a must stop when on Isle of Arran.

COMMENTS FROM THE FORWARD TEES: Corrie has a variety of views including the mountains (including Goat Fell Peak) and the Firth of Clyde. The course is set on the side of a hill and plays in the trees opening into a meadow. The yardage on this small course is short, but the holes demand creative shots. There are trees and mounds in the fairway and shots over other fairways to keep you focused. The longest hole, the 6th, is only 320 yards long, but it slopes left to right and goes uphill into the wind and has heather on the right. A round here is challenging and rewarding, as is a sweet in the tearoom after a round.

DALMALLY GOLF COURSE
Old Sawmill, Dalmally, Argyle PA33 1AE
www.dalmallygolfclub.co.uk   No phone
Parkland, 4528 yards, par 64, £15/day

AMENITIES: None, I'm not even sure there are toilets in the small club office. Honesty box course.

COURSE COMMENTS: Built in 1987 by club members and maintained by them, the Dalmally GC is an out-of-the-way 9-hole track worth a stop if you're passing, even if it's just to play the third hole. Several holes follow the River Orchy, but the par 3 third, *Orchy Splash*, plays across the river. The fairway doglegs right around a bend in the river, so the hole can play as a dogleg par 3. You could take the adventuresome route through an opening in the trees along the riverbank. The green is 150 to 160-yard carry across the bend of the river. The rest of the holes are fairly ordinary, but if in the area have a round and see if you've the balls (golf balls, that is) to hit the green at *Orchy Splash*.

DOON VALLEY GOLF CLUB
1 Hillside, Patna, Ayrshire KA6 7JT
No web   01292-531607

Parkland, 5886 yards, par 70, £7 for 9, £12 for 18

AMENITIES: Small clubhouse built in the late 50s. No golf shop, but trolleys are for hire.

COURSE COMMENTS: Founded in 1927, this hilly 9-hole course has some funky holes and views of the village and River Doon. Cross the rail tracks to get from the clubhouse to the course. The course is very welcoming to visitors. In the parking lot as we were getting ready to play, two locals visited as they came off the course. One said about us, "They're Americans and they've come to play our course!" As we played we met a local playing behind us. When he found out we were Americans he stopped and pointed out the routing of the course--he wanted us to enjoy his course. A problem we noted was that there were no rakes in the bunkers (found out local kids will steal them)--smooth the sand out as best you can and try to stay out of the next one. A piece of advise we got from a member was that on many holes it's best to lay up short of the gullies so you can see where you're going on your next shot. *Coulters Neuk*, the 135-yard par 3 fifth, is one of the most interesting holes we've played. A large ditch or canyon with a small burn runs diagonally the length of the hole with a mature tree half way to the green on the right. The result is that the hole is almost all carry to a small green protected by one bunker right. Over the green is a steep drop-off. To the right is OB. Ladies play a tee on the right which avoids the canyon, but makes the hole 177 yards long with OB right and the tree and canyon left. If you want a break from the big courses in the Ayrshire area, Doon Valley is not a bad choice.

THE DRAGON'S TOOTH GOLF COURSE
Glenachulish, Ballachulish PH49 4JX
www.dragontooth.co.uk 01855-413202
Parkland, 5003 yards (18), par 67, £18 for 18

AMENITIES: A few golf essentials available where you check in. Cafe/coffee shop serves golfers' snacks and lunches, and has views of the 9th green and the loch. The course is part of an activity centre which includes Segway Experience, rafting, boating, and canoeing.

COURSE COMMENTS: At only ten years old the 9-hole Dragon's Tooth GC (named for a local peak) is an interesting parkland track set beside Loch Linnhe near the Glencoe area. Designed by Robin Hiseman (who's designed many courses in Dubai) in 2002 the course affords views of two munros (mountains over 3000 feet tall)--Sgorr Dhearg and Sgorr Domhnuill--with the Dragon's Tooth in between, as well as views of Loch Linnhe and across. Being so close to the loch the tree-lined course can be windy and be sure to ask if you need to worry about midgies (nasty little biting no-see-ums). Seven bunkers, all greenside, are in play. Except for a shallow bunker on one, all the others are penal--have to be hidden from the road by local ordinance. Four holes have burn crossings and the 5th also has a pond. The river is in play off the men's tee on the 18th (many holes have two sets of tees to make a more interesting 18). The greens are varied in design and size, but most are flat with subtle borrows. All greens have been built to USGA specifications. We thought most of the holes were interesting, but several especially caught our attention. The 2nd/11th, a 139-yard par 3, presents a tee shot which must negotiate over a burn, a path, and between trees to find a long narrow green. It's a tough shot on the 2nd and even tougher when played off the 11th from 185 yards. Next is the par four 3rd/12th at 287/350 yards. Drive straight toward the loch on a fairway which drops about ten feet at the 100-yard marker. The green is left (large trees stop any thoughts of driving the green from either tee) and has no bunkers. A pond and burn about 200 yards from the tee are the main problems at the 5th/14th, a par 4 of 297/327 yards. The hole doglegs left around the pond. It's best to be short of the water and have a short iron into the green protected by one bunker left. The 8th is a 367-yard par 4 while the 17th is a 474-yard par 5. On both holes the tee shot is down to a burn. On the 8th a good shot of 220 yards will carry the burn hidden from the tee. The burn will be more visible and in play on your second shot on the 17th. The green is tucked right and has a vicious fronting bunker and OB behind. Bogey is a good score, especially your first time around. The golf manager, Fiona, will help you get started on this fine holiday track.

COMMENTS FROM THE FORWARD TEES: This course, near Ballachulish and Glencoe, is a 9-hole course along A823 to Oban and Loch Linnhe with A82, the more major road, on the other side of the Loch. Dragon's Tooth has a separate set of tees for a second nine that changes some holes significantly and will have a second handicap. I played the first nine with a yardage of 2234, the second nine is 2339 yards equaling 4573 yards for the 18 holes. As a 9-hole course it has only one par 5, the 4th. There are three par 3s with yardages ranging from 122 to 169. For some ladies the red tees will be too easy and take all the challenge away and they should probably play the yellow tees. This is a well maintained course and in a beautiful setting with views from every hole. Be sure to find the "Dragon's Tooth" in the mountains to the southeast, especially visible from the 4th and 6th holes.

DUNDONALD LINKS GOLF COURSE
Ayr Road, Gailes, Ayrshire KA11 5BF
www.dundonaldlinks.com 01294-314000
Links, 6340 yards, par 72, £95

AMENITIES: Very adequate temporary clubhouse with a fairly large golf shop (good prices), offices, changing rooms, and a cafe/bar which serves good food. The course is currently better than the clubhouse, but the clubhouse is more than adequate. Good practice range.

COURSE COMMENTS: Purchased by Loch Lomand Golf Club in 2003, the old Southern Gailes was redesigned by Kyle Phillips (Kingsbarns) and renamed Dundonald Links in honor of the history of the area. The championship calibre course has been a qualifier for the British Sr Open and is quite popular thus quite busy--be sure to book ahead. Dundonald

Links is eminently playable by all levels of golfers, but will be a challenge even to the best. Eighty-four bunkers, mixed fairway and greenside, are in play and are penal enough that it's often difficult to advance your ball forward. Five holes have water troubles, mostly a small burn, but the 14th does have a pond left. The burn is not big, but must be planned for. The mix of large and small greens is well-matched to the play of the hole and are well-conditioned. The wind, gorse, and heavy rough are the other challenges at Dundonald, but the lovely dunes, some trees, the commuter train separating Dundonald from Western Gailes GC, and views of the firth are pleasant pluses. All holes on the course are fun to play, but a few stand out in our notes. The 3rd at Dundonald is a par 5 of 510 yards. The hole is straight with a bend to the right about 100 yards out from the green when the burn which has run the length of the hole crosses the fairway. Only one bunker left worries long drivers, but the swaled green has two traps in front and one behind. The 6th is a relatively simple par 3 of 135 yards, except for the burn which crosses in front of the green and stays close to the left side and the two bunkers (one in front and one behind). The green has several tricky pin locations. Simple! The 360-yard par 4 ninth is a slight dogleg right with two nasty bunkers right in the way of long drives. Second shots must contend with a burn directly in front of the green as well as two right front. The green is one of the flattest on the course. On the back we liked the 120-yard par 3 eleventh. Here the tee shot is over a waste area to a small green fronted by three traps. One small pot bunker behind is particularly evil--if I were in it I'm not sure I could ever get out without a hand-wedge. Fun short hole if you stay out of the sand. A straight ahead par four (360-yards) with only one fairway bunker right is the 13th. A ditch runs the length of the hole on the left and a burn crosses in front of the two-tiered green. The 17th, a 385-yard par 4, is a distinct dogleg left with three bunkers on the inside of the turn after a 180-190 yard carry to reach the fairway. Four more bunkers, three of them fairway, complicate second shots, but the green, although fairly small, is quite flat. The final hole is a long, narrow par 5 of 515-yards studded with six bunkers. The real decision comes at the third shot for most of us. Mounding right and left, a bunker left and one behind, and a burn 25 yards in front of the green demand a precise shot. Strong, fair finish to the round. Dundonald is a challenging championship course which fits in nicely with the other grand golf (Troon, Western Gailes) in the area.

COMMENTS FROM THE FORWARD TEES: We were lucky enough to play Dundonald on a bright sunny day. There was a breeze that increased later in the day, but the wind certainly could have an impact on this course as it blows in from the Firth of Clyde. Dundonald is a true links course and many holes are separated one from another by unaltered sand dunes, reminding me of time spent in the dunes along the Oregon coast. The holes are so cleverly laid out one might not realize how close the holes are one to another. This course is a great golf challenge which also affords chances for many successes, too. Several holes are narrow and lined with large dunes, dune grass, and heather--careful shot making is required. From the forward tees the total yardage is 5560 yards with a par of 72. There is water on a few holes, but of special note are holes the 9th and18th with water around the green. I also really liked the par 3 sixth with water on two sides and an uphill sloping green. Precision is key to scoring at Dundonald. This golf course is a good stop when in the area.

HILTON PARK, ALLANDER COURSE
Auldmarroch Estate, Stockiemuir Road, Milngavie, Glasgow G62 7HB
www.hiltonpark.net 01419-565125
Parkland, 5483 yards, par 69, £20-30

AMENITIES: For both courses: The lovely, modern clubhouse has a spikes bar and a formal dining room. Friendly staff and good food. A small, but well-stocked golf shop has all your golfing needs.

COURSE COMMENTS: Opened in September of 1928, the Allander course is the design work of famed Scottish architect James Braid.   The lovely tree-lined courses didn't always look the way they do now.   The courses began because during World War I two Glasgow area clubs were forced to close by the Ministry of Defense.   Members of the two clubs joined to purchase land near Milgalvie about 12 miles from Glasgow.   The two courses opened within three months of each other with the Allander course the second to open.   Today's lovely tree-lined course has views of the nearby Campsie Fells.   Playing in the hills which are never too severe, but it does mean the it's hard to find a flat lie and that having an electric trolley is a distinct advantage.   The course has several blind drives, but they are marked well.   As you'd expect from a Braid designed course there are plenty of bunkers (18 has no fairway bunkers, five on 17 , and 4 on 7)— not every hole had a bunker but several have multiple— thankfully, none are too severe.   Greens are small to moderate in size with subtle slopes.   There are two burn crossings and on two holes a burn runs along the side.   Water, though, is never much of a problem.

There is much to like on the Allander Course starting with *Craigaqllion*, the 544-yard, par 5, 3rd.   This dogleg right hole has trees all along the right and plays downhill with no bunkers to bother your efforts.   Longest hole on the course, but a good birdie or par opportunity.   Next is a nice 181-yard par 3 called *Fickle*.   This uphill one-shotter has a grass bunker in front of the green (it has always been a grass bunker) and one sand bunker on the right.   The Allander burn also runs along the right.   *Burncrooks*, the number one stroke index hole, is a 372-yard par 4.   The hole is relatively flat until the approach which is down with a sharp dogleg right just before the green—like a shepherd's crook.   There are no bunkers guarding the green, but a small burn run just right and behind the green.   You can go for the green over trees and the burn, but the prudent play is to lay up to a gap in the trees and pitch on.   On the back we liked the 12th, *Earl's Seat*, a nice short par 4 at 282 yards.   A burn crosses about 150 yards out on this short downhill two-shotter with a slight dogleg left just before the green. There are no bunkers protecting the green, but it is a quite elevated plateau-green with runoffs on all sides. The 14th, *Garvel Bridge*, provides some great views from the top of the course. The 334-yard par 4 plays downhill to a left-sloped fairway and the green is protected by two fronting bunkers and trees are close behind. As tough as it sounds, it is a good birdie opportunity. It's nice that the course comes back to the clubhouse after the ninth, and the day we played we shared the course with some local roe deer.

FROM THE FORWARD TEES: This a nice tree-lined course set on rolling hills with the Allander Burn running along and through the course. The yardage from the front is 4978 yards with a par of 70. There are two par 5s on each side where the 11th is very long at 512 yards, but it plays downhill. There are four par 3s of reasonable length and all are interesting, challenging holes. Three of the par 3s are uphill with raised greens—typical of James Braid courses. I especially liked the130-yard15th where you tee off over the Allander Burn uphill to a raised green. There is much walking up and down hills, but few sidehill lies. Pars and bogies are very possible for ladies on this course.

HILTON PARK, HILTON PARK COURSE
Same details as Allander Course
Parkland, 6002 yards, par 70, £20-30

AMENITIES: Same as Allander Course.

COURSE COMMENTS: The Hilton Park Course is the first of the Braid courses completed at Hilton Park (June, 1928). During World War II much of the course was closed by the MOD and nine holes were never reopened. The redesigned holes keep much of the feel of a Braid course. In the past twenty years about ten thousand trees we're planted to give definition, wind shelter, and to improve drainage (on both courses). In fact, now that the trees are mature, the club is contemplating a thinning program. This course is the more tree-lined of the two and yet still affords lovely views of the

Campsie Fells, several mountains (Bens Lomand, Venue, More, Ledi, and Vorlich), and down to Glasgow. Some members we spoke to say that this is the hillier of the two courses, but we didn't notice a great deal of difference. The 37 greenside bunkers on the course are more penal than the bunkers on the Allander. There used to be some fairway traps, but they were taken out because of complaints. The current committee is looking into putting a few back. The greens, while larger than on the Allander, are still not overly large, but they are more sloped. Burns or ditches are in play on seven holes, but are only a real concern at the 1st and 17th. We saw plenty of wildlife on the Hilton Park course including curlews, pheasants, and roe deer. Members say that kestrels, partridge, and short-eared owls can also be seen.

While there are no weak holes on the Hilton Course, a few did catch our attention. The 1st, *Craigengaun*, a 483-yard par 5, is a tough but interesting starting hole. This slight dogleg left starts out downhill with trees on both sides. The crux of the hole is a burn crossing 100 yards from the green which has a fore bunker left and another on the right side of the green. The relatively large green putts very true. A good start is a par here. *Kyber Pass* is the 6th, a 216-yard single-shot hole which goes down and then up to a raised green. The green is protected by mounds left and two bunkers right. Par is tough. The 7th hole, called *Allander*, a very good short two-shotter (266-yard par 4) follows the the long par 3. Big hitters can try to drive the raised green, but the bunkers left and right may not be worth the risk. The small green is even trickier to hit with second shots. On the back don't be fooled into thinking that *Deil's Dozen*, the 153-yard par 3 twelfth, is easy. Five surrounding bunkers and a sloped front make this hole demanding. We loved the name of the par four 320-yard 14th —*Mugduck*—even though we don't know what it means. The hole is a nice downhill dogleg right with trees lining the fairway and two bunkers at the green. A birdie (perhaps a duck) opportunity. The 17th, *Muckle Drop*, is a dramatically downhill 184-yard par 3. The problems here, besides picking the correct club, is a burn before the green, three bunkers around the green, and mounds on both sides—otherwise, it's an easy hole. Try to play both these fine courses, but if you only have a chance for one, our pick would be the Hilton Park Course.

FROM THE FORWARD TEES: This course is 500-600 yards longer than the Allander, but the fairways are a bit wider and it has a more open feel. Most holes are tree-lined and well separated from each other. On holes 1, 10, and 17 a burn crosses the fairway and is particularly bothersome from the Forward Tees. The course is fairly long at 5519 yards with at least one long par 5 on each side. the 4th is the hardest par 3 on the front. It plays 166 yards uphill with a raised green. On the back the 17th is 163 yards downhill which is quite tricky because of the burn crossing and bunkers around the green. This is a great course with good variety.

IRVINE GOLF COURSE (BOGSIDE)
Bogside, Irvine KA12 8SN
www.theirvinegolfclub.co.uk 01294-275626
Moorland, 6116 yards, par 70, £50

AMENITIES: The lovely venerable clubhouse has a pleasant lounge which looks out to the 18th green. Serves light meals all day. The club has a small, well stocked golf shop.

COURSE COMMENTS: Like many Scottish courses, including Gleneagles and Cruden Bay, the Irvine Golf Course at Bogside owes its existence at least in part to the late 19th century rail expansion. The course was once a stop on the west coast line from Glasgow. Founded in 1887, the course was designed by famed architect James Braid and, though the course has been continually update, it is basically the Braid course you play today. Braid's handiwork is evident in the more than 115 bunkers in play. Most are deep and difficult to get out of--true hazards. Holes two and eighteen have ten bunkers each and only the fourth has none. With all those bunker there's no need for any water hazards. Greens are small to moderate and several have noticeable slopes. All are kept in good condition. There are some nice views of the surrounding hills, but the course is loveliest when the gorse and broom are in bloom. Besides the wind, always a condition of play this near the sea, blind holes and heavy rough add to the challenge of the traps.

We had heard some describe the course as "quirky," but we found the design features that might be quirky to some to be some of the most interesting holes on the course. A nice set of those interesting holes starts with the 3rd, a 307-yard par 4 called *Fullerton*. On this the first of a set of four "quirky" holes which all fit the land well, you tee off between patches of gorse to a fairway with five waiting bunkers. The green protected by another pot bunker is tucked behind a couple of mounds and is quite small. Next is the *The Moor*, a par 4 of 292 yards. No bunkers here, but OB and a hill on the left and gorse on the right complicate the drive. The green is raised and will be hard to hold with OB behind. No bunkers were needed. The 5th, *Sandface*, is visually very intimidating, but actually the 226-yard par 4 is easier to play than it looks. This short hole begs the bold to try to drive the green. The prudent play would be to lay up at about 170 yards out from the tee short of the steep "sandface" hill with a very large bunker at the bottom. The blind wedge to the green will hopefully avoid the three bunkers around the green. On the back side we like the 11th, a 454-yard par 4 (stroke index #2). *Grandstand* is a long two-shot hole which doglegs left around a nest of four bunkers. Three more fairway traps and three greenside traps bother approaches to the small green. The first shot at the 14th, *The Spectacles*, is to a fairly wide open fairway with six bunkers at the sides. Your next shot on this 431-yard par 4 is toward the spectacles, two bunkers set into a mound with the green behind. The green is large and two-tiered. You finish your round at the 18th, *Flagstaff*, a 312-yard par 4. A tee shot over two bunkers and to a raised fairway (175 yards) is the crux of the hole--that is if you discount the seven bunkers surrounding green. If this course is quirky, you can give me quirky every day.

FROM THE FORWARD TEES: Irvine GC is a heathland course about a mile from the Firth of Clyde. This lady friendly course, with rolling hills, heather, and grasses, has appropriate adjustments in tees. The overall yardage is 5661 yards with a par of 72. The course has only one par 5 (the second at 422 yards) and one par 3 on each side. A good short game is essential at Bogside because many approaches require precision. A good drive is needed to be able to have a shot at the elevated green at the 4th. The 5th has an even more elevated green and an intimidating bunker at the bottom of the hill. A stroke saver was invaluable the first time around. There are no toilets on the course, but it does come back to the clubhouse at nine. A fun course that requires your attention.

LAMLASH GOLF CLUB
Lamlash, Isle of Arran, North Ayrshire KA27 8JU
www.lamlashgolfclub.co.uk 01770-600296
Undulating heathland, 4510 yards, par 64, £22

AMENITIES: Modern clubhouse with views over the first and last from the upstairs bar/restaurant. Small pro shop will get you set up.

COURSE COMMENTS: Founded in 1889, the first 18-hole course was designed by Willie Auchterlonie in 1896. The course was later redesigned by Willie Fernie and then modernized in 1968. The hilly course is the oldest on Isle of Arran and the view from the top of the course "must be one of the best in golf." Several features characterize Lamlash GC. The views of Holy Isle in Lamlash Bay and the village are dramatic. The par 3s are tough. The 10th is a 215-yard dogleg left where you can't see the green because of a large ravine. Then the 11th, *Last Climb*, is a steep uphill 225-yarder. The 12th, *Lighthouse*, plays 215 yards across the top of the course. The fairway slopes steeply to the right with OB and gorse left. The next par 3 to mention is *Quarry*, the 233-yard 15th with a blind shot over an old rock quarry then downhill to the green. The course also has some wildly downhill shots.

Both the 5th and 14th have downhill carries of about 175 yards. Sixteen, *Wee Dent* is only 97 yards, but the drop is so dramatic that the front of the green can't be seen from the tee. The 9th, *Mullaig Mhor*, is a 270-yard par 4 where the green can be seen from the tee, but the landing area can't--it's all downhill. One player commented, "Some exacting holes, with tight fairways and small greens." Though not championship golf, the course is fun to play.

COMMENTS FROM THE FORWARD TEES: This is a very challenging course to walk because of the hills. The hills create some of the hazards--others include a ravine, quarry, gorse, a burn, and trees. If that's not enough the views can distract you, too. For ladies the best course management will be needed. Several hole have hazards to be negotiated from tee to green. There are also some blind approaches to greens. This course unlike many others has visitor tees for ladies. Also there are several short par 4s for ladies that are par 3s for men. The over all yardage is short at 3643 yards, but there is more than enough challenge here. An interesting fun course to play.

LOCHGILPHEAD GOLF CLUB
Blairbuie Rd., Lochgilphead, Argyll PA31 8LE
www.lochgilphead-golf.com   01546-602340
Moorland, 2056 yards, par 32, £20 for 18

AMENITIES: Small clubhouse is only open weekends. There is an honesty box for when no one is around. No golf shop and no trolleys.

COURSE COMMENTS: The 9-hole Lochgilphead course plays on the side of a major hill, with a steep uphill climb on the 3rd, down on the 4th, up again at the 5th, and way down on the 6th. Problems are the hill, sidehill lies, and water on four holes. The course is more interesting than it looks at first with several intriguing holes. The 3rd, *Mount Druim*, is a 131-yard par 3 which plays straight up the hill--at least two clubs longer than the measured distance. Another interesting par 3 is *Graveyard*, the 177-yard 5th. Again it's an uphill hole with trees along the right side. Going down you have the 6th, *Rifle Range*, a 392-yard par 4. The hole begins with a dramatic downhill tee shot which plays longer than it seems. Second shots must contend with a burn just in front of the green and OB (and sheep) behind--I visited the sheep when we played. The most unique hole at Lochgilphead is the 8th, *Cuilarstitch Bends*, a two-shotter of 264 yards. Your tee shot is a lay up over a bog area. The approach then needs to clear a burn in front of the green. Lochgilphead is a course we would visit again.

MACHRIE BAY GOLF COURSE & TEAROOM
Machrie Bay, Isle of Arran
www.machriebay.com   01770-840329
Links, 4556 yards, par 66, £15 day

AMENITIES: Pay in the tearoom which has breakfasts, hot and cold drinks, sandwiches, soups, and sweets, open from 10 a.m. until 5 p.m. No golf shop.

COURSE COMMENTS: Machrie Bay GC offers very basic golf in a lovely setting along the Kilbrannan Sound. It's not a destination course by itself, except that Walter Hagen while visiting Scotland to play in the Open dropped in at Machrie Bay. He had wanted to play the more famous links of Machrie on Islay. They brought him to Machrie Bay instead. The story goes that he was very gracious when he played. The links at Machrie Bay are flat and straight, except for a couple of holes. The 1st, *Kilbrannan*, a par 4 of 262 yards, plays between the Kilbrannan Sound on one side and Arran's main road on the other. You need to start out straight. The 2nd, *The Hummocks*, is a 162-yard par 3. Your semi-blind tee shot (you can only see the top of the flag) must clear a valley contained by two large hummocks. The last, *Road Hole*, is a par 4 which plays downhill 250 yards to the main island road about 200 yards from the tee. Your second shot must cross the road to find the green about seven feet below road level. There's a bailout area to the right if you don't want to go for the flag. One player's comments, "Small, but quite interesting," sums up the course which is a good warmup for Shiskine up the road.

MACHRIHANISH GOLF COURSE
Campbelltown, Argyll PA28 6PT
www.macgolf.com   01586-810213
Links, 6235 yards, par 70, £60

AMENITIES: The very comfortable clubhouse, which serves some of the best food in the area, looks out to the first tee across the street. Complete golf shop next to the first tee.

COURSE COMMENTS: The Championship links at Machrihanish was the design work of Old Tom Morris in 1879. When he saw the land Morris commented, "The Almichty maun hae had gowf in his e'e when he made this place." More recently, Michael Bamberger in his 1992 book *To the Linksland* likened Machrihanish to golf Nirvana. These aren't the only comparisons between Machrihanish and Heaven. If it weren't so out-of-the-way, Machrihanish would be on everyone's top play list. Make an effort to visit this outstanding 18-hole links course and you won't be disappointed. Another comment heard repeatedly, and one we found to be true, is that the staff and members at Machrihanish are super friendly. This is links golf at it's best, an Old Tom Morris course where accuracy off the tee is vital, as is proper clubbing to the well-maintained greens. Numerous bunkers (many quite penal), dune grass, blind shot, and coastal wind and weather will always be conditions of play at Machrishanish.

As hard as it may be to select featured holes at a featured course, we have to try. There's no better place to start a round of golf than the first hole at Machrihanish. It's a hole which draws universal praise. Tom Watson, five time Open Champion, has called it perhaps the best first hole in Scottish golf. The hole is a prime example of risk-reward golf. *Battery* is a 428-yard par 4 where the tee shot must cross the Atlantic Ocean if the tide is in or the Machrianish beach if it's out. How much ocean or beach you choose to tackle is the risk; and the reward for a better shot is a shorter second. The second shot (length will depend upon how heavily you bailed on the first shot) must negotiate two fore bunkers to an otherwise unprotected green. A good start on this hole can make the rest of your round. Another of the typically strong holes is the 9th, *Ranachan*, a 353-yard par 4 that starts with a blind tee shot. The second shot must find a green protected by three pot bunkers left and one back. A particular favorite is the 13th, *Kilkivan*. This 370-yard two-shotter begins with a straight tee shot, but the second must carry a large cross-bunker 50 yards out from the back-sloping green, guarded on both sides by pot bunkers. The course plays with only one par 3 and no par 5s on the front and two 5s on the back.

Machrihanish is links at its best: wind, rain, sun, ocean views, gorse, heather, rough, and bunkers, bunkers, bunkers. One incident that pleased us at Machrihanish happened after a round. We had played ahead of a local couple and pulled further ahead as we went along. As we were putting our clubs in the car before going into the clubhouse lounge, the couple behind us came in and chatted with us in the parking lot. They commented about how fast we played "especially for Americans" and said, "You're welcome to come back anytime." Scots do expect and appreciate quick play.

COMMENTS FROM THE FORWARD TEES: The setting for Macrihanish is one of the best in Scotland, along the sea and set in the dunes of the Kintyre Peninsula. The course is a first rate links course which takes course knowledge (a stroke saver or course guide is a good idea) and planned shots. There is much trouble to find on this course and with links rolls I often found the many deep bunkers especially around the greens. The wind also affects the shots. Ladies start with a long challenging par 5, but there is only one par 5 on each side. There is one par 3 on the front and 3 on the back. The yardage is less and the par on the back nine holes is 3 stokes less, but I didn't find the back that much easier. Two of the par 3s on the back are over 160 yards long and not easy. It's a demanding course, but one I go back to.

MACHRIHANISH DUNES GOLF COURSE
Machrihanish, Argyll PA28 6PT
www.machrihanishdunes.com 01586-810000
Links, 6268 yards (White Tees), par 72, £80

AMENITIES: The Starter/Halfway House has a few golf essentials and serves good sandwiches, soups, and snacks. In the village the Old Clubhouse Pub is a good bet for drinks or a meal. The club has a complete golf shop behind the Old Clubhouse Pub in what was the original house for the Machrihanish greenskeeper. Full range of logoed supplies is available. The course is part of The Village at Machrihanish Dunes complex which includes the golf course, the Old Clubhouse Pub, golf shop, the Ugadale Hotel, the Ugadale Cottages, and the Royal Hotel in Campbeltown.

COURSE COMMENTS: The 2009 David McLay Kidd (Bandon Dunes, St Andrews Castle, Tetherow) designed course plays adjacent to the original Machrihanish GC and is touted as "the world's most natural golf course" because so little land was moved to build the course. Machrihanish Dunes is indeed a special course starting with the site which is designated as an Area of Special Scientific Interest, protecting Burnet moths, marsh orchids, and other flora. Routing of the course avoids certain areas meaning there are some long walks between holes (up to 200 yards). The course itself is quite spectacular with about 50 bunkers in play. All the bunkers, except one, are natural--they were created by the more than 200,000 rabbits which inhabited these dunes and there are still an estimated 30,000 about the course. The bunkers, which have been left natural except for some clean up, are quite penal--history tells us the rabbits have no love for golfers. In a bunker is at least a one-shot penalty, if not more. Five holes (2, 6, 7, 14, and 15) have the beach and sea in play. The course has marked a couple of other areas as water hazards, but they are more marshy than watery. About half the greens are moderately sized and the rest are large. Consistent with other Kidd designed courses, the greens are quite swaled--you almost never have a straight putt--and several are distinctly tiered. Machrishanish Dunes is one of the loveliest links courses we've ever played with views of the Atlantic from several holes on one side and the Kintyre hills on the other. Wind and weather will always be a condition of play on the links. Numerous blind fairway and approach shots and typical exaggerated links bounces mean that having a caddie or forecaddie (guide) to show you the way is money well spent. Our guide, Welshman Owen Morgan, did so good a job directing us around the course that neither Anne nor I ever got in a bunker and we both scored close to our handicaps on a truly difficult course. The group of big hitters behind us, the ones who didn't take a caddy, told us later about all the trouble they got into and all the balls they lost by not having a guide. Owen told us that the course is manageable with a Stroke Saver after a time or two around with help.

The day we played we started on the 10th hole and finished on the 9th which they told us was to be the new routing. There are no weak holes at Machrihanish Dunes, but the ones that caught our attention most started with our second hole of the day, the 11th, a par 4 of 423 yards--I'll use the white tee distances but this holes, for example, could play anywhere from 375 to 483 yards and still be a par 4. On this dogleg right drive to fairly generous fairway which is also relatively flat--relatively! After a slightly blind drive (use the aiming post) the prudent play is to lay up short of the wildly swaled green and try to get up and down. The 13th is a testing short (253-yards) par 4 with a long narrow green. Plenty of humps and bumps can send your shot off line, but with some luck you could be chipping for an eagle or putting for a birdie, but only if you avoid the pot bunker left of the green. Next is the first of back-to-back par 3s as you turn to the sea. The amoeba-like green on this 131-yarder has many tricky pin placements and two bunkers front left. Here short is better than long. A good par 5 is the 17th at 556 yards long. The hole is fairly straight, but a large bunker on the left 200 yards out and three more around the green will cause problems. The green is one of the smaller on the course, but is also probably the flattest. After nine holes you return to the

Starter/Halfway House where you can make a quick stop or more extended lunch break. The 1st hole is a good start to the challenging back nine we played. The 366-yard par 4 is blind the whole way--you will not be able to see the green until 60 yards from it. Use the aiming post behind the green as your target. The slight dogleg left fairway has plenty of contour. One bunker left guards the moderately swaled green which is down in a bowl--that's why you can't see it until you're on top of it. Our guide, Owen Morgan, said of the par four 391-yard 4th, "It's a par 5 pretending to be a par 4." The tee shot is blind--aim over the pole and favor the left side. One bunker on the left about 70 yards from the huge green is all the protection this multitiered putting surface needs. A testing short two-shotter is the 379-yard 8th. In fact, a British golf magazine called it the toughest hole in championship golf--in the world! Your blind drive must find a ribbon of very undulating fairway. The fairway ends about 250 yards out where you cross a ravine by a bridge. The approach shot is over a wetlands to one of the smallest greens on the course. Finally, don't be fooled by the scorecard on the 360-yard 9th. We learned that when they measured the hole length it was "as the crow flies," not as the golfer plays. The dogleg left adds 80 or 90 yards to the real length of the hole. Stay right of the post on yet another blind drive and try to reach the top of the hill--any shot short bounces further right than you want to be. Second shots should be over two traps in the middle of the fairway to a massive green with two more protecting traps. In this routing the last holes are two seriously difficult holes in a row.

Machrihanish Dunes is definitely a championship track, yet it is fun and eminently playable (with the help of guide) by the average player.

COMMENTS FROM THE FORWARD TEES: Machrihanish Dunes is truly a championship course with many challenges. It has all the usual links characteristics, including constant wind and often rain squalls. These conditions add to the challenge of needing to hit low running shots. The course would be even more difficult without a caddie or guide (at least the first time). There are many holes with hidden slopes, bunkers, or marshy wet area to be avoided. From the forward tees the total yardage is 5285 yards with a par 72. There are three par 3s and three par 5s. The par 3s are manageable distances, but with bunkers, wind, dune grass rough, and links rolls they aren't easy. The par 5s are long, from 415 to 494 yards long. We were also told that the course is usually unpopular with American women because it requires long carries off the tee. I don't consider myself a long hitter, but I didn't have much trouble getting to the fairways. I loved playing this testing course and would never pass up a chance to play Machrihanish Dunes.

MAYBOLE GOLF COURSE
Memorial Park, Maybole, Ayrshire KA19 7DX
No website   01292-612000
Parkland, 2635 yards, par 33, £8

AMENITIES: Community bowling green and swimming pool next to the course, but no real clubhouse or golf shop.

COURSE COMMENTS: Maybole GC is a very traditional town 9-hole course which opened in 1924. The course is short, inexpensive, and has views of the Carrisk Hills (look for the fantastic view of ancient graveyard to the northeast). Short and inexpensive doesn't mean uninteresting--there are good holes on this little course. Fairways are tight and undulating, but the rough is not tall or hard to play from. The 5th, *Monument* (named for the World War I monument to those from the parish who gave their lives in that war which is near the tee), is a par 4 of 340 yards. The narrow fairway plays uphill (aim about 15 yards right of the monument) with a blind second shot over a burn. The green is protected by a grass bunker. The 8th is a very interesting 275-yard par 4 dogleg right. Your tee shot faces a cross bunker about 190-200 yards out and the green is tucked behind a stand of trees. The hole is short with many ways to find trouble. Maybole is not destination golf, but if you're in the area and only have time for nine or want a break from the Troons and Turnberrys give it a shot.

SEAFIELD GOLF COURSE
Belleisle Park, Doonfoot Road, Ayr KA7 4DU
www.ayrseafuiekdgiolfclub.co.uk   01292-441258
Parkland and links, 5481 yards, par 68, £19

AMENITIES: Tam 'o Shanter Pub on the premises serves light snacks and drinks.   A well-stocked golf shop serves this and the Belleisle course.

COURSE COMMENTS: The original 9-hole Seafield course opened in 1904 as the design work of James Braid--those holes are now 6-13.   Shortly after the course was expanded to 18, again by Braid.   The first five holes are parkland, the next eight are links, and the remaining five are back to parkland.   The course is characterized by some great short par 4s.   The 2nd, *Loup the Burn*, a 362-yard par 4, begins with a blind tee shot which needs to stay short of the road and the burn.   Try to stay left on your drive or your second shot will be blocked by trees.   *Roon the Wa'*, is one of the fine short par 4s, only 297 yards.   More intimidating than difficult, this hole sweeps right in an arc with a rock wall left (OB) the whole length.   Mounds and rough right make finding the fairway important.   Another interesting short two-shotter is *Doon 'n Roon*, the 259-yard 14th.   A large fir which hangs out into the driving area makes the shot from the elevated tee more demanding.   The green is drivable with a fairway wood, but trees left and a trap right add to the adventure.   *Braid's Plateau*, the 16th, is only 265 yards long and plays slightly downhill from the tee toward a burn (should not be in play) and then steeply up to a green protected by three bunkers, only one of which is visible from 70 yards out.   A classic Braid design with trees in the middle of the driving area.   On the 17th your blind drive must end up short of the burn about 250 yards out--the difficulty is the hole is downhill from about 150 out from the tee.   At the burn there are numerous trees to get in the way of your second shot to a green fronted by two traps.

Easier to get on than the Belleisle Championship course and easier to play, Seafield is still a fun track, and will be better after completion of current revision projects.

COMMENTS FROM THE FORWARD TEES: I enjoy the challenges at Seafield with its links and parkland holes. The course is more difficult than it looks, with a burn crossing six holes, and hills, slopes, and mounds in several fairways. The course is popular with the locals and was busy the day we played. We paired up with two locals which added to the fun-- who needs a stroke saver when there is a local to tell you what's around the bend. The three par 5s are more than 400 yards and par 3s range from 122 to 199 yards, but the difficulties will be water carries, long carries, and sloping approaches. I walked off the course wanting to play it again.

SHISKINE GOLF AND TENNIS CLUB
Shore Road, Blackwaterfoot, Isle of Arran KA27 8HA
www.shiskinegolf.com   01770-860226
Links, 2996 (12 holes), par 42, £20 round, £33 day (2 rounds)

AMENITIES: New clubhouse, Felicity's at the Clubhouse opened in March of 2010 and food service is even better than before. Whenever we'd eaten at the old tearoom we had been pleased with the food, quality and variety, but everything is even better now. The old starter's office has been turned into a small, but well-stocked golf shop under the direction of PGA professional Douglas Bell.

COURSE COMMENTS: Shiskine is our favorite course in the world. In good weather or in bad, the course will always challenge and delight. Shiskine is a 12-hole links course which plays along the shore of the Kilbrannan Sound and beside Drumadoon Head. The original 9-hole course was designed by Willie Fernie of Troon in 1896. In 1912 it was decided to expand the course to 18-holes. Willie Park Jnr was commissioned to build the new course. The Fernie course was scrapped, except for the 5th and the 9th, and new holes were built including six which played up on the side of

Drumadoon Head. During World War I, 1914-1919, the hill holes were left to revert to grass and bracken because of a lack of work force to maintain them. After the war the club decided that besides being difficult to maintain, the hill holes didn't meet the standard of the rest of the course. Thus was born the world's first planned 12-hole course. It's a number that visitors find just about right. If you want to go around twice in a day (the most the club will allow), 24 holes is also a very doable number.

The course is a stunner with grand vistas of the Kilbrannan Sound, Drumadoon Head, rocks filled with seabirds, pleasant farmland, and the Kintyre Peninsula across the water. One of the most enjoyable features of Shiskine is that every hole is absolutely unique from every other hole-- wonderful variety. While mostly flat, there are some hills and raised tees and greens which add interest. Blind tee shots on seven of the 12 holes demand confident shot-making (or blind luck). Bunkers aren't a problem at Shiskine; the few there are on the course are not penal. Gorse and fescue rough is a different matter. The biggest problem on the course is the wind and weather. If you hit a day without wind or rain, as we have a time or two, you may just want to play forever. If the wind is up and the rain is coming in sideways it's a different course, but still one worth a go.

I'm tempted to describe in detail every hole on this great course, but it's probably best to let you discover much of it for yourself. Be sure to pick up a stroke saver in the golf shop before you go out; with all the blind shots it is almost a necessity the first time you play. Holes three and four are a fantastic combination. The 3rd, *Crow's Nest*, is a 128-yarder seemingly straight up hill. A unique signal lets you know when the group ahead has cleared the green. Take an extra club, aim at the aiming post, and hope you can hold the green surrounded by heavy rough. For those who can't reach all the way to the top there is a shelf about half way up so you can make two pitches. Once at the top you next play back down to the 4th green and the sea. *The Shelf* is a 146-yard one-shotter which plays down to a large flat green. If there's no wind take about two clubs less. If the wind is up, into you, behind, or quartering, good luck--make your best guess and have a go. *Hades*, the drivable 222-yard par 4 eighth, is an opportunity for eagle or birdie with a good drive, or a high number if you find the gorse left and behind. Next is the 9th, *Drumadoon*, at 506 yards it's the only par five on the course. The drive here is fairly open, but a deep burn makes the approach to the elevated green tough. Drumadoon is the most difficult hole on the back six (remember, it's a 12-hole course). Everyone who plays at Shiskine recognizes its quality, so even if it is fairly isolated it will be busy most of the time. Be sure to call ahead, but be aware that the club only takes tee times 24 hours in advance in the summer.

COMMENTS FROM THE FORWARD TEES: T h i s continues to be one of my favorite courses in Scotland. It is unique because it has only twelve holes. What makes it really special is that it truly has twelve very different holes. Each hole is a test of skill and planning. Weather here can be unbelievably beautiful, sunny and calm or windy, cold, and wet. A burn runs through the course and the seashore is in play on four holes. The course is not long but don't be fooled by the shorter yardage, you will be too busy planning your shots. The holes that require the most planning for me are the holes with dunes, hill, and hummocks to hit around and over. The 3rd is the first real thought provoking hole. It is a short 118-yard par 3 but to reach the green one must hit up to the green which is 60 feet above you. The green also slopes right to left and sits on a small shelf. The next is also a par 3 back down to the green and I find it easier to play than it looks especially if the wind is not in your face. The 5th has a small dune covered in grass right in the middle of the fairway where my first shot likes to land. Then comes the 7th which is a 164-yard par 3 with a 50-foot hummock to clear. You must not be too long or a burn gets your ball. There are more challenges on the rest of this course. Take the time to visit this wonderful course. I just love it.

SPEAN BRIDGE GOLF CLUB
Station Road, Spean Bridge, Inverness-shire
www.speangolf.org.uk   07747-147090
Moorland, 4542 yards, par 68, £18 for all day, £10 for 9

AMENITIES: Practically no amenities--toilets or trolleys--when we played several years ago, but the club built a new clubhouse in 2009 which looks very nice and more visitor friendly.

COURSE COMMENTS: The course, built by members in the 1950s and now maintained by members, fits the land well.   The 9-hole track has some moderate hills and several blind shots, but is not a difficult walk.   There are no bunkers on the course. The course has some interesting holes including the 7th, a 287-yard par 4. Here the downhill tee shot must avoid a small burn about 190 yards out.   The 8th then goes uphill 312 yards. Stay out of the trees on the right on the tee shot.   The approach is to a plateau green tucked to the right.   Ball placement is key on this hole.   The first and the ninth are par 3s; all the rest are moderate length par 4s. If in the area, the course is worth a visit.

COMMENTS FROM THE FORWARD TEES: I had to lighten my bag and carry my clubs because I could not rent a trolley, but it was worth it. The course is visually very interesting, but has some hills with short but steep ups and downs. Spean Bridge is a short course at only 1884 yards.
I did enjoy the course, even though I wasn't as precise as I needed to be on several shots.

TURNBERRY, KINTYRE COURSE
Turnberry, Ayrshire KA26 9LT
www.turnberry.co.uk   01655-331000
Links, 6194 yards, par 71, £135

AMENITIES: The lovely historic Turnberry Clubhouse, opened by HRH the Duke of York in 1993, is open to all visitors.   Great photo displays on upstairs wall.   The Tappie Toorie Lounge has lovely views over the course and serves a full menu (expensive). People watch golfers finish the Kintyre 18th. The golf shop in the clubhouse has a full range of clothing and accessories--it's where you check in for golf.

COURSE COMMENTS: The Kintyre Course at Turnberry is world class links and an Open Qualifying course. Designed originally by James Braid in 1923, it was redesigned by Jimmy Alexander in 1954. A final upgrade was done by architect Donald Steel in 2001 when the course was renamed the Kintyre. Even though this is the second course at Turnberry, the first is the Championship Ailsa course, Kintyre is a grand links challenge and will be very busy in season; off season there's a good chance you can walk on. The views from the course are fantastic--the Turnberry Lighthouse, Ailsa Craig, Isle of Arran, Kintyre Peninsula, and other islands. The challenging golf, though, is what you are really there for. More than 80 fairway and greenside bunkers will command your attention. Most of the traps are playable, but several are quite penal. Water is a problem on only two holes: a burn is in play if you are off-line right on the 17th, and seriously in play on the 1st as the burn crosses the fairway 100-150 yards from the green. Most of the moderate to large greens have interesting contours and several are distinctly tiered. Only the 3rd is relatively flat. All are good to putt. Besides the bunkers and the bit of water, the coastal winds and ever-present gorse are the other main challenges. It's hard to highlight a few holes when all the holes at Kintyre are wonderful, but we narrowed it down to our favorites. The 1st, *Barley Rigs*, a 517-yard par 5, is a great starter. The long dogleg left has fairway bunkers right and left which can complicate the drive, but it is really the burn which winds across the landing area of most second shots that is the crux of the hole. Most would be wise to lay back and have a 120-150-yard third into the sloped green with one large bunker right. *Sandy Loo*, the 376-yard par 4 fourth has seven bunkers which play havoc with both your drive and approach shots on this tough dogleg left. The green is deeper than it looks from the fairway and is tiered. A very entertaining short hole is the 8th, *Kintyre's Cove*, a 280-yard par 4. Drive to the top of the hill, about 190-200 yards from the green.

From there it's all down hill to a green sloping away. Two bunkers short add interest. The views are terrific, be sure to bring your camera. With marsh and a bunker left, you will want to stay right with your drive at *Misk*, the 414-yard 13th. A nest of three traps left come into play on second shots. The tiered green has one protecting bunker on the right. The final three holes at Kintyre make a great finish. The 16th, *Paddy's Milestane* (the Irish name for the Ailsa Craig) is a testing short, 125-yard, par 3. The very undulating green that is guarded by two bunkers makes up for the lack of length. Next is *Lea Rig*, a dogleg left to right 418-yard par 4. Two bunkers and a burn on the inside of the turn add difficulty to the drive. Avoid those troubles and it's clear sailing to the large swaled green with two traps on the left. The par 5 finishing hole, *Kintyre Hame*, has eleven bunker dotted its 495-yard length. Stay left with your drive to avoid the right hand fairway bunkers. Three left and two more right will bother second shots. Once you get past the two fore bunkers and two left greenside, the putting is tricky on the very subtly sloped green. It's a lovely finish that will be watched by those in the clubhouse lounge. The Kintyre course at Turnberry is not inexpensive golf, but compared to the prices at other big courses (Kingsbarns, Castle Stuart, Gleneagles) it's almost a bargain.

FROM THE FORWARD TEES: The day we played the Kintyre course was a beautiful sunny fall day with only a light sea breeze. The setting is outstanding and sometimes the views are so dramatic it was hard for me to concentrate on the golf. This links course is definitely a playable challenge. The course from the forward tees is 5643 yards and has a par 73. The front side has one par 5 and the backside has four par 5s (par 38). My favorite hole was the 8th, *Kintyre's Cove* with the green set in a rocky cove hidden from view until you are within 70 yards at the top of the hill. The eighteenth doglegs right and has a very swaled green set in front of the clubhouse windows. I chipped up onto the green for about a 15 foot putt. I heard a knock on the clubhouse window. A group of men golfers were standing there clapping and giving me a thumbs-up. What a fun way to finish such a good course.

WEST KILBRIDE GOLF COURSE
33-35 Fullerton Dr., Seamill, West Kilbride KA23 9HT
www.westkilbridegolfclub.com 01294-823911
Links, 6146 yards, par 71, £52

AMENITIES: Pleasant clubhouse lounge looks out to the 18th green and the 1st hole. Bar meals served all day. The nice small golf shop has everything you need for a round.

COURSE COMMENTS: Starting as a 9-hole course designed by Old Tom Morris in 1893, West Kilbride expanded to a full course with a redesign by James Braid in 1905. The course is busy, but very accommodating to visitors. The links course is set between the Ayrshire farmland and Firth of Clyde and is generally flat with typical links undulations. With lovely views across the firth to the Isle of Arran, West Kilbride plays mostly inland on the out holes and six of the inward holes play along the beach. There's plenty of trouble to find on the course studded with more than 85 bunkers--many deep. Typical of Braid's designs many of the fairway bunkers are difficult to advance forward. A drainage ditch is in play on three holes, but it causes the most trouble on the first where it crosses directly in front of the green. Greens are moderate in size with one double green, the 6th and 17th. All have subtle slopes, are kept in good condition, and fairly easy to putt. Wind, as with all links courses, will be a condition of play.

Besides the views of Arran, the firth, and the village there's is much to like about West Kilbride starting with the second. *Wildcat*, a 341-yard par 4, doglegs right around a large hill--big hitters can try to cut the corner and hope for a bounce down to the fairway. One bunker guards the relatively small flat green. Next is *Yonderfield* the 479-yard par 5 third. The fairway slopes right to left for the first half of the hole. Bunkers left and middle will bother second shots while two bunkers and a mound will affect approach shots to the smallest green on the course which is protected further by two bunkers left front. It's a classy challenge. The sixth hole, called *Mound*, is a par 4 of 345 yards. Your slightly right angled tee shot must avoid one bunker on the right as the fairway rises (the mound). Second shots are to the courses only double green (shared with 17) which is protected by four traps. On the back we like the 11th, *Dykeside.* This short (253-yard) two-shotter has four fairway bunkers which challenge your drive. There are two more traps left and right at the green. Next is *Whinhurst,* a fine 162-yard par 3. It's all about the bunkers here--six of them surround the green. Anything too near the the bunkers will run off the green and into sand. It's a tough short hole. The last hole we picked as a favorite is the 16th, *Hunger-em-oot.* On this 324-yard par 4 a small burn (drainage ditch) about 150 yards off the tee shouldn't be trouble except perhaps for ladies, but it will be in your mind as you drive. The crux of the hole is avoiding the four fairway bunkers and three greenside bunkers. West Kilbride is a lovely links course where the members are friendly and the challenges are fair.

FROM THE FORWARD TEES: The course is a true links course on the shore of the Firth of Clyde. The views include the Isle of Arran and north to Great Cumbrae. An easy walk, the course is a bit longer than others at 5781 yards for the red tees. With a par of 73 (36/37), there are two par 5s on each side and a total of three par 3s (two on the front and one on the back). The course is very playable from the fairway, but there is plenty of trouble off the cut grass--there are numerous bunkers and a couple of burn crossings. It is a course you can score on, though.

WHITING BAY GOLF CLUB
Golf Course Road, Whiting Bay, Isle of Arran KA27 8QT
www.whitingbaygolfclub.org.uk 01770-700487
Hilly parkland, 4405 yards, par 63, £18

AMENITIES: Pleasant clubhouse with lounge which serves sandwiches and light meals. Outside seating for good weather. Buggies are available and might not be a bad idea on this hilly track. No golf shop.

COURSE COMMENTS: Whiting Bay Golf Club, built in 1895, is one of the older courses on Arran. The course is quite hilly, but affords great vistas of Ayrshire, Ailsa Craig, the Holy Island, as well town and the shoreline. Bring your camera. The golf will be exciting as well. Besides the elevation changes (barely any flat lies here), the wind can be a major factor of play. All the holes are challenging regardless of length. The 7th, *Braes'n'Dunes*, is an uphill 235-yard par 3 which plays like 270 yards or more. If the wind is against you might feel like playing two woods to reach the par 3! On the short 314-yard par 4 twelfth you should lay up at the bottom of the hill, about 190 yards. The second shot is then blind to a fairly open green. The 11th at 208 yards has a stone fence and forest left and the ground between the tee and the green slopes steeply right, but the view out to Holy Island is spectacular. You finish at 18, a 430-yard par 4. Watch for other golfers since the 2nd crosses the 18th fairway. The hole is all downhill and your second shot needs to land at least 30 yards short of the green; even in wet conditions the ball will roll onto the very swaled green. Whiting Bay GC is one of the reasons we love the Isle of Arran.

PUBS, RESTAURANTS & TEAROOMS

Balgarth Hotel Restaurant on Danure Road in Alloway close to the new Robert Burns Museum. Dine in the hotel dining room or conservatory. Hotel has a broad pub-style menu with Thai and cajan selections. Nice service.

Bread Meats Bread on Vincent Street in downtown Glasgow. A lively, crowded burger diner specializing in all kinds of burgers, poutines, and special sandwiches. Good food, nice staff, fun place. Can be a long wait for a table.

Brig o' Doon House Hotel (restaurant) in Alloway on the River Doon. Located just in front of the bridge over the River Doon (Robert Burns' Brig o' Doon from the poem "Tam O'Shanter"), the hotel restaurant provides great meals for just above pub prices. One of the best dining choices in the area.

Brodick Bar and Brasserie (bistro/restaurant) at the north end of the village of Brodick on Isle of Arran. Recently remodeled the Brassarie continues to serve excellent meals off a large entertaining (chalkboard) menu. One of the best bets on the island.

Carradale Hotel (pub/restaurant) in Carradale on the Kintyre Peninsula, just up from the golf course. Pub meals from an extensive, upscale pub menu and inexpensive set price two or three course dinners make the Carradale Hotel a good stop when in the area.

Catacol Hotel Pub at Catacol on the northwest coast of Isle of Arran. Sited directly on the Kilbrannan Sound looking across to the Kintyre Peninsula, the Catacol Hotel is a rustic hotel and pub. Food is basic, tasty pub fare and the locals are friendly.

The Chartroom II Bistro and Arduaine Restaurant at the Loch Melfort Hotel near Oban. Next to the Arduaine Gardens (NTS), the hotel has two fine eateries. For more casual (and cheaper) dining try the Charthouse II Bistro famous for its fresh langoustines and fish chowder. The more formal Arduaine Restaurant serves set price meals with some unique items.

Coasters (pub) on the seafront in Oban. This is a good place to catch the local flavor and have a drink. Not really an eatery.

The Drift Inn (pub) in Lamlash on Isle of Arran next to the bowling green. The pub food is good and the place is usually very busy.

Eilean Mor (restaurant) on the main island road through Brodick, Isle of Arran. Bistro-style restaurant with wood tables, some with views of the bay. You can't miss the restaurant with its distinctive red facade. Large menu, good food, especially pizzas, and friendly staff are the drawing cards.

Glenisle Hotel Restaurant on the main street of Lamlash, Isle of Arran, facing the bay. Modern (recently refurbished) lodge-style dining with several small eating areas and a large dining room. The menu is limited but the food is delicious. There is a pleasant lounge for coffee or drinks after dinner.

Lagg Inn (pub/restaurant) in Kilmory on the southern end of Isle of Arran. Established in 1791, the inn is a little out of the way, but worth the effort to visit. The very interesting menu is served both in the pub and the more formal restaurant. Interesting food at fair prices. Take the short hike (500 meters) up to the ancient cairns behind the inn.

The Lighthouse (cafe/restaurant) in the village of Pirnmill south of Lochranza on Isle of Arran. Cafe by day and restaurant on weekend evenings, The Lighthouse has a well deserved reputation for good food. Be sure to book for an evening meal, especially if a little out of season, since they won't open if there are no bookings.

Loch Fyne (pronounced Fine) Oyster Bar (restaurant) on the west side of Loch Fyne about nine miles from Inveraray. Excellent variety of quality seafood, and a seafood shop and garden store.

Machrihanish Golf Club Lounge (pub) at the golf club about six miles northwest of Campbeltown. There are only a few times that we'll recommend a golf club lounge for eating, although usually golf club food is good. Machrihanish's lounge is one of the special ones. Some of the best food in the area and the lounge is open to non-golfers as well.

Morris's Steakhouse (restaurant) on the bay front in Largs. Touted as the best steaks in the area, Morris's was a disappointment. The food wasn't bad; it just wasn't anything special and the service was mediocre.

Muneroy Tearoom and Store on the road through Southend. Tearoom serves snacks, full meals, and lovely cakes. Decorated with kitsch in every corner. Nice atmosphere with coal fire and Irish music.

The Old Clubhouse Pub across from Machrihanish GC. The pub is literally in the old Machrihanish GC clubhouse, which for years has been a low-scale pub of another name. Newly refurbished by the owners of Machrihanish Dune as part of their complex, the pub is a lovely golfer's hangout and serves upscale pub fare at upscale (though not outrageous) prices.

Pierhead Tavern on Shore Road (the main road around the island) in Lamlash on Isle of Arran. Tasty pub grub in large portions, especially the haddock and chips. The new dining room is a strong addition.

Sea Bed Restaurant at the Anchor Hotel on the harbour at Tarbert. Both the restaurant and pub bistro serve the same extensive menu which is heavy on seafood. Everything we've had is excellent and the service always fine.

Stable's Restaurant on Bank Street in Fort William. Nothing fancy, but the window tables do have a good view and the food was tasty.

Suie Lodge (pub) in Glen Dochart near Crianlarich. We found Suie Lodge by accident--nothing else in the area was serving at 3:00 in the afternoon. It was our good fortune. The pub serves homemade food and specializes in local game. Good food and friendly people.

The Waterfront Seafood Restaurant on the docks of Oban harbour. Housed upstairs in the old Fisherman's Mission, the restaurant specializes in fresh seafood, of course, and offers great views of Oban Bay. To tell you how good the food is, we thought it still smelled good after we were stuffed and on our way out.

Wildings Hotel (restaurant) in Maidens by Turnberry GC on the Ayrshire coast. We had a great meal here several years ago. The restaurant now serves only set price lunches and dinners.

LODGINGS

The Anchor Hotel
Harbour Street, Tarbert, Loch Fyne, Argyll PA29 6UB
01880-820577 www.lochfyne-scotland.co.uk £90

Conveniently located in the heart of the village on the harbour, the Anchor Hotel has recently been refurbished and offers lovely rooms at reasonable prices--ask for the sea view, a little higher but well worth it. Serves a great breakfast with good choices.

The Broom Lodge
5 Broomfield Place, Largs, Ayrshire KA30 8DR
01475-674290   www.broom-lodge.co.uk   £55
With good views of The Cumbraes, Arran, and Bute, The Broom Lodge has a great location and comfortable rooms, although we had a few small problems with our room the night we stayed. Breakfast is hearty and tasty.

The Burlington
Shore Road, Whiting Bay, Isle of Arran KA27 8PZ
01770-700255   www.burlingtonarran.co.uk   £55
Built as a guest house in 1904 in the Arts & Crafts-style with Edwardian features, The Burlington has comfortable rooms and reputation for fine food (book ahead for an evening meal). The restaurant is part of Scotland's "Slow Food" movement (organic and locally grown) with a three course dinner for about £25.

Craigard House Hotel
Low Askomil, Campbeltown, Argyll PA28 6EP
01586-554242   www.craigard-house.co.uk   £90
Craigard House Hotel is a recently converted Victorian mansion with an interesting history. Accommodations are first class throughout and the food, both breakfast and evening meals, are top rate. The house began as a whisky distiller's home and then was run as a maternity home by the local Council from 1942 to 1973. In 1998, after extensive remodeling, Craigard House opened as a small hotel. An elegant and historic stay when playing Machrihanish and southern Kintyre courses.

The Glenisle Hotel and Bistro
Lamlash, Isle of Arran KA27 8LY
01770-600559 www.glenislehotel.com £116
In the heart of the charming village of Lamlash, the Glenisle opened in 1849. In 2008 the hotel and bistro underwent a major remodel. The rooms are nicely appointed and the breakfast is delicious. A good choice if our favorite B&B, Lilybank, next door isn't available.

Grammar Lodge
32 St John Street, Campbeltown PA28 6AU
01586-553355 www.grammarlodge.co.uk £80
Converted grammar school with large open rooms and special amenities like drying facilities (you can get wet on the Kintyre courses). One of the best showers we've had in a B&B. "In a class of it's own."

Greenan Lodge
39 Denure Road, Doonfoot (by Ayr) KA7 4HR
01292-443939 www.greenanlodge.com £70
Greenan Lodge is a large modern B&B with huge rooms (our double was actually a suite) and a lovely guest lounge. Located on the main coastal road between Turnberry and Ayr, the lodge is convenient to most of the tourist sites in the area (five minutes drive from the new Burns Museum) and all the golf courses. Howard is a knowledgeable golfer and Helen a friendly host. Breakfast is delicious.

Kilmichael Country House Hotel
Glen Cloy by Brodick, Isle of Arran KA22 8BY
01770-302219 www.kilmichael.com £163
Believed to be the oldest house on the Isle of Arran, Kilmichael is as rich in historic associations as it is in elegant accommodations. The five star facility has been featured as a Best of Britain Hotel and is past winner of the Taste of Scotland's "Country House Hotel of the Year." The tariff is not cheap, but then nothing is cheap about Kilmichael House. Rooms are nicely appointed and each has a distinct style. We

stayed in a lovely room which was once the stable and were greeted with fresh flowers and a generous tipple of malt whisky. The restaurant, which has been called "Arran's finest," is highly recommended (though it is expensive). Breakfasts are excellent and the service deserves its five star status. Certainly, Kilmichael House is one of Scotland's premier lodgings.

Lilybank Guest House

Lamlash, Isle of Arran KA27 8SL
01770-650000 www.lilybank-arran.co.uk £65
Situated on the shores of Lamlash Bay overlooking the Holy Isle, Colin and June Richardson's Lilybank Guest House has an ideal location for the golfer wanting to play the several courses available on the Isle of Arran or just to explore the sites of the island or both. Most rooms are ensuite and have bay views. The dining room as well overlooks the bay and breakfast is delicious.

The Warren

Machrihanish, Capbeltown PA28 6PT
01586-810310   www.machgolf.com/accommodation/The-Warren £ Reasonable
Built originally as a golfing lodge in the 1890s, The Warren is a great location for playing the wonderful links at Macrihanish or the new Machrihanish Dunes. Rooms are lovely and spacious and the breakfast is delightful. Bryan and Judy McClements are great hosts, ready to see to all your needs. Phone contact is best.

ATTRACTIONS

Brodick Castle (HS), Brodick, Isle of Arran. Home of the Hamiltons since 1503, the castle overlooks Brodick Bay and the Firth of Clyde, while behind it stands Goatfell Peak, the tallest point on the island at 2866 feet. Brodick Castle is a fine example of a Victorian Highland estate with a lovely garden.

Culzean Castle and Country Park (NTS), near Ayr. The former Kennedy estate was redesigned at the end of the 1700s by neoclassical Scottish architect Robert Adams. The setting is awe-inspiring as the castle hangs on the cliffs overlooking   the Firth of Clyde and the Isle of Arran. There is plenty to see in the interior and on the grounds of Culzean (pronouced "cullayne") Castle.

Crossraguel Abbey (HS), near Maybole. The abbey, built in 1244 as a Clunic Monastery (one of only two in Scotland), has several parts still in good condition. The tower house is mostly complete with good views of the surrounding countryside from the upper floor windows. The abbey is a good place to search for mason marks, marks in the stones left by the masons who cut and placed the stones.

Isle of Arran Shops, Brodick, Isle of Arran. The island, known as Scotland in Miniature, possesses some interesting shops to explore. There's a fine chocolate shop in the heart of the village of Brodick, and just north are two more special shops. Arran Aromatics specializes in locally made soaps and lotions, while Island Cheese Company is famous for its hand-crafted cheeses.

Robert Burns' Museum and Cottage (NTS), Alloway. The new Burns' Museum is very well done with interesting exhibits. The Scottish national poet's birth house is only a short walk away and shows the living conditions of a tenant farmer family in the mid-1800s. Just up the street across from the museum is Alloway Kirkyard and Brig o'Doon--all with strong Burns associations.

Stones of the Isle of Arran (HS). The Isle of Arran hosts numerous standing stones, stone circles, and pictish stones, and most are easily accessible. The cairn at Torrylin (in the south near Kilmory), Moss Farm, and Machrie Moor stones (near Blackwaterfoot) are fascinating.

Chapter Ten: The Best of Scotland

The Ring of Brodgar, Orkney Islands

Golf Courses

In each chapter we've described the out-of-the-way golf courses we've played during our trips to Scotland. What we haven't done is much comparison among courses. To do that we present our top ten favorite courses. Remember, like everything else in this book, our choices are subjective. This is our list. With that caveat here are our favorite (not necessarily the best, but what we like the best) Scottish hidden gems:

10. Fortrose and Rosemarkie GC, Black Isle. So much draws us to this course--the challenging holes, the views of the Firth of Moray, the history of the golf on the land, and the history of the linksland it's built upon. We definitely plan our Scotland trips around playing Fortrose.

9. North Berwick West Links, East Lothian. Some may be surprised that we would place one of the most famous courses, an Open-qualifying venue, so low on our list of favorites. North Berwick is a great course I would play anytime, but there are others I like better.

8. Crieff Ferntower GC, Crieff, Perthshire. Crieff Ferntower is a long parkland track which is both fair and demanding. The lovely course playing along the knock is fun to play and very reasonably priced for the quality of the course.

7. Dundonald Links, Ayrshire. The Loch Lomand group has produced another winner. Dundonald is a spectacular links course in the area of Troon and Western Gailes. Playable by all level of golfers (choose the appropriate tees), the course will fairly challenge you at every hole.

6 (tie). Machrihanish GC and Machrihanish Dunes GC, Machrihanish, Kintyre. Machrihanish is a beautiful venerable Scottish links course with an absolutely world-class first shot over the Atlantic. Machrihanish Dunes is wild, dramatic, and natural. Both courses are challenging yet fair, and the isolation of these two courses is both their charm and drawback.

5. Turnberry, Kintyre Course, Ayrshire. This is a great links course, challenging yet fun to play. Nice variety in the holes and world-class conditioning make this a course we'd play anytime.

4. Crail Balcomie Links, Crail, Fife. The age and history of the course is part of the draw. For me it is the combination of first playing the great links holes and then strolling around a point to end with some tough parkland-like holes. Balcomie is a course we go back to time after time.

3. Boat of Garten Golf and Tennis Club, Highlands. What's not to like about Boat? It's tough (rough, bunkers, trees, elevation changes, tricky greens) and it is fair. Hit it well at Boat and you get rewarded. Hit off line and pay the price. Length helps, but accuracy is more important. The setting is stupendous, filled with mountain and river views, birch forests, and a steam train chugging beside the course. After you finish a round at Boat the clubhouse has a great lounge for a malt, a meal, or a brew.

2. Royal Dornoch GC, Highlands. Truly championship golf as tough as it can be and still be playable by the average player. Prettiest in the spring and early summer when the broom and gorse blooms bright yellow, the course is always lovely and wonderfully conditioned. Players like Tom Watson aren't wrong when they say that Royal Dornoch may be the best out-of-the-way test of your golf skills in the world.

1. Shiskine Golf and Tennis Club, Blackwaterfoot, Isle of Arran. If I could play only one course for the rest of my days it would be Shiskine. Twelve holes is a very good number and twenty-four (two rounds) is not bad either. Every hole at Shiskine is so different from every other that it make a round seem unbelievably full. The views are unrivaled and the golf challenging--I always feel that birdies and bogies or worse are real possibilities on every hole. I have found no better golfing adventure anywhere.

STOP FOR A BITE OR A BREW

In these chapters we've listed more than seventy-five pubs, restaurants, bistros, or tearooms. We believe that they are all good enough to recommend to our friends. Which ones, though, would be best? After much discussion, reading notes and journals, and wracking our memories, we've come up with a list of special recommendations.

Best Golfer's Pub:
Eagle Hotel, Dornoch
Old Aberlady Inn, Aberlady
Claret Jug, St Andrews
The Old Clubhouse Pub, Machrihanish

Best Seafood:
Mussel Inn, Edinburgh
Loch Fyne Oyster Bar, Loch Fyne
Waterfront Seafood Restaurant, Oban
Anstruther Fish Bar, Anstruther
Crown Hotel Pub, Portpatrick

Best Pub Menu:
Moulin Inn, Moulin near Pitlochry
Port Bar, Lake of Menteith
Brodick Brasserie, Isle of Arran
Cavens Pub, Dumfries

Best Beers:
Traquair Arms, Innerleithen (Traquair Ales)
Moulin Inn, Moulin near Pitlochry (Moulin Brewery)

Most Historic:
Clachan Inn, Drymen
Brig o'Doon House Hotel, Alloway
Dreel Tavern, Anstruther

Best Golf Course Food:
Macrihanish GC, Machrihanish
St Fillans GC, St Fillans

Best Golf Course Clubhouse Pub:
Royal Dornoch GC, Dornoch
Fortrose and Rosemarkie GC, Fortrose

Best Tearoom:
Abbot's House, Dunfermline
Old Tudor Coffee Shop, Auchterarder
Water Mill Cafe, Blair Atholl

Best Cafeteria:
Storehouse Restaurant and Farm Shop, Foulis
      Ferry
Speyside Clootie Dumpling and Heather Garden,
      near Grantown-on-Spey
House of Bruar, Bruar near Blair Atholl

Best Restaurant:
Osteria, North Berwick (Italian)
Yann's, Crieff (French/European)
Deil's Cauldron, Comrie (Scottish/European)
Sutherland House, Dornoch (Scottish)
The Rowan Tree, by Aviemore (Scottish)
Anderson's, Boat of Garten

OWER AT LAST

Our lists are done, but yours should just be getting started. Pour over the maps and guide books. You know you'll want to see Glasgow and Edinburgh. You'll probably want to play the Old Course, Troon, Turnberry or Carnoustie-- but don't limit yourself to just playing the famous and thus missing some of the best Scottish golf. To make your trip complete start a list of the other courses you may want to play:

Crieff, Crail, Fortrose, Reay, Royal Dornoch, Royal Aberdeen. Make a list also of sites you want to visit: Blair Castle, Clava Carns, Melrose Abbey.

**Your Hidden Gems Scotland adventure awaits.
Slainte Mohr!**

INDEX OF GOLF COURSES

Made in the USA
Lexington, KY
30 June 2018